The Best
Bicycle Tours
of
Eastern Canada

The Best Bicycle Tours of Eastern Canada

Twelve Breathtaking Tours through

NOVA SCOTIA

NEWFOUNDLAND

PRINCE EDWARD ISLAND

NEW BRUNSWICK

QUÉBEC

ONTARIO

Jerry Dennis

An Owl Book

Henry Holt and Company   New York

Copyright © 1991 by Jerry Dennis
Maps by Gail Dennis
All rights reserved, including the right to reproduce this book or portions
thereof in any form.
Published by Henry Holt and Company, Inc.,
115 West 18th Street, New York, New York 10011.
Published in Canada by Fitzhenry & Whiteside Limited,
195 Allstate Parkway, Markham, Ontario L3R 4T8.

Library of Congress Cataloging-in-Publication Data
Dennis, Jerry.
The best bicycle tours of eastern Canada : twelve breathtaking tours
through Nova Scotia, Newfoundland, Prince Edward Island, New
Brunswick, Québec, and Ontario / Jerry Dennis.—1st ed.
          p.   cm.
"An Owl book."
Includes index.
1. Bicycle touring—Canada, Eastern—Guide-books.   2. Canada, Eastern—
Description and travel—Guide-books.   I. Title.
GV1046.C22C363   1990
796.6′4′09713—dc20   91-18866
                                                                      CIP
ISBN 0-8050-1492-6

Henry Holt books are available at special discounts for bulk purchases for
sales promotions, premiums, fund-raising, or educational use. Special
editions or book excerpts can also be created to specification.
For details contact: Special Sales Director, Henry Holt and Company, Inc.,
115 West 18th Street, New York, New York 10011.

First Edition—1992

Book design by Claire Naylon Vaccaro
Printed in the United States of America
Recognizing the importance of preserving
the written word, Henry Holt and Company, Inc.,
by policy, prints all of its first editions
on acid-free paper. ∞

1 3 5 7 9 10 8 6 4 2

Facing title page: *The coastline of the Northern Peninsula
in western Newfoundland.*

·CONTENTS·

CONTENTS · vi

· ACKNOWLEDGMENTS ·

I'm grateful to many people for their assistance during the research and writing of this book, but would especially like to thank John Klepetka for his companionship, advice, and mechanical help while in Newfoundland and Prince Edward Island; Michelle Cortright for her patience and enthusiasm; and Tom Carney for his valuable suggestions and moral support.

Thanks are due also to Gary Forshaw and Anne Cascadden of the Canadian Consulate General's office in Detroit for suggesting many outstanding places to cycle in Canada and for arranging local contacts in those places. Thanks as well to their colleagues in the provinces, especially Tammy Stevenson in New Brunswick, Lynda Hanscome in Prince Edward Island, and Kay Coxworthy in Newfoundland.

Thanks to Trek USA for invaluable technical suggestions and for the generous loan of several fine bicycles.

Thanks also to Steve Tracey and Ron Barger for working through the complex channels necessary to supply the ultimate sag wagon, a 27-foot motorhome.

Finally, thanks to my wife, Gail, and our sons, Aaron and Nicholas, for their enthusiastic support and assistance during a very busy twelve months. This book is affectionately dedicated to them.

· MEASUREMENTS ·

Measurements of distance in this book conform to the metric system, and are consistent with Canadian road signs, maps, and publications. Other measurements conform to U.S. units. Following is a table containing the units of measurement you will find in this book and their approximate conversions.

CONVERSION TABLE

kilometer	.6	miles
meter	3.3	feet
centimeter	.4	inch
square kilometer	.4	square mile
pound	.4	kilograms
ounce	31	grams
gallon	3.8	liters
acre	.4	hectare

To convert Fahrenheit temperatures into Celsius:

$$?F° - 32 \times 5/9 = ?C°$$

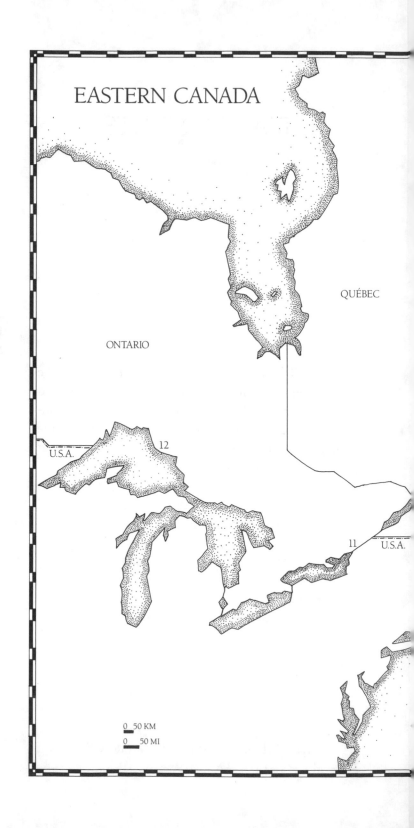

N

LABRADOR

NEWFOUNDLAND

PRINCE
EDWARD
ISLAND

10

NEW
BRUNSWICK

9

5   6

2

*Atlantic
Ocean*

8   7

1   NOVA SCOTIA

ROUTE KEY
1 Annapolis Valley
2 Cabot Trail, Cape Breton Island
3 Gros Morne National Park
4 Avalon Peninsula
5 Blue Heron Drive
6 Kings Byway Drive
7 Fundy National Park
8 Grand Manan Island and the Quoddy Loop
9 Gaspé Peninsula
10 Charlevoix / Ile d'Orléans
11 St. Lawrence Shore / Thousand Islands Parkway
12 North Shore / Lake Superior

New Brunswick's Blacks Harbour.

· INTRODUCTION ·

Travel writers have a guilty little secret. We want everyone to believe our job is a job like any other, that like everyone else we dread stepping back on the treadmill come Monday morning. Give us an opening, and we'll tell you about writer's block and jetlag and the pressure of deadlines. If we're feeling particularly eloquent (and we often feel particularly eloquent), we'll explain at length our role as the eyes and ears of society, guiding hardworking, duty-pressed people to places where they can hope to find renewal and respite. It sounds noble and grown-up and responsible, but don't believe a word of it. Our secret is this: we're in it for the fun.

My friend John Klepetka saw the truth one remarkable morning on the west coast of Newfoundland. We had biked through the hills of Gros Morne National Park and descended to a section of the coast open to winds howling across the entire vast expanse of the Gulf of St. Lawrence. Contrary to what many cyclists consider a law of nature, the wind was not in our faces, but at our backs, blowing at perhaps 60 kilometers per hour. Ahead of us stretched 240 kilometers of deserted, treeless, flat-as-a-ballfield coastline. For 3 or 4 or 5 hours (who could think of time at such a time?) we cruised with almost no effort across Newfoundland's strange, remote coastal barrens, on a newly surfaced, absolutely flat highway that was almost devoid of automobile traffic. "Tough, eh?" John asked at some point, grinning, and my facade collapsed. I broke out in song and laughter. I yodeled. I shouted that nobody had the right to expect such great fun in the name of employment.

It's been said that the best way to write a book is to simply write what you would like to read. I set out to write this book because I wanted to know more about bicycling in eastern Canada, a place that has fascinated me all my life, yet any books I could find on the subject were not what I wanted to read. I did not want a Fodor's Guide, with lists and schedules and the easy enthusiasms of travelese. The available bicycling guides were outdated, inaccurate, superficial, or were written by people who had obviously never visited the routes they described. There was no sense of place in those descriptions, no hint at the character of the land and the people who lived there. They told me the distances between cities and the easiest routes to the major tourist attractions, but left me with no idea whether I would like what I found there.

I suspected that eastern Canada was an excellent place to bicycle, but there was no way to find out except to spend a summer there myself, exploring. My suspicions turned out to be entirely justified. This huge and diverse region contains so many fine bicycling destinations that my job quickly became the enviable one of weeding out the merely fine from the absolutely excellent.

Because I believe that it is better to know a few places well than many places slightly, my intention from the beginning was to select a dozen of the best bicycle tours in the six eastern provinces, then explore them and describe them in intimate detail. Those choices were based on simple prejudices: I like to ride in varied and attractive surroundings, in the kind of country that demands attention, in places where traffic is light and roads are in good condition, and where towns and villages offer more substance than glittery tourist shops, convenience stores, and fast-food restaurants. Even in a region representing considerably less than half of Canada, the 12 tours finally selected cover a lot of ground, from the most eastern points of North America in Newfoundland, to the fishing villages of the Fundy coast, to the pastoral farmlands of Prince Edward Island and French-speaking Québec, to the remote and lovely Lake Superior shoreline. No two trips are alike; each, in fact, is so different from the others it is easy to imagine they are set on separate continents rather than in separate provinces of the same nation. They vary topographically and aesthetically, and demand widely varied bicycling expertise. To use a phrase that might have come right out of the pages of Fodor's, there should be something here for everyone.

Canada, with its area of more than 9.9 million square kilometers (3.8 million square miles), is the second-largest nation on earth, smaller only than the Soviet Union, and contains a sizable percentage of the last wild and unexplored country in the northern hemisphere. It is the fact of those many thousands of square kilometers of wilderness that defines the character of Canada and impresses it on the minds of visitors. All that wild country to the north is apparent even in its cities, and Canada's cities are among the busiest and most sophisticated on the continent. The wilderness clears the air and outlines the boundaries. It gives perspective to the entire land.

Like the United States, Canada has long been a melting pot of races, religions, and nationalities. Its native people have blended in the last four centuries with its immigrants to create a rich and varied society. The residents of any city or village might be descended from an amazing variety of people: Micmac Indians, Basque fishermen, French fur traders, British colonists, American Loyalists, German mercenaries, Irish farmers, Portuguese fishermen, African slaves who escaped the American South and were smuggled north in search of sanctuary.

The result is a diversity of cultures, traditions, and language unique in the world.

Such qualities give Canada an exotic, foreign air far out of proportion to its distance from the United States, and help make it an outstanding choice for a bicycle vacation. A recent poll of *Bicycling* magazine readers identified it as by far their most popular foreign destination. Certainly, part of the appeal is its proximity to the U.S. border: no other country is so easy to visit or so near the population centers of the eastern seaboard. But just as significant, it's a place where a bicyclist is made to feel welcome. At least 8.2 million Canadians bicycle, according to the Canadian Cycling Association, and even those who don't participate in the sport seem to appreciate it far more than their neighbors to the south. Except in the largest cities, the pace of daily life is slower, more sympathetic to bicycles than automobiles. Motorists, as a rule, are considerate. Some will wave as they pass. Such a friendly, relaxed atmosphere, placed among some of the most spectacular scenery in North America, makes for world-class recreational biking.

It's enough to make a travel writer sing.

Using This Book

Ideally, this book should be used both as a starting point for planning a trip and as a travel guide while on it. My hope is that it will be read first in its entirety, at leisure, in the comfort of an easy chair at home, and used to decide which trip or trips are most suitable for individual purposes. Length and difficulty are only the most obvious factors to be considered before embarking on any trip. More subtle considerations such as availability of services, road conditions, the nature of the terrain, and wind and weather conditions can make the difference between a fully enjoyable and a fairly enjoyable bicycle vacation.

I hope also this guide is used on the road and that it becomes dog-eared, dirty, and scribbled with notes. I prefer to see it stored in panniers than bookshelves, and to know it was read by the light of campfires as often as by the light of floor lamps.

The book presents twelve chapters of tours—two chapters for each of the six eastern provinces. Every chapter commences with a capsule summary listing the beginning and end of the trip, the roads it travels, what provisions for lodging a rider can expect to find, the length of the trip, and some idea of its difficulty. Preceding the first chapter for every province is an introduction to that province, covering historical, cultural, and geographical features that I think are useful and entertaining, and including such practical considerations as weather, language difficulties, traffic laws, as well as sources of additional information. The route descriptions themselves are presented in logical sequence, commencing at the suggested beginning of a trip and proceeding to the end, with side trips, observations, and digressions noted along the way.

I don't pretend to have visited every bed-and-breakfast inn, hotel, restaurant, or café along every route. Where I stopped, and was impressed, I say so and don't hesitate to give some recommendations for memorable meals and lodging. More often services are mentioned in general terms and are supplemented with the telephone numbers (often toll-free) of each province's tourist bureaus. Recommendations and even reservations are available from any of those numbers.

Likewise, I have avoided listing prices for individual services unless, as in the case of ferry transportation, it seems important to the budgeting and planning of a trip, or, as in the case of fresh cod from Newfoundland's wharfs, when it is almost too good to be true. Those prices listed were the latest available in autumn 1991, and unless otherwise noted are in U.S. dollars. In general, prices for lodging and restaurant meals are roughly equivalent to those in the United States.

As mentioned in "Measurements" (page ix), distances in this guide are measured in kilometers and meters. For an approximate conversion to miles, multiply the number of kilometers by 6/10. To convert meters to feet, multiply the number of feet by 3.3. A conversion table containing approximate conversions of other units of measurement that you will find in this book appears on page ix.

Each trip is divided into segments of about 80 kilometers, organized so that whenever possible a segment begins and ends at a town or park where campgrounds and other possibilities for lodging are available. Eighty kilometers per day is not a grueling schedule for a reasonably well-conditioned bicyclist under most circumstances, although there are 80-kilometer sections of the routes that are extremely difficult to complete in one day. Those sections are noted in the text.

About the Maps

In most cases the maps include only those roads relevant to the trip described. On Prince Edward Island, for instance, where a great number of roads are packed into a relatively small area, most of the least important and least useful of them have been left off to keep the maps as uncluttered as possible and still be useful. They work best as general references to keep oriented while reading the text and should be supplemented, on the road at least, with the excellent provincial road maps available free at tourist information centers throughout the provinces.

Crossing the Border

The boundary between the United States and Canada is one of the easiest to cross in the world. In most cases it involves little more than a brief interview with a border official who asks where you're from, where you're going, how long you're planning to stay, and whether you are carrying restricted items like alcohol, tobacco, or firearms.

It is not necessary for U.S. citizens to carry visas or passports to enter Canada, but identification is required. Customs officials recommend a birth certificate, voters registration, or passport, and say that a driver's license may be refused as inadequate. Also, anyone under 18 traveling unaccompanied by an adult must have written permission of a parent or guardian to cross the border. Citizens of other countries who are residents of the United States must bring their alien registration card to gain entry to Canada. Duty is charged on certain items, most notably cigarettes, tobacco, and alcoholic beverages. Visitors to Canada are permitted to bring up to 200 cigarettes, 2 pounds of tobacco, 40 ounces of alcoholic beverages (for those 19 years of age or older), and a 2-day supply of food (this regulation appears to be lightly enforced). Taxes will be charged on supplies of items in excess of those amounts.

Money Matters

Prices in Canada vary a great deal, but certain items are heavily taxed and are therefore quite expensive. A 7 percent federal goods and services tax, implemented in January 1991, applies to virtually all purchases in Canada. In some cases, however, that tax replaced a "hidden" manufacturing tax of 13 percent and has actually reduced prices. It's worth noting that foreign visitors are eligible for a rebate of the goods and services tax on accommodations and many consumer products. Information and rebate forms are available at most federal offices, including border points of entry.

Some products are considerably more expensive in Canada than in the United States. Photographic film, for example, is sometimes triple the price in Canada. At a time when gasoline could be purchased in the United States for $1.10 per gallon, it cost an average of 65.9 cents per liter (about $2.50 per gallon) in Canada, making it prudent for motorists to enter the country with a full tank. Bicycle accessories and parts of all kinds are almost always more expensive in Canada. Those prices are softened somewhat for U.S. residents by an exchange rate that favors the U.S. dollar (as of this writing) by about fifteen percent.

If you never leave home without traveler's checks, you might consider using those issued by Canadian banks. They're available from banks and travel agencies in the United States, but sometimes require special order, so allow several days for delivery. In spite of all company claims to the contrary, cashing U.S. traveler's checks can be a chore. Banks in Canada are generally open only from 10:00 A.M. to 3:00 P.M., Monday through Friday, and typically charge a service fee of $2 or $3 for cashing checks (the fee is the same whether you cash $10 worth or $1,000 worth). In remote areas and small communities, clerks sometimes have difficulty calculating the exchange rate, will sometimes offer a lower rate than in larger cities, or will simply refuse U.S. checks. For those reasons, it's also wise to carry Canadian rather than foreign currency. I met people in Newfoundland who had never seen a U.S. one-dollar bill; others were reluctant to accept U.S. currency because it meant a trip to the bank before it could be converted to usable funds. It's a good idea, nonetheless, to bring at least some U.S. currency, since many motels and restaurants, as a promotion to attract U.S. tourists, advertise exchange rates as much as 5 or 10 percent more favorable than the official rate.

While I highly recommend eating out in Canadian restaurants, be prepared to see a 10 percent food tax added to your bill. Otherwise, dining prices throughout most of eastern Canada are comparable to those in the United States.

VISA, MASTERCARD, AMERICAN EXPRESS, and all other major credit cards are recognized and accepted in Canada. Don't worry about being charged U.S. dollars for an item or service purchased in Canada: the correct exchange rate (which varies by slight amounts every day) will be adjusted on your monthly credit-card statement.

Transportation

Major airlines link most Canadian cities with the United States, and will accommodate cyclists and their equipment if certain precautions are taken. Most consider a bicycle as freight, not luggage, and charge a fee accordingly. Air Canada, for instance, charges a fee of $25 one-way to transport a bike. The airline will not accept it at all, however, unless the handles are loosened and turned sideways to take up less space, the pedals are removed, and the bike is packed in a sturdy container or in one of the bike bags Air Canada can provide for $3. Veterans of air transport say shipping damage can be avoided only by packing your bike carefully in a durable carrier—the bags provided by the airline might reduce scratches but do little to protect fragile components when a heavy suitcase is thrown on top of them. Good cases aren't cheap, however. Hardshell models available from Bike Kase, Bike Tote, Bike Travelier, Pedal Pack, and Peloton Industries retail for $300 to $495. Less durable fabric bags with platform bottoms are available from Athlon, BikPro, North Sails, Performance Bicycle Shop, Rhode Gear, and Tri Tech Sports and cost from $170 to $375.

Canada's primary passenger railroad, VIA Rail, offers an interesting alternative for cross-country and interprovincial travel, and an alternative way to enter the country from the United States. VIA Rail connects with Amtrak lines from New York and Washington to Niagara Falls and Montreal, and from Chicago and Detroit to Windsor. Bicycles are treated as baggage but will only be accepted for transport if the train is equipped with a baggage car (most are), and then only if the bike is dismantled and boxed in the same manner as required by airlines. Information about reservations, fares, and schedules is available through travel agents or by calling these toll-free numbers: 1-800-665-0200 (from the western United States), 1-800-387-1144 (from the midwestern United States), 1-800-561-3949 (from the southern and eastern United States), and 1-800-361-3677 (from New York, Connecticut, and Rhode Island).

Every car- and passenger-ferry operating in the Maritimes is willing to accommodate bicycles and bicyclists. Good thing, because ferry transport is a fact of life in eastern Canada. Information about fares, regulations, and reservations is provided in the introductions to the individual provinces.

Road Construction

Road construction in Canada is another unavoidable fact of life. Unlike the United States, where enormous sections of highway are often torn up in one sustained burst, Canada does its roadwork in a more piecemeal fashion. It is unusual to find sections of more than 8 or 16 kilometers under construction at one time. More often, much smaller segments are in the process of being resurfaced, graded, widened, or rerouted. When a section of Canadian road is torn up, it is *really* torn up. The roadbed is often cobbled with stones far too rough for skinny-tired bicycles, and there is often no real order to the temporary lanes, resulting in an anything-goes attitude among drivers. Sometimes a flag-person guides traffic, but cars often simply wind their way along wherever they can. It's impossible to guess where roadwork will occur next, but I've tried whenever possible to note roads and sections of roads that are in particularly bad condition. It's likely those sections will be under construction in the near future. On the other hand, highways noted as recently resurfaced or otherwise in good condition are not likely to be bothered for a number of years.

Campgrounds

All six of the easternmost Canadian provinces are well equipped with a variety of national, provincial, and private campgrounds. Information about available services, seasons of operation, and other features of those parks is included in the text. Because camping fees are so variable, I have not listed them in the text. In general, expect overnight fees for unserviced campsites (usually equipped with a fire pit or grill and picnic table) in national parks to range from $8.50 to $12.50 per night. Provincial park fees are usually less, ranging from $6.00 to $10.50. Private campgrounds, which are most often oriented toward recreational vehicles in need of electric hookups, can charge a tent-camper as little as $5 and as much as $18 per night, and will sometimes charge additional fees for the use of hot showers.

Seasonal Considerations

The climate of the eastern provinces is tempered considerably by the Atlantic Ocean, Gulf of St. Lawrence, Bay of Fundy, and Great Lakes, which cool coastal regions in the summer and warm them in the winter. Inland reaches, however, especially in Newfoundland, Québec, and Ontario, are much colder in winter and much warmer in summer. Bicycling season lasts from May through October, but you can expect to find decent weather in April and early November some years. Keep in mind that black flies and mosquitoes can be a nuisance, especially in May and June; copious supplies of repellent are advised.

Although summer comes to much of eastern Canada by late May, the tourist season lags considerably, making May and June excellent times to tour uncrowded roads. July and August will find the provinces more crowded, with roads busier and some campgrounds frequently filled. By many standards, however, even the busiest season is not particularly busy. September might be the finest month of all for a bicycle tour in most areas. Tourists have returned home, leaving the roads empty except for local traffic; the weather is mild and pleasant; and autumn colors will be approaching their peak brilliance by the end of the month.

Rain is unavoidable in eastern Canada during the

spring and summer. While total amounts can't compare to far western Canada or the Pacific Northwest of the United States, it's wise to be prepared for several days of rain per week. When planning an itinerary, allow a little extra time for rain-outs. As boring as it is to spend a day trapped inside a tent, it's still (usually) preferable to bicycling in a downpour.

Languages

In Canada's larger cities it is possible to hear a great variety of languages being spoken, but throughout most of the eastern provinces English and French predominate. French is the official language of Québec and is so deeply rooted in the culture that it is unusual to hear English spoken or to see English printed on road signs, advertising, or newspapers. Pockets of French-speaking Canadians are found as well in all the other eastern provinces, especially in northern and western New Brunswick and along the west coast of Cape Breton Island in Nova Scotia. English-speaking travelers should refer to the introduction of the Québec chapters for more information about communicating in French Canada.

What to Bring

· BICYCLES ·

If you're traveling by automobile and have the carrier space for both mountain bikes and road bikes, by all means bring both. Mountain bikes are great for city travel and for the innumerable short side trips possible along the tours in this guide. Equipped with slick tires to reduce road friction, and perhaps an aerodynamic handlebar to put a rider into a more streamlined riding position, a mountain bike can be converted into a passable touring bike. But only passable. If you plan to ride primarily on paved roads, you will be glad for the extra performance, lighter weight, and higher speed of a touring bike designed for road use. In spite of claims by bike manufacturers, there is as yet no true all-purpose bike. "Crossover" or "hybrid" models, though useful for city transportation or short jaunts to the grocery store, are neither good off-road bikes nor good road-touring bikes.

Deciding which road bike best suits your needs may not be easy. There are three basic categories of road bikes: racing, touring, and sport/touring. Racing models are excellent for triathlons and other competitions, and for all-around fitness and training, but are usually a poor choice on an extended tour, especially if you need to load them with gear. They are typically lighter than touring models, have shorter wheelbases and steeper frame angles, and have very stiff frames that are efficient at transmitting muscle energy into speed but result in a relatively rough ride.

A touring bike, ideally, should combine the speed, efficiency, and high performance of a racing bike with the durability and strength of a pack mule. The longer wheelbase and relaxed frame angles result in a less responsive but far more stable ride on a bike designed for hauling big loads long distances. Braze-ons allow a variety of choices of racks and panniers. Saddles are often heavily padded with foam or gel and are more comfortable than the thin leather pads of racing bike saddles.

Sport/touring bikes combine some of the features of racing and touring models, and are generally lower priced than both. Their frames are stiffer than those of touring bikes, but more relaxed than racing bikes, making them an excellent choice for occasional racers and weekend riders who need to carry moderate loads for touring and light camping. Many manufacturers offer triple cranks and 21-speeds, offering low gears that you'll appreciate in hilly terrain.

If you prefer not to bother transporting your own bicycles, rentals are often available in the most popular tourist regions of eastern Canada. It's encouraging to note that more and more cycle shops are offering quality road and all-terrain bikes (ATBs) for rental. McQueen's Bike Shop in Charlottetown on Prince Edward Island is a case in point. It offers a variety of touring bikes and ATBs for $55 to $70 per week and can recommend some excellent tours in the region. For lists of other shops offering rentals, contact the regional tourist offices.

· BIKE PARTS AND TOOLS ·

Because many of the tours described in this book are in fairly remote country, it is essential to be equipped with a basic inventory of spare parts and the tools necessary to install them. Bicycle shops can be found in almost every sizable city but are rare in small communities. To prevent a minor breakdown from becoming a major hassle, you might want to equip an under-saddle wedge pack with the following items: pliers, crescent wrench, Allen wrenches, spoke wrench, brake wrench, tire levers, standard and Phillips screwdrivers, replacement tube and tube patch kit, lubricant, and towelettes for cleanup. On the road, be sure also to include a frame pump.

In the more remote sections of eastern Canada spare parts can be difficult to find (and expensive if you can find them), so it is important to bring along such basic replacement parts as spokes, tire tubes, foldable tires (such as the lightweight, Kevlar-bead models), extra chain links, brake shoes, and a length of brake cable.

· CLOTHING AND ACCESSORIES ·

Cycling clothes are not designed simply to make a fashion statement. The point of tight-fitting jerseys and Lycra shorts with chamois seat pads is to keep a cyclist comfortable and aerodynamic. A loose, flapping shirt can slow you considerably, and 6 hours of pedaling in bluejeans can produce chaffing in the crotch and other related horrors.

It makes excellent sense to spend some time shopping for adequate clothing. Most well-equipped bike shops have changing rooms, and knowledgeable sales people will help make sure you get the clothing you need in sizes that fit. They can also guide you through the dizzying world of modern fabrics, defining and listing the advantages of polypropylene, Lycra, Gore-Tex, Coolmax, Thermax, Hydrofil, Capilene, and Versatech. Good cycling clothes are light, comfortable (they stretch when you stretch, and in the right places), and durable, and will wick perspiration away from your body to help keep you cool and dry.

It's important to bring along clothing suitable for all weather conditions. Cycling shorts and a jersey will suffice for most summer days, but a pair of full-length tights, a cotton undershirt, and a light windbreaker for early mornings or sudden cold snaps will be welcome. Some experienced cycle-tourists in Canada insist you should plan on one day of rain for every 2 days of sun. That seems pessimistic but gets the point across. Carry a good lightweight rain jacket made from Gore-Tex, Thintech, or any of the other modern miracle fabrics that are lightweight and allow heat and perspiration to escape while repelling rain. The jacket should be designed for bicycling, so that it covers buttocks while you're bent over on a bike, is generously ventilated, and won't bunch under the arms or in the shoulders. Full-length rain pants designed to be worn over shorts or tights are optional, but can be invaluable if the rain occurs in cool weather. A handy item is a pair of lightweight neoprene shoe covers to keep feet and shoes dry in the rain.

Footwear is always an important consideration, whether on the road or lounging around a campsite. Stiff-soled cycling shoes with pedal guides on the soles, plenty of ventilation, and short laces that won't get caught in chains and gears are more comfortable on long trips than ordinary sport shoes and help improve pedaling efficiency. A pair of tennis shoes are fine for lounging in camp or strolling around town, but you might consider packing a pair of light hiking boots if you plan to do even semiserious exploring on foot.

Padded cycling gloves reduce the pressure on the ulnar nerve in the palm and are nearly a necessity for a long trip.

Sunglasses are important not only for comfort but safety, and will protect your eyes from glare, wind, dust, and sand. Any number of excellent glasses are available; check the displays at bike shops or in mail-order catalogs.

A pair of lightweight (even folding) binoculars can be useful, especially along coastal regions where whales and seals are likely to be seen basking offshore, or in remote areas where moose, reindeer, and other notable wildlife can often be spotted. If you have the space to carry them, regional field guides to wildlife and flora can add to your enjoyment in unfamiliar country.

A lock of some sort, unfortunately, is as necessary in Canada as it is elsewhere in the world. Check out the vast variety of locks available at any cycle shop, and choose one that is tough yet lightweight and compact.

· CAMPING EQUIPMENT ·

Because little grievances like sticky zippers and ill-fitting tent poles tend to become magnified on extended trips, it's always a good idea to use the best equipment you can afford. The longer the bike tour and the more nights spent in a sleeping bag and tent, the truer that becomes. Good equipment is quick and enjoyable to set up, lasts many years, and weighs less than budget gear. Weight is a major consideration. A few ounces here and there can add up to a surprising difference on a fully loaded bike, a difference that becomes immediately noticeable on the first long ascent.

I like the romance of sleeping under an open sky and the simplicity of not having to bother with a tent, yet experience has made me admit finally that it's no fun to bed down in the open when sleep is interrupted (as it so often is) by insects, wind, rain, sleet, and snow. The tents designed in the last decade or so have made it so easy to carry and erect a shelter that there's little reason not to take one along, even if you're determined to use it only in emergencies. A single person has the choice of any number of lightweight designs. Look for one that weighs about 3 pounds, is easy to set up, folds down (poles included) into a compact package, has plenty of ventilation using no-see-um netting, and has a rain fly and waterproof floor. A model large enough to sleep two will of course weigh a bit more and take up more space in a pannier. Excellent, high quality tents cost from $165 to $225 (or much more). Keep in mind that with camping equipment—maybe even more than most other things—you get what you pay for. Still, if you don't plan to use a tent frequently, and simply want a decent, durable model light enough for bike touring, manufacturers like Peak and Eureka! offer one- and two-person lightweights that retail for $100 to $130.

Sleeping bags are probably the source of more arguments than any other item of camping equipment. Traditionalists argue for goose down and list such indisputable advantages as light weight, superior insulation, extended loft life ("loft" means fluffiness), and the ability to be stuffed into a package the size of a hamburger bun (well, almost). Powerful arguments. Still, recent improvements in fillers like Quallofil, Hollofil, and PolarGuard have created a new breed of synthetic bags that are nearly as light as down, nearly as warm, and stuff into tote bags nearly as small, for notably less price. Plus—and this is the argument that makes me lean toward synthetics on long trips in rain-prone regions—they can be dried quickly and easily, whereas wet goose down wants to stay wet forever. Whatever your choice of materials, for a summer trip in eastern Canada, bring a "three-season" bag rated for temperatures down to about 20 degrees. The temperature probably won't drop that low after April and before November, but some communities in the region have reported frost every month of the year. Be prepared, as the Boy Scouts say; you can always leave your bag unzipped when it's balmy outside.

In addition to a good bag, you'll probably want some kind of sleeping pad. Cheap inflatable air mattresses are a nuisance—noisy to sleep on, slow to inflate, and almost certain to leak. More substantial pads of closed-cell foam or deluxe pads, like the self-inflating Therm-a-Rest (open the air valve when it's unrolled, and the compressed foam expands, drawing air inside; close the valve to keep the air trapped), are bulkier but make up for it by putting a durable, comfortable, waterproof, insulated barrier between you and the cold, cruel world.

A ground cloth of nylon or plastic to place under your tent floor will extend the life of your tent. It can also be used for a makeshift shelter to cover your bike and gear in a sudden rainstorm.

Cooking kits should be light but durable, and all the components should nest together into a compact, non-rattling package.

Cooking over an open fire might be the ultimate outdoor culinary technique—a fine dusting of maple ash, after all, can be tasty as fresh-ground pepper—but during midsummer forest-fire alerts, and in places like New-foundland's Avalon Peninsula where firewood is just a dream on the horizon, a camping stove becomes a virtual necessity. Like backpackers, bicycle tourists have a need for lightweight, compact stoves that work under all weather conditions and are safe enough to use inside a tent during a thunderstorm. There are many stoves to choose from, ranging from one-burner models as delicate as Swiss watches, to powerful two-burners that can boil a quart of water in 3 minutes. Fuel should be a major consideration. Butane models are quick to light and are convenient, but replacement cartridges can be difficult to find in small communities. White gas is more commonly available, and extra fuel can be easily stored in tight-lidded plastic bottles in your panniers. The best (and most expensive) stoves, the so-called multifuels, burn practically any flammable liquid. Good outfitting shops should have a broad selection of stoves to choose from. Expect to pay $40 and up.

· PANNIERS AND PACKS ·

Camping gear always varies with individual needs and preferences, but regardless of the type or amount of equipment, a sound and efficient method of carrying it on a bicycle is critical to the success of a lengthy tour. Panniers are the equivalent of a hiker's backpack, and should be selected with an equal amount of care. Shop for a system of panniers and racks that is sturdy, light-weight, and accessible, with enough pockets and zippers so you don't have to empty everything just to get at the map you left on the bottom, and that will distribute the weight of your camping equipment evenly around the bicycle. A pair of rear panniers can carry the bulk of the gear, and should be loaded carefully to keep weight as even and low to the ground as possible. A handlebar pack is convenient for carrying rain gear, cameras, and personal items, but should not be overloaded or it will affect the front stability of your bike. A small saddle wedge attached beneath your seat—expandable models are available that can hold an amazing volume of stuff—and a fanny pack worn around your waist can also be useful for carrying personal items such as wallets, keys, sunscreen, and insect repellent.

For light touring, such as inn-to-inn trips, a handle-bar pack is probably sufficient for carrying a few personal items, some snack foods, and a change of clothes. I like the Cannondale models, with their quick release system so you can carry the bag with you into a restaurant or store.

· FOOD AND BEVERAGES ·

Finding enough drinking water should seldom be a prob-lem in eastern Canada, not because of the abundance of lakes and rivers, but because the tours described in these pages pass through so many villages and past so many campgrounds, picnic areas, stores, restaurants, and other places where a bicyclist can traditionally hope to find a spigot or pump that gushes safe water. Unfortunately, in

Canada as elsewhere in North America (and the world, for that matter), the water in lakes, rivers, and streams may well be home to parasites like *Giardia lamblia*. For those days when safe drinking water might be in short supply, it's imperative that lake and river water be boiled or treated chemically before consumption. Bringing water to a rollicking boil for 5 minutes or more is the simplest way to kill *Giardia* and most pathogens, but it can be a time-consuming job to build a fire, heat the water to boiling, then wait for it to cool. A little organization helps: if you suspect finding enough water will be a problem, boil a few quarts in the evening and before you go to sleep cover the container to keep insects and dirt out; by morning it will be cool and sediments will have settled to the bottom.

If you feel you absolutely must carry a system for purifying water, there are a number of alternatives. The various chemical treatments (most use iodine in liquid, crystal, or tablet forms) do the same job as boiling in much less time, but they usually leave the water tasting like leftover chemical soup. Portable filtration systems are expensive ($40 to $175—available at most outfitting shops), but they quickly and efficiently filter bacteria, tapeworms, flukes, and *Giardia* cysts, and can treat water at rates of one pint per minute, or faster.

On the road, unless your trip is a very short one, you'll need to carry at least one and preferably two water bottles. Cages mounted on braze-ons on your bike frame are the most common way to carry the bottles, although some riders choose to tuck them into panniers or carry them on harnesses around their backs.

For variety and as a source of on-the-road carbohydrates, a supply of fruit juice (some experts recommend you dilute it 1:3 with water) will be welcome. If you're riding long days in difficult terrain, energy drinks like Gatorade not only prevent dehydration but help restore depleted stocks of glycogen, where carbohydrates are stored.

A cache of nutritious, high-carbohydrate snack foods

can help get you through those sometimes unbearably long stretches between meals. Some good choices that fit easily in pockets and can be eaten while you ride include energy bars, oatmeal cookies, fig bars, bananas, dried fruits, and muffins.

Freeze-dried and other specialty foods are almost certain to be more expensive the farther you get from major population centers and will be impossible to find in most of the lightly inhabited rural areas described in this book. Bring a good stock of such foods with you, especially if you plan to be on the road for extended periods and need the lightweight, space-saving advantages of freeze-dried meals. Canadian supermarkets often stock dried fruits, soups, and other staples, but their availability varies from region to region.

Safety

Many Canadian cyclists seem less concerned about headgear than riders in the United States, but this is definitely not a time to apply the adage "when in Rome . . ." Take a helmet; wear it.

The choice of helmets is an individual one and will depend on your priorities. Hardshell models are made of ABS or other high-impact plastic, and while generally the sturdiest helmets, they usually weigh 13 ounces or more— too heavy, according to many bicyclists. Foam-only helmets are currently the most popular designs, partly in reaction to the weight problem of hardshells. They're usually molded from expanded polystyrene (EPS), the same foam plastic used in beer coolers, and covered with a netting of Lycra for style and to help hold the foam together in an accident. Thinshell (also known as microshell) models are rapidly gaining favor with many riders; they use an EPS body coated with a thin, high-impact plastic shell that gives additional security without adding much weight. Although the lightweight and comfortable foam-only models are currently the most popular helmets, many riders are taking a careful look at plastic-coated designs. Unprotected foam is easily dirtied and punctured, and may also be less safe in an accident than hardshells or thinshells. A recent study at Wayne State University in Detroit concluded that foam-only helmets grip the pavement during a fall and can cause serious neck injuries.

Another factor to take into account is ventilation. During hot weather an inadequately ventilated helmet can cause even the most safety-minded rider to stash it in a sidepack. Vent size and placement vary considerably from manufacturer to manufacturer. One of the best ways to compare helmets is to refer to *Bicycling* magazine's annual "Helmet Buyer's Guide," published in the May issue. Or ask other riders how they like their helmets, and whether they find them cool in hot weather.

Most of the best-known manufacturers—including Bell, Etto, Giro, Matrix, Paramount, Pro-Tec, Rhode Gear, Specialized, and Vetta—offer both thinshell and foam-only helmets that are comfortable and cool in hot weather. Price ranges from $35 to $90, with an average of about $50 for a safe helmet that looks good and wears well.

Safety on the road depends on much more than a good helmet. It's essential to adopt defensive, alert bicycling habits. Always ride on the far right side of a road or street; obey the same traffic laws as motorists; signal your intentions but don't count on hand signals to magically open lanes. Mirrors—attached to a helmet or to handlebars—can take some of the anxiety out of riding along busy roads, and help give fair warning of approaching semitrucks and erratic drivers. Reflectors can be installed on panniers and seat packs to increase your visibility at dusk and in darkness. Flags, though they're clumsy and create drag, are not a bad idea in heavy traffic.

A compact, basic first-aid kit should be an essential part of any bicycle tourist's gear. Gauze, adhesive tape, and antiseptic ointment are sufficient to treat minor cuts and the road burn that's an inevitable result of most bicycle accidents. It's a good idea to include aspirin, Tylenol, or other nonprescription pain relievers. Everything should fit easily in a handlebar pack or saddle wedge, so it remains accessible.

Medical Care and Emergencies

Hospital and ambulance service is available throughout the eastern provinces, and is always available to nonresident visitors. If you are not a Canadian citizen, be sure to find out if your health insurance policy is valid in foreign countries; not all are. If you are on special medication, bring an adequate supply as well as prescription information in case of the need for refills. For emergency telephone assistance, dial "0" ("911" in major cities).

Conditioning

Getting in shape for a bicycle vacation can be as simple or as complicated as you want it to be. For casual cyclists, the good news is that it isn't necessary to follow the strict training regimen of a racer to prepare for a 2-week bicycle vacation. If you schedule only short distances the first few days, and are prepared for some sore muscles in the mornings, by the end of the trip you can be feeling fit and trim and ready for 160-kilometer days. Still, it is a good idea to spend some time on a bike before your trip, even if it's only commuting to work or taking an hour every evening to ride around the neighborhood. Such light training will go a long way to prepare your buttocks, hands, and leg muscles for the more difficult work ahead.

In addition to bicycling itself, getting in shape involves eating sensibly. Serious cyclists in training try to maintain a diet of about 60–65 percent carbohydrates (breads, potatoes, pasta, fruit, etc.), 20–25 percent fat (dressings, sauces, nuts, dairy products, etc.), and 15 percent protein. While such a strict diet isn't a prerequisite to a bicycle tour, it can increase endurance and make the trip more enjoyable. Luckily, a bicyclist's diet doesn't include tiny portions. It's recommended, for instance, that you load up on carbohydrates for a few days before the beginning of a trip, eating large, guilt-free meals of Chinese food, pasta, bread, potatoes, and other high-carbohydrate, low-fat foods. Carbo-loading builds up stockpiles of glycogen in your muscles, thus increasing your body's ability to store and use carbohydrates.

The best conditioning tip is probably common sense. Get accustomed to riding a bicycle and make sure your equipment and clothing are comfortable. If you're overweight, try to lose a few pounds. If you plan to camp as you go, take a few day-long and weekend tours with your panniers loaded to get accustomed to the ride and to increase your confidence in traffic. Even if you plan a cushy inn-to-inn luxury vacation, it's wise to get accustomed to riding with your bike loaded with full water bottles and a handlebar bag filled with clothing, cameras, and any other gear you plan to carry along.

Package Tours

A number of bicycle-touring companies offer organized tours in eastern Canada, many of them covering ground described in this guide. Typically on such a tour, itineraries are prescheduled and meals and lodging are provided, freeing a cyclist to travel light. Some companies offer bicycles and accessories; others expect you to arrive with your own equipment. In most cases, support vehicles are on hand (often patrolling the route) in case of mechanical breakdown, injury, or fatigue. Lodging is often at bed-and-breakfast inns, and meals are at restaurants specializing in local cuisine. Besides the convenience of having someone else do the planning and organizing, the most attractive feature of such a tour may be social: spending a week or 10 days with a group of people who share a love of bicycling and an appreciation for fine scenery is almost certain to be rewarding.

Among the companies that offer tours in eastern Canada are:

- **Blyth & Company Biking and Walking Trips** (6-day tour of Prince Edward Island); phone 1-800-228-7712 (from the United States), 1-800-387-5603 (from Ontario), 1-800-387-1387 (from elsewhere in Canada).
- **Classic Bicycle Tours and Treks** (1- to 2-week tours of Prince Edward Island, Nova Scotia, and Québec); phone 1-800-777-8090.
- **Covered Bridge Bicycle Tours** (2- and 6-day tours in New Brunswick); phone 506/849-9028.
- **Down East Tours** (various tours in Nova Scotia and Newfoundland); phone 902/765-8923.
- **Freewheeling Bicycle Adventures** (5- to 10-day tours of Nova Scotia); phone 1-800-341-6096 (from the United States) or 1-800-492-0643 (from Maine only).
- **Maine Coast Cyclers** (6-day tours of Prince Edward Island); phone 802/496-4603 before June 1, 207/236-8608 after June 1.
- **New England Bicycle Tours** (6-day tour of Prince Edward Island); phone 1-800-233-2128.
- **Sunset Bicycle Tours** (5-day tour of Prince Edward Island, and 9-day tour of P.E.I. and the Magdalen Islands); phone 902/892-0606.
- **Vermont Bicycle Touring** (9-day tour of Nova Scotia); phone 802/453-4811.
- **Vermont Country Cyclers** (one-week tour of Nova Scotia); phone 802/244-8751.

Phone numbers and addresses of other tour companies are available from the tourism bureaus of the individual provinces and in the advertising sections of magazines such as *Bicycling*, *Outside*, and the Canadian publication *Explore*. Another good source of information is All Adventure Travel, a travel agency in Boulder, Colorado, that specializes in bicycle tours and other adventure trips around the world and acts as a clearinghouse for many individual tour companies. Its catalog, "Biking and Hiking Travel," lists several Canadian tours. Contact this agency at P.O. Box 4307, Boulder, CO 80306; phone 1-800-537-4025 or 303/939-8885.

In general, expect prices for package tours to range from about $750 per person for a 5- to 7-day tour, to $1,500 per person for a 14-day tour (prices include all meals and lodging, but do not include transportation to and from the tour site), often with slightly lower prices for late-season tours in September and October. A deposit of $200 to $400 per person is usually required for reservations. Most companies offer rental bicycles (usually 10- or 12-speed sport/touring models, although some offer only all-terrain bikes) for $75 to $125 for the entire trip and include helmets at no charge.

Further Information

Additional general information about traveling in Canada is available from the individual provinces (phone numbers and addresses are listed in the chapters). A good source of general bicycling information is the Canadian Cycling Association, 1600 James Naismith Drive, Suite 810, Gloucester, Ontario K1B 5N4.

A Brief Glossary of Bicycling Terms

Aero-bar. An extension to the handlebar designed to allow a rider to rest his or her weight on the forearms in a more aerodynamic position.

Braze-on. A threaded nut, welded to a bicycle frame for attaching water cages, racks, and other accessories.

Chainring. The front sprocket on which the chain rides.

Crankset. The assembly that includes the right and left crank arms attached to the pedals, and one or more chainrings.

Derailleur. A device that moves the chain from one sprocket or chainring to another in order to shift gears.

Drafting. Riding immediately behind another bicycle to take advantage of the reduced air resistance.

Granny gear. The lowest gear, used only during the steepest ascents.

Headset. The assembly on a bicycle where the moveable front fork is attached to the frame.

Pannier. A pack or bag designed to be mounted or suspended on a bicycle to carry camping equipment and other gear.

Quick release. A mechanism that fastens a wheel to the frame for quick removal without tools.

Rack. A wire frame mounted to a bicycle and used to support panniers.

Saddle. The seat of a bicycle.

Saddle wedge. A small pack designed to fit beneath a saddle.

Sag wagon. A support vehicle, usually equipped with spare parts, first aid supplies, extra clothing, snack foods, and beverages.

Switchbacks. Zigzagging or hairpin curves on a road, especially on steep hills.

Toeclips. Metal cages attached to pedals to keep the feet from slipping off and to increase pedaling efficiency on the upstroke.

· NOVA SCOTIA ·

In both the geographic and the aesthetic senses, Nova Scotia is in the heart of the Maritime Provinces. Its combined area of 55,491 square kilometers (21,425 square miles) protrudes roughly north to south, bounded by the Atlantic on the east and the Bay of Fundy and Gulf of St. Lawrence on the west, and joined to the mainland at New Brunswick by a 24-kilometer umbilical in the center. It is often said Nova Scotia in outline resembles a lobster, a fanciful image made apt considering that commercial fishing is the primary economic activity of the coastal regions. No portion of Nova Scotia is more than 56 kilometers from ocean, and since the entire ragged coast of 7,400 kilometers is home to rich and diverse quantities of sea life, fishing—for lobsters and other seafood—is central to the concerns of residents and visitors alike. When you visit, in other words, you should plan on eating fish.

The landscape of Nova Scotia proper and Cape Breton Island has three distinct personalities: the coastal fringe with its fishing villages and rugged, rocky coastline;

the wilderness forests of interior regions such as Kejimkujik National Park and Cape Breton Highlands National Park; and rich agricultural lands, particularly those of the Annapolis Valley.

Portions of all three regions are described in chapters 1 and 2, featuring the Annapolis Valley in southern Nova Scotia and the Cabot Trail in northern Cape Breton Island. Altogether, Nova Scotia adds up to one of the most interesting and attractive of Canada's provinces.

Weather

Weather varies dramatically from southern Nova Scotia to the highlands of Cape Breton, and each of the two widely spaced trips described has its own particular weather conditions. In general, however, you can expect moderate climate, tempered by proximity to the Atlantic and the Bay of Fundy. Average daytime summer temperature in the capital city of Halifax is 72 degrees F.

Language

Nova Scotia's population of 874,000 is descended from a variety of cultures, including Micmac Indians, French, English, Irish, German, Scottish, Portuguese, Dutch, Greek, and Asian. English is spoken virtually everywhere, although there are pockets of French-speaking Acadians—most notably on the west shore of the highlands region of Cape Breton.

Traffic Laws

The speed limit on most provincial highways is 80 kilometers per hour. The speed limit in residential and urban districts, unless otherwise posted, is 50 kilometers per hour.

Cycling Laws

Cyclists in Nova Scotia must obey the same traffic laws that apply to motorists and are especially reminded to ride on the right side of roads, signal direction changes, and stop for traffic lights and stop signs.

Miscellaneous

Nova Scotia Tourist Information Centres are a good place to get assistance and information before traveling in the province. They're located on the ferries from Bar Harbor, St. John, and Newfoundland, as well as at twelve Nova Scotia cities, including Amherst (near the New Brunswick border), Annapolis Royal in the Annapolis Valley, Digby (near the ferry service from St. John, New Brunswick), and Port Hastings (just over the causeway into Cape Breton Island).

For More Information

For general information about Nova Scotia, and to take advantage of the province's "Check In" system of guaranteed reservations at campgrounds, motels, hotels, resorts, and inns, use the following toll-free numbers:

From the continental United States: 1-800-341-6096
From Maine: 1-800-492-0643
From Nova Scotia, New Brunswick, P.E.I.: 1-800-565-7105
From Newfoundland and Québec: 1-800-565-7180
From Ontario: 1-800-565-7140 or 1-800-565-7180
From Canada's western provinces: 1-800-565-7166

Or write: Check In, Suite 515, 1800 Argyle Street, Halifax, NS, Canada B3J 3N8.

For ferry information and reservations, contact Marine Atlantic at P.O. Box 250, North Sydney, NS, Canada

B2A 3M3; phone 1-800-341-7981 (from the continental United States, except Maine), 1-800-432-7344 (Maine), 1-800-565-9411 (Ontario and Québec), 1-800-565-9470 (New Brunswick, Nova Scotia, Prince Edward Island), 1-800-563-7701 (Newfoundland and Labrador).

For further information about Cape Breton Highlands National Park, write to Park Superintendent, Ingonish Beach, NS, Canada BOC ILO; or phone 902/285-2691.

1

Annapolis Valley

Begin/End: Annapolis Valley to Wolfville
Road: Hwy. 1, Hwy. 221
Accommodations: Hotels and motels, bed-and-breakfast inns, private campgrounds
Length: 161 kilometers (100.6 miles)
Difficulty: Easy to moderately easy

Even a hardcore fan of remote, mountainous places is likely to fall in love with the Annapolis Valley in southwest Nova Scotia. This is civilized country, a fact I noted with mixed feelings at the beginning of my trip, when I still wished to be alone in spectacular surroundings. Yet, as I rode the quiet, mostly flat roads that run the length of the valley, I found myself becoming more and more enchanted with its small farming communities, its meticulous farmhouses, and its pastoral, long-settled landscape. By the end of the trip I was not missing mountains at all.

The valley of the Annapolis River (which includes the valleys of the Cornwallis, Canard, and Gaspereau rivers) is the most prosperous agricultural region of Nova Scotia, and offers some of the finest, easily paced bicycle touring in the Maritimes. Many of the roads follow the rivers closely, taking the easy course along the valley bottom, resulting in flat or near-flat routes along much of the length of the 128-kilometer Annapolis Valley. Cradled between the low, rounded ridges of North and South Mountains, and only a few kilometers inland from the Bay of Fundy, the valley in places resembles famed agricultural river valleys of Europe. Its location and geography give the region an average of 55 more sunny days per year than the rest of the Maritime Provinces, a feature that contributes to making it the fruit-growing center of Nova Scotia. Small farms and orchards are scattered along the length of the river, alternating with spruce and fir forests and, in the lower valley, tidal marshes that have been drained and diked to convert them into pastures and meadows.

Acadia, the name given by the French to the entire region now known as the Maritime Provinces, was colonized by France beginning in 1605 when Samuel de Champlain helped establish the first permanent settlement at Port Royal on Nova Scotia, along the south shore of the Bay of Fundy. In later decades French settlers spread throughout eastern Canada and settled as far west as Québec and Montreal.

Access to the Annapolis Valley is relatively uncomplicated. At the southwestern end of the province, a 2.5-hour ferry ride from Saint John, New Brunswick, to the Nova Scotia port of Digby puts you within easy cycling distance of the lower valley. Farther south, at the major port of Yarmouth, ferry service from Portland and Bar Harbor, Maine, makes it possible to drive a vehicle from the United States, and either park in Yarmouth and proceed from there on bicycle or drive north to the start of the Annapolis Valley at Digby or Annapolis Royal. The eastern end of the valley, near the cities of Wolfville and Hantsport, is within 80 or 100 kilometers of Halifax and its international airport, and is within easy driving distance of the New Brunswick border.

Although no convenient highway loop is readily ap-

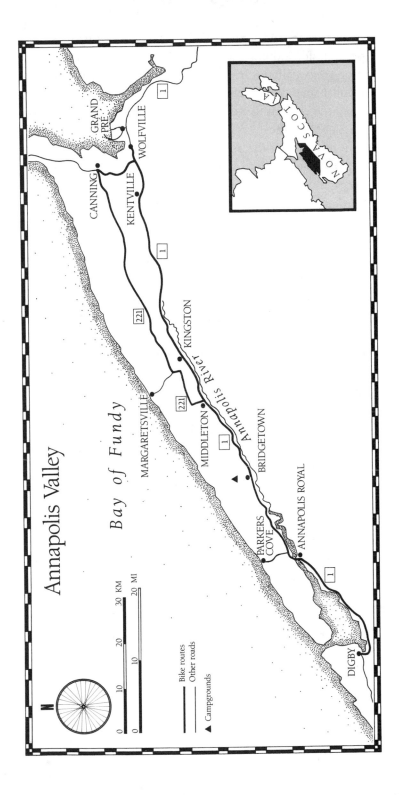

parent in the Annapolis Valley, several alternatives are possible for looping back without riding the same route. Along most of the length of the valley three roads run parallel (but almost never visible to one another), making it simple enough to ride the length of the valley east, say, on Route 1, the Evangeline Trail, then return on Route 201 or even on the region's nearest approximation to a superhighway, Route 101 (two to four lanes of controlled access—the major truck route of the region, and not a particularly pleasant ride for cyclists). But because the roads are within a couple of kilometers of one another for most of their lengths, and because so many connecting roads weave back and forth between them, this chapter describes only a one-way trip on Hwy. 1 and Hwy. 221, which are the most scenic roads in the valley, with a few suggestions for side trips and detours. A return trip to the starting point is possible on Acadian Bus Lines, which has stations in most sizable towns along the route. As with bus service everywhere, however, it is sometimes difficult to arrange transport for a bicycle, especially during busy summer seasons.

It would be logical to follow the Annapolis River downstream through the valley to take advantage of the slight descent, but prevailing west winds make it more practical to travel from west to east, up the valley. Essentially the trip described below begins at Annapolis Royal and ends at the town of Wolfville (pronounced "Woof-fle" by its residents). Numerous accommodations are available in both towns, including many attractive bed-and-breakfast inns, as well as historical and cultural attractions that make the communities fine starting and ending points. Camping is somewhat limited, although there are a fair number of private campgrounds spread out along the route.

DIGBY TO ANNAPOLIS ROYAL—32.4 KILOMETERS (20.1 MILES)

The 2.5-hour ferry crossing from Saint John, New Brunswick, is the simplest way to reach southern Nova Scotia from the mainland. Saint John sprawls across peninsulas

Farms in the Annapolis Valley, Nova Scotia, with the Annapolis River visible in the distance.

at the mouth of the St. John River, and its streets can be confusing. The ferry landing is well designated, fortunately, with traffic signs marked "To Digby." Get reservations as early as you can; I waited until the day before my crossing and nearly didn't get on—only a late cancellation made enough space available. The ferry company asks that reservations be made at least a few days in advance, and that you arrive at least one hour before departure to pay for your ticket (reservations don't require a deposit), but you'd be wise to arrive at least half an hour earlier still. I arrived at the dock at 9:20 for the 10:30 boat and was among the last in line. It amounts to a lot of waiting around: the last automobile on the ferry is also the last off, since vehicles are loaded at one end of the boat and unloaded at the other end.

The ferry is large and very comfortable. Access to motor vehicles is not allowed once the ferry sails, but on board are staterooms (for an additional price) and spacious, heated lounges and a cafeteria. Other amenities include a gift shop, post office machines, and video games. Even with a full load of vehicles, the lounges, decks, and cafeteria are uncrowded. Prices in the cafeteria and lounges are not as high as you might anticipate, considering you're a captive customer. The cafeteria serves a basic breakfast, lunch, and snacks for about the same price charged at most family-style restaurants. Soft drinks, beer, wine, and cocktails are available at a bar and cost about the same as at mainland establishments in Canada. The largest lounge, with comfortable, airline-like seats arranged in rows of three or four (with enough room to stretch out and sleep, as many passengers do), is the most spacious of the rooms and affords a fairly good view over the bow and the sides of the boat. Not that there's much to see. The morning trip is often—if not usually—through the famed pea-soup fogs of Fundy, but during late summer the fogs diminish and whales, seals, and other marine animals are often sighted during the crossing.

The ferry landing on Nova Scotia is about 3 kilometers north of **Digby** at a wharf located safely inside the turbulent Digby Gut—the current-driven channel where the Annapolis Basin empties into the Bay of Fundy. From the wharf to Digby is a mostly flat route along a wide, two-lane road with paved shoulders, about half a meter to a meter wide, lined with a number of bed-and-breakfasts and motels. Digby is a fishing village (best known for its scallops and smoked herring) of 2,500 people, with the usual services and shops downtown—including Robertson's Bikes, a small but highly recommended bicycle repair shop—and a shopping center on the outskirts of the community. A tourist information center downtown can be helpful. Much of the town has a good view of the Annapolis Basin and Digby Gut.

On the southern edge of Digby go east on Hwy. 1, where it is a two-lane highway with no shoulders. The entire length of Hwy. 1 from here is known as the Evangeline Trail, in reference to the epic poem by Henry Wadsworth Longfellow about the 1755 expulsion of the Acadians from Nova Scotia. The route emerges for a short way with busy Hwy. 101, here a divided four-lane with paved shoulders. It is the only expressway in the region and the primary truck route, so expect heavy, fast-moving traffic. After about one kilometer, take the Hwy. 1 exit to Smith's Cove.

Hwy. 1 from here is a two-lane paved road with no shoulders, in fairly good shape (with some cracks and patches—also watch for several difficult railroad crossings). The speed limit through this area of resorts, cottages, and scattered residences is 70 kilometers per hour. The terrain is slightly rolling, the road winding among the low hills and offering clear views of the bay and the extensive mud flats visible at low tide. A few hotels and restaurants specializing in lobster and other seafood are scattered along the way to Smith's Cove.

Within 7 kilometers of Digby the houses spread out and the road begins to climb slightly and wind along the river valley. Just past the town of Smith's Cove (where there are few services), Hwy. 1 merges with four-

lane 101 for another one-kilometer stretch. At the intersection, an interesting side trip south follows the Bear
River upstream 5.6 kilometers over rolling hills to the
town of Bear River. Residents of this picturesque village
nestled among steep, wooded hills call it the Switzerland
of Nova Scotia. Originally a shipbuilding community re-
nowned throughout the Maritimes, it was settled in the
eighteenth century by Loyalists, including a contingent
of Hessian mercenaries who had been hired by the British during the American Revolution. Today the town is
primarily supported by a tourist trade attracted to craft
shops, galleries, and restaurants. The tiny downtown
district crowds a narrow road and bridge over the Bear
River, which varies in depth by as much as 6 meters
depending on the stage of the tide. The town, though
small, is crowded with most services, including a bank,
post office, drugstore, grocery, laundromat, and several
hotels and restaurants. It's home, also, to the largest can-
dle works in the Maritimes, and to a good bakery with
the inviting name Sugar and Spice and All Things Nice
Bakeshop.

Back at Hwy. 1, the merge with 101 crosses the border into Annapolis County and the unofficial beginning
of the Annapolis Valley. Take the Hwy. 1 exit east—the
first exit after crossing the mouth of the Bear River—
toward Annapolis Royal.

This section of the route follows the lower Annapolis River, where it widens to one and a half kilometers
or more in width before entering the Annapolis Basin.
For the next 32 kilometers the river is bordered by diked
marshlands converted to agricultural fields. The road
continues to be two lanes, well surfaced, with no shoulders, and winds through slightly rolling country scattered
with houses and patches of hardwoods. It remains moderately developed with houses and small businesses. As
in many parts of the Maritimes, ice cream shops here are
adorned with signs advertising the usual malts, shakes,
and cones, plus clams and shrimp.

The town of Cornwallis is a Canadian Forces Base

with a large shipyard and wharf. A single grocery store along the highway is the only service available.

Beyond Cornwallis the road continues to be lined with widely spaced houses. The route is fairly hilly, though none of the hills are very steep or long.

Clementsport, with a population of 381, is a small farming and fishing village best known for its exports of clams. The old church of St. Edward (circa 1788) is now a museum and is located on the high hill above town, where there is a fine view of the Annapolis River and Basin. To continue to Annapolis Royal, stay left at the intersection and cross the Moose River on Hwy. 1.

After Clementsport the terrain opens into farmlands and meadows, with frequent, long views of the river. Houses and occasional bed-and-breakfast inns are spaced along the route, through mostly undeveloped country of meadows and thickets of second-growth forest.

A large amusement park and picnic area are located just off the road east of Upper Clements. Beyond that busy commercial cluster, the road passes through large open meadows the remaining 8 kilometers to Annapolis Royal.

ANNAPOLIS ROYAL TO MIDDLETON— 48 KILOMETERS (30 MILES)

The town of **Annapolis Royal** (pop. 738) is one of the loveliest in all the Maritimes. A quaint, picturesque village rich in history, it was established in 1605 and claims (as do a number of towns and cities in eastern Canada) to be the oldest established community in Canada. As you enter the heart of the community, Fort Anne National Historic Park, the oldest such park in Canada, is clearly visible across nicely maintained parklike lawns, and contains the remnants of earthwork fortifications and a gunpowder magazine dating back to 1708; earlier structures on the site were first built by the French in 1643.

Today, the residential center of the town is highlighted by immaculate Victorian houses along deeply shaded, tree-lined streets. Some of the large, historic homes have been converted into what are very likely the most attractive bed-and-breakfast inns in Nova Scotia, and perhaps in all the Maritimes. On Upper George Street, such outstanding inns as the Garrison House Inn, Queen Anne Inn, Hillsdale House, and St. George House are located near the 4-hectare Annapolis Royal Historic Gardens where about one and a half kilometers of footpaths lead through extensive botanical gardens.

In the downtown area and its vicinity are gift and craft shops, live theater, museums, restaurants, a farmer's market, and Mad Hatter Books, a good bookstore with emphasis on titles of regional interest.

Hwy. 8, a major two-lane that exits Annapolis Royal from the south, leads to the wild interior of the province, most notably to Kejimkujik National Park, 48 kilometers away. This 380-square-kilometer park offers excellent hiking and canoeing on a large trail system and a network of lakes connected by portage trails. Cycling is limited to 16 kilometers of road that skirt the eastern edge of the park and the shore of Kejimkujik Lake.

Hwy. 1 in Annapolis Royal leaves the north side of town over a causeway across the Annapolis River. On an island midway across the river is the Annapolis Tidal Generating Station, the largest electric generating plant of its kind in the world. Operated by Nova Scotia Power Corporation, the station generates electricity by using giant turbines turned by water flowing from a reservoir after the tide has receded. Public tours are available.

Just beyond the causeway, Hwy. 1 bears right (east). For an interesting side trip to Port Royal National Historic Park, the reconstructed site of the first French settlement in Canada, take the left fork at the intersection. The 10.5-kilometer ride is on a mostly flat, two-lane road with no shoulders that follows the Annapolis River a short distance, then cuts inland. Interesting houses with more examples of ornate Nova Scotian architecture and elaborate gardens line the way. Just beyond the intersection, the town of Granville Ferry has a pair of interesting bed-and-breakfast inns, the Moorings and Bayberry House, as well as a café and gift, jewelry, and craft shops built in the European style directly to the edge of the street. The countryside beyond the village opens quickly into meadows and farmlands beside the river, with a great view of farms and hills across the valley.

The Port Royal Habitation was settled in 1605 by French fur traders—the first European settlers north of Florida in North America—and was destroyed in 1613 by an expedition of English soldiers from Jamestown, Virginia, bent on eradicating all French settlements on the Atlantic seaboard. Port Royal National Historic Park is a reconstruction of the settlement on its original site, complete with authentic furnishings and equipment, and attended by knowledgeable tour guides dressed in period costumes.

On Hwy. 1 north of Annapolis Royal, the road continues to be two lanes wide, but with paved shoulders about half a meter wide. Traffic is fairly heavy from here to Bridgetown, though the paved shoulder and the relatively slow pace of Nova Scotian drivers help make it an enjoyable ride. Along the entire 22.5-kilometer distance to Bridgetown, Hwy. 1 is lined with scattered houses, small businesses, and occasional light industry. The countryside remains gently rolling and partially wooded. The river narrows above the reservoir at Granville Centre, and winds along the valley floor where it is lined with marshes and diked meadows.

At intervals, numerous roads (both paved and gravel) turn north off Hwy. 1 toward the coast, 8 kilometers away. While most of the paved roads lead to interesting coastal villages, be warned that they get there by crossing the North Mountains, a long range of wooded hills that run east to west between the Bay of Fundy and the Annapolis Valley. Most of the roads involve a continuous climb of about 3 kilometers, and though they offer the opportunity for a wonderfully long, steep descent, it only comes, of course, after a terribly long, steep ascent.

Nonetheless, if traffic on Hwy. 1 is a problem (and it can be, at least during summer and especially on summer weekends), you might consider the alternative of turning north on Parker Mountain Road about one and a half kilometers after the Tidal Generating Station on the Annapolis River, and cycling the difficult and hilly 8 kilometers to **Parkers Cove**. This route is also an attractive alternative to the valley in midsummer when temperatures are usually at least 10 degrees cooler near the water. Parkers Cove is a tiny fishing community, interesting because it is so unpretentious: it is simply what it is, a village entirely dependent on the Bay of Fundy for its livelihood. The only services are a seafood diner and a small grocery store. Although lobsters and other seafood can be purchased directly at the dock in the center of town, it is a village that makes little attempt to lure tourists. That may be because it has no need to. Although it does not appear to be a prosperous community, a retired fisherman who lives in Parkers Cove told me that commercial fishermen of Nova Scotia today can make a very good living off the sea—his sons, he said, pay as much as $50,000 a year in income tax—though it is always a precarious and uncertain occupation. That precariousness showed in his own face, brown as leather and furrowed by years of exposure to the sun and wind. In typical Nova Scotian understatement, speaking in the lilting accent of the Maritimes, he explained that "winters can be fairly rough, depending on the heft of snow we get." Yet, regardless of the difficulty of the seasons, the work goes on, with the fishermen operating within 11 kilometers of shore during the winter, when high winds make it prudent to stay close, but required by law to fish 11 kilometers or farther offshore during the summer to give the inshore fishery a rest. The catch is mostly haddock, scallops, and lobster.

Take the coastal road north from Parkers Cove. It follows the shoreline closely, and between Parkers Cove and Hampton offers good views of the Bay of Fundy.

As a side trip, the route is marginal—interesting but not as spectacular as many other portions of the Nova Scotia coast. Great views of the ocean are possible, but the residences are mostly run-down or tasteless modern ranch homes. Although some old, shake-shingled houses and barns are scattered among the newer ones, many of the most attractive buildings have been deserted and are in decay. None of the villages between Parkers Cove and Hampton offer services.

The shoreline here is rocky but not abrupt; during low tide the rocks are covered with knotwrack, rockweeds, and other seaweeds. The road is fairly flat between the towns, but dips sharply into valleys whenever tributaries empty into the ocean. Traffic is very light. At Hampton, turn south on Hampton Road to Bridgetown, and be prepared for a steep climb back up the North Mountains.

At the crest, on the south side looking over Bridgetown, **Valleyview Provincial Park** is a good place to stop overnight if you're camping. Even if you're not camping, however, stop to see the spectacular view it affords of the Annapolis Valley. There are overviews at both the picnic area and the camping area in the park, with the picnic area offering the broadest view of the valley, a view that extends all the way to the Annapolis Basin.

Descent from the provincial park is quick and steep, and made tricky by several hairpin curves. The road flattens in the valley. A little under 10 kilometers from Hampton, Hampton Road enters the town of Bridgetown.

If you choose to stay on Hwy. 1 and not take the side trip to the coast, the 19.5-kilometer route from Annapolis Royal to Bridgetown is pleasant, the road continuing mostly flat through farmlands and orchards (apples, mostly), with frequent views of the winding Annapolis River, its marshes, and the old dike system that converted salt marshes to pasturage. Small businesses and houses give way gradually to farms and farmhouses. A few minor hills are fairly long but not steep. The traffic, though relatively heavy in summer, is usually moderate because most through traffic and trucks follow nearby Hwy. 101. It's interesting that three major roads (and often four) run parallel to one another in the valley, yet they are almost never within sight of one another. It is especially surprising since the valley is seldom more than 3 to 4 kilometers wide and is not overgrown with extensive woodlands.

Scenery in this portion of the valley is classic: in the mornings fog from the Bay of Fundy sometimes spills over the top of North Mountains; the Annapolis River is visible just to the south of Hwy. 1, hazed in mist, winding lazily through meadows and dense thickets. Farmhouses and outbuildings are set back from the road and surrounded by groves of trees and rolling meadows. Fields of lupines, daisies, and irises are in abundant blossom all summer.

In **Bridgetown** (pop. 1,095), Hwy. 1 passes beneath enormous shade trees and is lined with elaborately decorated Victorian houses, hotels, motels, and restaurants. Other services include such bed-and-breakfast inns as Newcombe Brook Farm, the Coach Stop, and Chesley House, and gift shops, local arts and crafts, banks, groceries, a bakery, and a railway station. For a good lunch or snack, try the James House Tea Room. A public park with picnic tables stretches along the river near the center of town.

Like other towns in the valley, Bridgetown has a distinctly different character from the villages on the coast. It was originally settled because it was the first place on the Annapolis River that could be forded during low tide. Today its quiet residential streets and nicely kept yards and gardens suggest a far more leisurely life-style than the hardscrabble life of fishermen. The valley towns are farming communities and in some ways are reminiscent of prosperous, long-established towns in the cornbelt of the United States. Streets are well maintained and lined with sidewalks shaded by large healthy maples and oaks. Houses are spacious and ornate, with meticulous paint schemes.

East of Bridgetown, Hwy. 1 loses its paved shoulder and becomes busier and less quaint. The remaining 22.5 kilometers to Middleton are over similar flat, slightly rolling country. The river becomes much shallower and narrower, with discernible current now that it is above tidal influence. It winds sharply through the valley and is less often visible from the road. The speed limit along most of the route is 80 kilometers per hour, but drivers are generally patient and tend to give cyclists plenty of room.

Lawrencetown, the home of the Nova Scotia College of Geographic Sciences, has two bed-and-breakfast inns (Marian's and the Wight House), a grocery store, convenience store, tiny regional library, drugstore, hardware store, restaurant, and post office.

MIDDLETON TO WOLFVILLE VIA HWY. 221 — 81 KILOMETERS (50.5 MILES)

Middleton (pop. 1,850) advertises itself as "The Heart of the Valley." It is the service and shopping center for a much larger population in the surrounding rural region, and supports far more businesses than its population alone would warrant. Most services are available, including a hospital, banks, public library, and tourist information center. An interesting museum is housed in the oldest consolidated school in Canada.

From Middleton eastward the Annapolis Valley begins to change in character, becoming more densely populated—at least along Hwy. 1—and crowded with communities that grow progressively larger. The terrain changes as well, becoming hillier, with rolling slopes overgrown with woods and underbrush and fewer of the long vistas that characterized so much of the lower river.

Hwy. 1 out of Middleton continues to be busy and without paved shoulders and is far less pleasant to cycle than in the lower valley. It enters a commercial corridor that is nearly continuous from here on, filling the distances between towns.

A more enjoyable route through the upper valley is found on the quiet rural roads to the north. Leave Hwy. 1 and the Evangeline Trail at the center of Middleton, traveling north on County Road 362 (known as Commercial Street within the town limits) about 3 kilometers to the junction with Spa Springs Road. Turn right here and continue east 8 kilometers, traveling parallel to Hwy. 1, to the intersection with Stronach Mountain Road. Turn left, go about a kilometer and a half, then turn right onto County Road 221. From here Hwy. 221 parallels Hwy. 1 for the remainder of the length of the Annapolis Valley.

A good side trip to the coast is possible on Hwy. 362 to **Margaretsville**. Take the left turn onto 362 off Spa Springs Road and head north into the hills. This may be the easiest crossing of the North Mountains, through shallow passes that avoid any major climbs. The route is continuously hilly, though never very steep, and leads to a gradual, slowly winding descent to the ocean. Margaretsville is a very small, attractive fishing village scattered with well-maintained white seafarers' houses. In town are Periwinkle Seafood Take-Out and a small grocery store, but no other services. From the road are views of stark rock bluffs down the shoreline east of the village. The route to East Margaretsville (and the return loop to Hwy. 221) is along a well-maintained county road with gradual and infrequent hills, and provides good views of the ocean past grassy meadows. Occasional stretches of mature maples create a striking canopy effect over the road.

Whether you stay on Spa Springs Road and 221 or take the short side trip to the coast at Margaretsville, the remainder of the trip to the upper end of the Annapolis Valley is a lovely, relaxed ride on quiet country roads. County Road 221 can be followed east as far as Kingsport, on the shore of Minas Basin, and connects with the easiest routes to Wolfville. The road passes through farmlands and apple orchards, over slightly rolling hills, through a lightly inhabited but prosperous region of agricultural Nova Scotia. The road itself is average in size, without shoulders, but the surface is well maintained and traffic is limited almost exclusively to local residents. Farms are large enough to be scattered, and traffic therefore is very light. This portion of the valley is dominated by meadows and pastures, with forested hills of spruce creeping to their edges from the slopes to the north. The hills appear smokey in morning mist, and it's easy to imagine how remote and untamed this country was before European settlement. Note that where gravel roads meet Hwy. 221 or where farm implements have driven on the road, the surface of the pavement can be scattered with loose gravel, manure, and clods of heavy clay soil.

The small towns along Hwy. 221 have no services other than occasional small grocery stores, many of them family-run country stores of a type too often driven out of business by modern supermarkets and party stores. Most are worth investigating. Although cracker barrels and potbellied stoves are long gone, you can still find unusual if not absolutely off-the-wall items for sale, many of them locally produced. Clerks tend to be friendly and talkative; in fact, some of the most interesting conversations of my own trip occurred across counters worn by generations of forearms. Inevitably the dialogue commenced with inquiries about bicycling and proceeded to the standard questions, "Where are you from?" and "So what do you think of Nova Scotia?" If you need other services, it is a simple matter to turn south on any of the numerous connecting roads that lead to communities strung out along Hwy. 1. Most are only a few kilometers out of the way and offer lodging and restaurants. **Kingston** (pop. 1,586) is typical, with most services (including Andy's Bikes on Main Street) and a shopping mall.

The portion of Hwy. 221 beyond Kingston enters somewhat hillier and slightly more inhabited country. Most of the tiny communities along here are merely gathering centers for the surrounding farms and have no services except an occasional general store. The country itself continues to be delightful, authentic, and unspoiled.

In Centreville, Hwy. 359 leads 5.5 kilometers south to **Kentville**, the largest community in the Annapolis Valley with 4,978 inhabitants. It offers all services, including a public swimming pool at Kentville Memorial Park, a tourist information center, and a hospital. This community and much of the surrounding area were settled by New England Planters who came to the area in the 1760s to claim the land vacated by the expulsion of the Acadians. Kentville is the location for each spring's Annapolis Valley Apple Blossom Festival and is home to some interesting pubs like Kings Arms, which is very British, and Paddy's, which is very Irish.

North of Kentville, Hwy. 221 continues east, through small but increasingly frequent villages to **Canning** (pop. 750), a well-established community settled by English Planters and today notable for bed-and-breakfast inns, like Pilgrim's Rest and Treetops, antique shops, a delightful tea parlor named the Bellhill Tea House, restaurants, and colonial homes. Other services include a bank, hardware store, and grocery.

At Canning you have the choice of proceeding due east for about 5 kilometers to Kingsport and a view of the Minas Basin, turning south on Hwy. 358 to continue to Wolfville, or going north on 358 to a spectacular high bluff known as the Lookoff. Although the road climbing to the top of the Lookoff is difficult—3 kilometers of ascent, much of it extremely steep—the payoff is great, with an unobstructed view of the entire upper Annapolis Valley, the Minas Basin, and the clay bluffs and salt marshes that ring it. The highest tides in the Bay of Fundy occur in the Minas Basin, and even from the Lookoff several miles inland you can see the expansive mud flats around the shore during low tide.

From Canning south on 358, expect to pass through pastures and hayfields into more densely inhabited country, with occasional subdivisions growing up near intersections, and convenience stores replacing the old ma-and-pa general stores of the less developed regions. About 5 kilometers south of Canning, 358 crosses the lower Cornwallis River, and almost a kilometer later joins a very busy Hwy. 1. Go east about 3 kilometers to Wolfville.

This portion of the Evangeline Trail is the busiest in the valley. Be prepared for heavy traffic and nearly continuous commercial development. **Wolfville**, with a population of 3,235, was settled originally in the late eighteenth century by New England Planters, and today is a prosperous, dignified-looking community with tree-lined streets and large Victorian homes. At the center of town is 100-hectare Acadia University, well-known throughout Canada for its fine theater arts program and other curricula. Check out the downtown bookstores (ah, the blessings of university towns), including the oddities and rarities at the Odd Book. Also downtown is Valley Cycle Centre, with bicycle rentals, outfitting, and repairs.

From Wolfville, a very interesting side trip can be taken to **Grand Pré** ("The Great Meadow") on the squat peninsula that juts into the Minas Basin northeast of town. From Wolfville, take Hwy. 1 approximately 5 kilometers east to Grand Pré Road, then travel north about one and a half kilometers to Grand Pré National Historic Park.

The original French settlement of Grand Pré was established around 1675 and by the beginning of the eighteenth century was one of the most prosperous Acadian communities in the Maritimes. By the early 1750s, however, British authorities in Halifax had become concerned that the Acadians posed a threat to British sovereignty and initiated, in October 1755, the infamous expulsion. That year most of the residents of Grand Pré were forcefully driven from their homes and loaded on ships that carried them to New England, Louisiana (where today's "Cajuns" are direct descendants of those early refugees), and other foreign destinations. Families were broken up, and virtually every possession that could not be carried was left behind. In all, over 10,000 Acadians were forced to leave Nova Scotia. Longfellow's sentimental poem *Evangeline*, which tells the story of the separation of two young lovers from Grand Pré, made the town and its unfortunate residents famous throughout the world.

The Grand Pré National Historic Site features large gardens and an impressive stone church. Beyond the historic site are thousands of hectares of rich meadows growing several feet below sea level. A total of 5,200 hectares of salt marshes were drained by the Acadian resi-

The hazards of low tide in the Minas Basin, at the head of the Bay of Fundy.

dents of Grand Pré using an ingenious dike system and converted into rich pastures and croplands.

At the end of Grand Pré Road, 4 kilometers from Hwy. 1, is Evangeline Beach with a public beach and parking area but no camping facilities. The beach is a good place to view the tides and explore the seemingly endless mud flats that stretch across the Minas Basin when the tide is low.

Return trips to Digby through the Annapolis Valley are possible using any number of strategies. For the quickest cycle ride back, take Hwy. 101, a four-lane divided highway most of its length that offers a direct, if not often scenic, trip down the valley to Digby or Yarmouth. Though it is a controlled access expressway, and very busy, bicycle traffic is allowed on its wide paved shoulders.

Another alternative is to take Hwy. 1 a portion of the distance back to Digby, then pick up Hwy. 201 on the south side of the Annapolis Valley. Like 221 on the north side of the river, it is a quiet country road, though less quiet and less attractive than 221.

2

Cabot Trail, Cape Breton Island

Begin/End: Baddeck
Roads: Hwy. 105, Cabot Trail
Length: 296.3 kilometers (184 miles)
Accommodations: Campgrounds, some motels and inns
Difficulty: Moderately difficult to very difficult

Separated only by a narrow strait from mainland Nova Scotia, Cape Breton Island seems to have developed an individual identity far out of proportion to its distance from the rest of Canada. Residents agree proudly, explaining they have always considered themselves Cape Bretoners first, Nova Scotians second, and Canadians third, an attitude that becomes immediately apparent when you cross the Strait of Canso and enter the island.

The island itself is dominated in the interior by sprawling Bras d'Or Lake—a saltwater lake connected by channels to the Atlantic, and large enough to accommodate oceangoing ships—and to the north of the lake by a large peninsula thrust into the Gulf of St. Lawrence. At the end of that peninsula, encompassing some of the most rugged terrain in eastern North America, is Cape Breton Highlands National Park.

The Cabot Trail circles most of the northern peninsula of Cape Breton Island and Cape Breton Highlands National Park, and was named for the explorer John Cabot, who first saw Cape Breton Island in 1497. The route around the national park has irresistible appeal to serious cyclists, and for good reason. Its 294 kilometers include some of the most challenging road riding in North America, climbing in several places from sea level to about 427 meters in continuous, grueling ascents. Cyclists intent on completing the loop as quickly as possible are certain to put their endurance and conditioning to a difficult test.

Those more interested in aesthetics than athletics will find the route rewarding for other reasons. The Cabot Trail is generally considered one of the most spectacular road routes in North America. For sheer beauty, the escarpments and deep valleys of the Highlands may be unequaled east of the Rockies. Mountains that roll across the interior of the peninsula tumble finally into the lonely and rugged coastline of the Gulf of St. Lawrence.

Needless to say, this is not a trip to be taken lightly. Cyclists planning to complete the entire route should be in at least moderately good condition and should be equipped with adequate bikes in good repair. Brakes, especially, must be in impeccable condition. Some of the descents are difficult, to say the least; on hairpin curves a snapped brake cable or failed pad could have disastrous consequences.

Generally, a clockwise circuit of the Cabot Trail is recommended, for a number of reasons. It takes best advantage of prevailing winds, putting them at your back when they're strongest; it allows you to take the inside track on the steepest and spookiest descents; and it means that several times you can ascend major hills on their long, gradual slopes rather than their more abrupt, steeper sides.

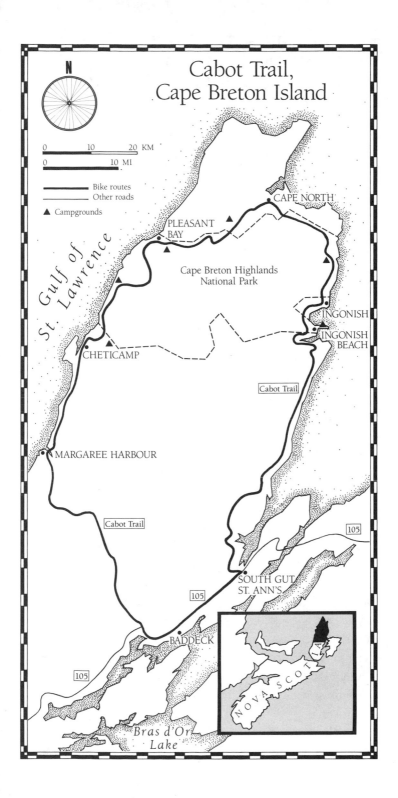

BADDECK TO CAPE BRETON HIGHLANDS NATIONAL PARK— 89.5 KILOMETERS (55.6 MILES)

There are any number of places from which to begin a trip on the Cabot Trail. To cycle only in the national park, begin at Cheticamp Campground at the southwest entrance, where vehicles can be parked at the visitors' information pavilion next to the campground. Park personnel will want to know your agenda, including approximate day of return and which campgrounds you will be staying at along the route. You'll be expected to pay in advance for sites at the several primitive campgrounds located within the park. Local police patrol Cheticamp Campground and the pavilion parking lot and will be notified that your vehicle is there.

From the standpoint of pure logistics, the best starting point for a complete circuit of the Cabot Trail is at the town of **Baddeck** on Hwy. 105, at the southern tip of the loop. Baddeck has a population of 965 and all services, including restaurants, hotels, stores, and bed-and-breakfasts. There are two private campgrounds on the outskirts of town. Overnight accommodations in Baddeck also include several luxurious alternatives, including Inverary Inn, MacNeil House, and the Silver Dart Lodge. The town is conveniently located whether you're arriving from the south, driving up from the mainland of Nova Scotia, or traveling from the population centers to the east at Sydney and Glace Bay. If you're arriving in the area by automobile, starting at Baddeck means you'll have to cycle only a few kilometers of highway you've already driven over. A clockwise circuit of the trail from Baddeck also allows you to loosen up and test your equipment through the relatively easy first third of the loop. By the time you reach the difficult ascents in the national park, you'll be more prepared for them.

The only complication at Baddeck is that there is no obvious place to leave an untended vehicle. Ask permission to park in a corner of the large parking area at the Alexander Graham Bell National Historic Park, or try either of the two campgrounds.

The Alexander Graham Bell connection to Baddeck is a strong one. The town has obviously prospered from association with the great inventor, who came to the area first in 1885 and spent most of the final four decades of his life there. Baddeck, on the shore of lochlike Bras d'Or Lake (pronounce it to rhyme with "Labrador"), reminded Bell of the Scottish highlands where he had spent his childhood. He and his family felt immediately at home here, in what his wife called the "gentle, restful beauty" of Cape Breton, and built an impressive mansion, "Beinn Bhreagh" (for "Beautiful Mountain"), which is still owned by the Bell family and is not open to the public, located on a headland across Baddeck Bay. Although Bell is best known for the invention of the telephone, he was a man of immensely varied interests and applied his considerable creative energy to a dazzling variety of subjects. Much of his most energetic experimental work took place in Baddeck, where he and a following of young associates performed ground-breaking work in aerodynamics, including the construction and flight in 1909 of the "Silver Dart," the first aircraft to achieve flight in Canada, and the development of efficient hydrofoils, one of which in 1919 set a then-world's record water speed of 112 kilometers per hour. The Alexander Graham Bell Museum in Baddeck offers a fascinating look at the life and work of this remarkable man.

From Baddeck, traveling west, Hwy. 105 is a busy two-lane highway with broad paved shoulders on both sides. Enjoy it while it lasts: there are few paved shoulders on the remainder of the Cabot Trail. From the highway you can see St. Patrick's Channel of Bras d'Or Lake. Filling much of the interior of Cape Breton Island, Bras d'Or contains depths up to 275 meters and is popular with recreational boaters who take advantage of its protected waters to explore the dozens of islands and long, reaching bays and inlets.

Eight kilometers from Baddeck, turn north at the official beginning of the Cabot Trail. The intersection is well marked with the distinctive Cabot Trail signs and has a grocery store and motel near the corner. The road here is typical, with two average-sized lanes and no shoulder. Traffic is fairly heavy in summer, at least by Cape Breton standards, but even on its busiest days it seems nearly deserted compared to popular tourist areas in the United States.

The countryside seems remote from the start, dominated by spruce forests and sizable, rounded hills. A fairly long ascent begins at Lower Middle River, but the road soon descends sharply into the town of Middle River and the first of several major river valleys. For much of the way to the coast, the road is only moderately hilly.

The terrain is quite hilly through the communities of Hunters Mountain and Lower Middle River, neither of which offers services. At Middle River, the road flattens somewhat in the meadow-dotted Middle River Valley. After the bridge over the MacLeods Branch River are a few scattered services, including a small grocery, a gas station, and a bed-and-breakfast inn.

Architecture in Cape Breton is markedly different from that in southern Nova Scotia. Compared to the stunning Victorian houses of Annapolis Royal and other mainland communities, Cape Breton's appear to be no-nonsense dwellings, with little ornament and few garnishes, the homes of hardworking people preoccupied with the demands of making a living. For an interesting discussion of architectural influences in Nova Scotia, and an explanation of the differences in housing styles in various parts of the province, see *Pride of Home: The Working Class Housing Tradition in Nova Scotia, 1749–1949*, by Joann Latremouille (Lancelot Press, Hantsport, Nova Scotia, 1988).

Through the Middle River Valley the road continues to be relatively flat, over a few low rolling hills, and passes close to the typically fast and lively Middle River. Wooded hills rise steeply along both sides of the valley.

Lake O'Law Provincial Park, a few kilometers past Upper Middle River, and about 26 kilometers from the intersection with Hwy. 105, offers picnicking and swimming on an attractive inland lake, but no camping. Some scattered businesses along this stretch (including take-out restaurants advertising lobster burgers—they're not as horrible as they sound) diminish the sense of remoteness found in the early portion of the ride.

After the park the road passes a series of fairly sizable hills from the valley of the Middle River to the valley of the Margaree River. The Margaree is one of eastern North America's most famous Atlantic salmon rivers, and is rich in angling history—a history well documented in the Margaree Salmon Museum in the town of North East Margaree. One longtime resident of the region told me the valley has changed much in 50 years, especially since the coming of paved roads, but that it has always been an area dependent on travelers attracted to the river and the salmon. It's worth noting that the fishing, after several decades of decline, is very good again as a result of stiff regulations and a moratorium on commercial netting of salmon.

The Margaree Valley here is wide and distinctive, with a broad, flat bottom and sides that rise steeply in wooded ranks. Farms are carved out in geometric patterns on the hillsides. The road winds among meadows and woodlands, with scattered houses and small businesses throughout, and has a definite downhill tendency as the river valley descends toward the coast. The route varies from relatively flat to rolling, with some stretches of steep, tightly bunched hills.

The towns of North East Margaree and Margaree Forks are spaced along several kilometers of the Cabot Trail, and together offer a few services, including a grocery store, service station, and private campground, and scattered housekeeping cottages, gift shops, and antique shops. From the forks of the Margaree River, where the west branch meets the mainstream, the valley is broader and flatter than above, and less inhabited. The road flattens considerably, with less obvious descent than in the hillier upper river valley.

Soon after the river widens into an estuary comes the first glimpse of the Gulf of St. Lawrence at the village of **Margaree Harbour**. The terrain changes dramatically from the hilly woodlands of the interior to coastal meadows and long, open slopes descending toward bluffs along the beach. The town itself begins with a restaurant at the causeway over the river's mouth, then continues with scattered restaurants, gas stations, stores, and homes. As in many of the open, coastal regions of the Maritimes, the town is widely dispersed, as if the open terrain eliminates any reason for congregating.

Beyond Margaree Harbour and its sister village of Belle Cote, the fairly flat route goes over some rolling hills and through open grasslands with meadows that descend to the bluffs above the ocean. Much larger bluffs are visible up the shoreline to the north. Even with a sprinkling of houses along this stretch, the coast is bleak, exotic, and strange.

The remaining 40 kilometers to the entrance of Cape Breton Highlands National Park continue through lovely coastline marred by carelessly maintained houses. The terrain continues to be mostly treeless and hilly, the road either rolling over minor hills or cresting downhill to follow stretches of flatlands. The road is in fair to good repair, with some sections of broken asphalt and crumbling edges. To the east is a great view of the first of the Highland mountain ranges.

The villages of St. Joseph du Moine, Grand Etang, and Point Cross were settled by Acadian refugees who had been driven from lower Nova Scotia by the British expulsion. Today they get by with a combination of commercial fishing and tourist industries. In season, the colorful buoys of lobster pots are clustered offshore. The towns are starkly visible, with both their good and bad sides plain to see in this open land where no trees obscure the view. It seems a place with few secrets. Some services are scattered along the route, as well as occasional gift shops, antique stores, and folk-art galleries.

With a population of 3,009, **Cheticamp** is the largest community on the northwest coast and is the western point of departure to Cape Breton Highlands National Park. Across a narrow harbor is long, low Cheticamp Island, where the first Acadian refugees settled in the region in 1755. The Acadian Museum, next to the prominent church in the center of the community, and a smaller genealogical museum at the north end of town give a good historical overview of the area and its early inhabitants.

Cheticamp is the last place where visitors can stock up on supplies before entering the national park, and offers most services, including grocery stores, restaurants, motels, housekeeping cottages, banks, and a hospital. It is not the most picturesque of Nova Scotia's fishing communities, having grown up largely, it appears, in response to the tourist trade attracted by the national park. Still, a number of local attractions are worth checking out, including whale-viewing cruises, and summer festivals such as the Festival de l'Escaouette in August, Fire Week in mid-July, and the Scottish Concert in mid-August. Many of the inhabitants of the town are descendants of French Acadians who escaped to Cape Breton during the expulsion and established fishing villages along the coast. Some lived in the village of La Bloque, now within the national park, and took up residence in Cheticamp when their land was absorbed by the park in 1936. Expect to hear the peculiar French idiom (spiced here and there with English words and phrases) in the grocery stores and restaurants. Almost everyone seems to speak English passably well, however, so a crash course in le français is not necessary to order a meal or cash a traveler's check.

CHETICAMP CAMPGROUND TO INGONISH BEACH— 105 KILOMETERS (65.2 MILES)

This leg of the Cabot Trail is the most difficult of the loop, packing a lot of major hills into a relatively short distance. Although it is only 105 kilometers long, plan on 2 days to complete it; more if you like to sleep late and stop frequently. Intermediate campgrounds are located within the park, and motels and housekeeping cottages are available in several communities along the way.

From the northern outskirts of Cheticamp and through the village of Petit Etang, you can look ahead to mountains—very steep, impressive, round-topped mountains with sheer cliffs and deep passes. At the entrance to the park, about 5 kilometers from Cheticamp, is Cheticamp Campground and a visitor center with an excellent bookstore specializing in local and natural history of the region.

Cape Breton Highlands National Park encompasses 958 square kilometers of the wildest and most rugged country in Nova Scotia and is one of the most spectacular parks in eastern Canada. From the coastal regions to the mountain slopes to the highland plateaus, nine distinctive land and forest regions can be identified, all shaped by glaciers and geological upheavals dating back 600 to 1200 million years. The high plateaus, covering about 90 percent of the park, are characterized by bogs and dry barrens overgrown with shrublike spruces and firs that have become stunted and deformed by winds and climate. Protected areas at lower elevations support boreal forests of mature balsam fir and black spruce, or mixed stands of maple, birch, and beech.

The Cabot Trail, which passes through each of the park's regions, circles an enormous interior accessible only by hiking trails, none of which completely traverse the interior. Trailheads are well marked and usually lead

The hills of Cape Breton Highlands National Park, at the heart of the Cabot Trail.

to lookouts, lakes, waterfalls, and other scenic destinations.

Weather in this jutting corner of Cape Breton is highly unpredictable. Park officials explain cheerfully that it is not unusual to pass through intervals of fog, rain, sleet, and sunshine in the space of a few hours. Temperatures average considerably lower than in mainland Nova Scotia and are influenced by the latitude, altitude, and especially the cold Labrador current of the Gulf of St. Lawrence. Rain and snowfall accumulations are higher than in most other portions of the Maritimes, although summer rainfall is not appreciably higher. Nonetheless, be prepared for rain and cold weather. Wind is the most dramatic weather influence. Prevailing west and southwest winds gain momentum across the gulf and hit the park with full force, howling up west-facing river valleys with the effect of a wind tunnel. Be especially cautious cycling around protected headlands where they are suddenly open to the force of the wind; it's possible to be blown off a bike by the sudden gusts. A park ranger laughed when I asked if cyclists had ever been blown entirely off the road by those winds. Then she grew serious and said, "But I suppose it's a possibility."

The mountains themselves are considered an extension of the Appalachian Range, and, as elsewhere in that range, have been rounded by exposure and erosion. Outcroppings of granite, sandstone, conglomerate, shale, limestone, and gypsum are visible in many of the larger valleys, especially where cut through by the park's major rivers, the Grand Anse, MacKenzies, Cheticamp, Aspy, Clyburn, and Warren Brook. In the interior, peaks reach 538 meters, and on the precipitous west coast rise from sea level to 370 meters in as little as one kilometer. That precipitous climb from ocean to mountain makes the west coast, not far from Cheticamp, the most challenging leg of the trip. Viewed from the coast, the road's winding switchbacks, climbing in serpentine coils, make an imposing sight. It's best to begin the trip after a dose of carbohydrates and a good night's sleep.

Near the park entrance north of Cheticamp, and adjacent to the visitors' center and bookstore, Cheticamp Campground is equipped with 162 serviced and unserviced sites, showers, picnic shelters, and other facilities. The campground is open year-round, though hookups and showers are open only from mid-May to mid-October. A number of hiking trails from the campground lead to waterfalls and rapids along the Cheticamp River, and to views of some of the spectacular canyon walls rising east and north of the campground.

Inside the park, the road is a two-lane highway slightly wider than before Cheticamp, without paved shoulders except on the inside of curves on the highest climbs. Traffic can be fairly heavy, especially when the weather is good on summer weekends, but vehicles tend to be relatively slow because most travelers are sightseers.

The first 4 kilometers after the campground the road is relatively flat, through a massive valley deep enough to be shaded most of the day. The flat route ends abruptly at the coast, where you start nearly at sea level and begin the first of several difficult climbs and exhilarating descents as the road traverses the face of the coastal mountains. This often-photographed section of the park is breathtaking, with the road snaking away for kilometers ahead—rising and descending along the coast like a necklace tossed on crumpled blankets. The slopes are wooded with conifers and mixed deciduous trees, and while not sheer, are steep enough to be dizzying, especially when you're descending on the outside of abrupt turns.

The road varies from about a meter to 100 meters above the water and offers almost continuous views of the ocean. During high winds the tops of waves are sheared off and blown in smokey trails parallel to the surface. Numerous scenic overlooks provide places for automobiles to pull over and park. They're welcome resting spots for cyclists but can also be hazardous as automobiles and campers congregate nearby, often turning unexpectedly on or off the road.

It's difficult to characterize the hills in this stretch. In general, if you're traveling clockwise, the ascents tend to be fairly gradual—about a kilometer to one and a half kilometers in length—whereas the descents are steeper and slowed by more dramatic switchbacks. There are exceptions to the pattern, however, and several extremely steep climbs are unavoidable. The road is in good condition, although a few unexpected potholes can be a hazard. Also watch for occasional fallen rocks where hillsides have been cut out to make room for the road.

A picnic area and unserviced historical exhibit are located on the site of the village of La Bloque, at a spot where the road descends nearly to water level. Originally an Acadian fishing village of about thirty families, it was vacated shortly after the creation of the park. Today little remains but the remnants of a concrete wharf.

Corney Brook Campground, located about 1.5 kilometers from La Bloque and 10.5 kilometers from the park entrance, has small, primitive sites on a small plateau between the road and the beach. Here I met a pair of cyclists from Boston who had the proper attitude. They had taken shelter from the wind and rain in a tiny tent, their bikes wrapped in plastic sheeting nearby, and were happily reading their way through a small stack of paperback novels. Fifteen meters away the surf pounded the shore. "We're in absolutely no hurry," they said. "Twenty miles a day, ten miles a day, no miles a day—we don't care. As long as we have enough to eat and read, let it rain."

Almost immediately after the campground the road begins a continuous gradual ascent, turning inland and following a steep river valley upward toward the top of French Mountain. In 5.5 kilometers the road climbs in relentless pitches and switchbacks to the plateau at the top of French Mountain, a height of 372 meters. Just beyond the crest of the hill is the first of several emergency roadside shelters equipped with telephones.

At the top of the mountain, crossing the extremely remote plateau region, the road is nearly flat, in good condition, with a wide gravel shoulder. Though at first it appears quite flat, the plateau is cut through with ravines and potholes and is overgrown with mosses, low shrubs, and miniature, grotesquely formed spruce and fir trees. Many tiny lakes and ponds are scattered across the plateau. About 3 kilometers inland from the crest of the hill is the highest elevation on the road, a peak of 455 meters, with a long view in all directions looking over the interior of the park.

Six and a half kilometers farther, after a series of rolling hills, is another emergency shelter. Views of the ocean ahead are overwhelmed by the impressively steep, sheer-sided valleys that drop away from the highlands. They can be viewed from a number of roadside lookouts.

Less than 3 kilometers from the emergency shelter the road begins an awesome 4-kilometer descent toward Pleasant Bay. The road winds sharply down 10- to 12-degree gradients, bending sometimes into 180-degree hairpins. A paved shoulder about half a meter to a meter wide and numerous pull-offs offer some security. Use plenty of brakes.

Just beyond the Mackenzies River the road leaves

the national park and enters a commercial pocket around the town of **Pleasant Bay**. Originally known by the French as Grande Anse and by the English as Limbo Bay, this area was uninhabited until 1819 when a shipwreck left a small community of Scottish settlers stranded on the shore. They spent the winter on the bay, near the mouths of three rivers—the MacKenzies, Pond, and Red—and found the place hospitable enough to make it a permanent settlement. Cut off by land from the rest of the province until 1932, the Scottish settlers and their descendants made their living by farming and commercial fishing. Trading was engaged in primarily with the community of Neil Harbour, which had been settled by Newfoundlanders on the opposite side of the Cape Breton Highlands peninsula. It was not until the completion of the Cabot Trail in 1932 that these and many other coastal communities in Cape Breton could make contact by land with the rest of the province. The entire route was not paved until 1962.

Today Pleasant Bay supports a population of about 300, many employed in the gift shops, restaurants, motels, bed-and-breakfast inns, and seafood take-outs that cater to visitors to the national park. The village is spread out along several kilometers of road, on the only flat terrain you'll see for awhile. Outside the town is a 300-year-old stand of sugar maples—one of the oldest in eastern Canada.

Beyond Pleasant Bay, within the park boundaries again, the route continues inland, traveling eastward along the Grand Anse River and the northern border of the park. The relatively flat valley floor continues for about 5 kilometers, gradually ascending a narrow, steep-sided valley with frequent sheer cliffs. Along the way is MacIntosh Brook Campground, with primitive sites and a picnic area beside the road.

At the head of the valley, about 6 kilometers east of Pleasant Bay, is the Lone Sheiling, a replica of the stone huts used by the Scottish farmers, or "crofters," who once tended their sheep in these hills. A short hiking trail leads through the maple forests near the hut.

Beyond the old hut the route grows more difficult, beginning with a 3.5-kilometer climb. Though long, this hill is not as steep as the earlier major ascents, and can probably be ridden in its entirety by cyclists in reasonably good condition. After a short stretch of alternating flat road, rolling hills, and brief descent, there is another short climb to the peak of North Mountain at 445 meters. Again, at this altitude, trees are stunted and low bushes are the dominant vegetation. On a cloudy day it's not unusual to pass through foglike cloud banks. An emergency shelter with phone is located near the peak.

A steep, 5.1-kilometer descent begins about a kilometer from the emergency shelter and quickly becomes fairly tricky, with switchbacks and short, very steep pitches alternating with nearly flat plateaus. Several overlooks provide a place to pull over and view steep wooded hills converging in different planes to the south and east. Below the highway are several remarkably deep gorges and canyons falling to the bottom of the valley of Southwest Brook, home to at least twenty-seven species of rare plants usually found only in subarctic Québec and high elevations in the Rocky Mountains. Botanists have theorized that the plants escaped the gouging of the last glaciers and have thrived in the moist hidden valley of the Aspy Fault, a line of bedrock cracked open by the collision of continents 250 to 400 million years ago.

At the bottom of the valley, beyond the north branch of the Aspey, Big Interval Campground with ten primitive sites is located beside the bridge over the South Branch of the Aspey. As at the other primitive campgrounds in the park, camping fees can be paid at Cheticamp or Ingonish (see page 73). Water must be boiled before drinking. About a kilometer beyond Big Interval the road leaves the park.

The 10.5-kilometer ride from the park boundary to the village of **Cape North** (pop. 152) is through a relatively flat valley of rolling hills where the bluffs along the valley sides gradually lose their height. Forests of birch, maple, and oak replace the spruce and fir of the higher elevations. A gentle descent of about 5 kilometers leads finally to the town Cape North.

At the western edge of Cape North is the intersection with the road north to the village of Bay St. Lawrence, near the northernmost point of Nova Scotia. Eight kilometers up the road, the base of Sugarloaf Mountain is believed to be the spot where John Cabot first landed in Nova Scotia in 1497. A reenactment of his landing is held on the beach each year on June 24.

The town of Cape North has a motel, gas station, restaurant, bakery, variety store, and ice cream shop. After a series of rolling hills through woods of hardwoods and spruce, the road comes to South Harbour, which has a few scattered services, including Danena's Restaurant—not much to look at on the outside, but a French country kitchen atmosphere on the inside with excellent home-cooked meals at reasonable prices.

About 5 kilometers from Cape North the road enters the national park again and immediately begins a long, gradual ascent punctuated by intervals of plateau. The hills are much smaller than to the north and west and support growths of hardwoods until near their peaks, where lines of stunted spruce are visible.

Neil Harbour, with most services and a hospital, is located a short distance off the Cabot Trail.

Approximately 5 kilometers south of the intersection with the road to Neil Harbour is a beach and picnic area at Black Brook. From here the road rises and falls along a rocky, craggy coastline. Though less spectacular than the large-scale mountains of the western shoreline, the eastern coast from here south is memorable and beautiful. Points of black, jagged rock jutting audaciously into the Atlantic have been given such names as Bluff Head, MacKinnons Point, Boiler Point, Shoal Point, Two Rock Point, and Lakies Head, and were important navigation aids to early sailors, as they are to the lobster fishermen who work this coastline today. Along the shore, hills are steep but not long—although expect some gradual climbs of up to one and a half kilometers—and are

The beach at Broad Cove Campground, on the Atlantic shore of Cape Breton Island.

occasionally topped by pull-offs with good views of the shoreline. The Atlantic here casts waves against pink or black rocks, the surf made startlingly white in contrast to the rich blues and greens of the deep water.

About 10 kilometers south of Black Brook Cove Picnic Area is another small picnic area, and almost a kilometer after that is Broad Cove Campground, with more than 250 serviced and unserviced campsites. The campground is equipped with excellent, clean restrooms and free showers—a wonderful luxury after 2 or 3 days of negotiating Cape Breton hills. There is also a heated activity building to take refuge in during bad weather. Facilities and campsites are open from mid-May to mid-October.

A .8-kilometer hike from the campground leads to a fine, protected beach bordered on both sides by jagged cliffs. During and after storms, when battered lobster pots and other treasures wash up on the beach, it's a great place to beachcomb. The water is too cold—and often too infested with stinging jellyfish—for enjoyable swimming, although bathers often swim in the warmer fresh water in the broad mouth of the creek that empties into the Atlantic there.

A short distance south of Broad Cove Campground the road passes out of the national park and into the town of **Ingonish**. The Ingonish area is a popular resort destination and the commercial headquarters of the eastern side of the national park. The towns of Ingonish, Ingonish Centre, Ingonish Beach, South Ingonish Harbour, and Ingonish Ferry are spread out along the shores of North and South Bays, which are themselves divided by a long, narrow peninsula called Middle Head pointing like an index finger into the Atlantic. The combined populations of all five communities is not much over 1,000, but they offer virtually all services, including restaurants, motels, cottages, laundromats, a bank, and a government liquor store. First settled by Portuguese fishermen in 1521 (the word "Ingonish" is thought to be derived from Portuguese), and later by French and English fishermen, the Ingonish area today relies primarily on tourism for its survival, although commercial fishermen still work from the wharfs along the two bays. If you're in the mood for luxury accommodations and gourmet food, you might consider staying at the Keltic Lodge on Middle Head, a fine old hotel now operated by the Nova Scotia Department of Tourism and Culture.

Don't think that this area is totally cut off from the wild side of Cape Breton Highlands: as I cycled along the shore of sparsely developed North Bay, I spotted a cow moose and her calf feeding in marshes at the base of Middle Head, just below an embankment where colorfully dressed golfers teed off on the fairway above.

Middle Head and a short section of road south of it pass through the national park again, past Ingonish Campground with 90 unserviced sites, showers, picnic shelters, and several picnic areas and public beaches. All facilities are open from June 25 to September 4, with limited winter facilities from October 15 to May 17.

The final park boundary is at **Ingonish Beach**, where there is an information pavilion as well as most services.

Generally, the villages in the Ingonish area and the remainder of the east coast are more attractive and less blatantly commercial than those of the west coast and the Cheticamp area.

INGONISH BEACH TO BADDECK— 101.8 KILOMETERS (63.2 MILES)

After Ingonish Beach the road circles Ingonish Harbour, at the base of high wooded hills dropping to the salt marshes at the mouth of the Ingonish River. The ski slopes here were the site of the 1987 Canada Winter Games.

At Ingonish Ferry (where there are no services), the road begins a gradual 6-kilometer ascent of Smokey Mountain, cutting inland a short distance along the river valley, then circling back to the shore side of the mountain. The climb is broken by occasional flat stretches and is never as steep as the ascents on the western shoreline. Pull-offs provide excellent views of the Ingonish shoreline and the Atlantic. The road is in good condition, without paved shoulders, and has been resurfaced so many times that the 5- to 8-centimeter drop at the shoulders can be something of a hazard. At the top of Smokey Mountain— named for the wisps of clouds often seen trailing over the peak—the 366-meter elevation gives a long view of the Atlantic. Lobster buoys along the shoreline look like distant rafts of waterfowl riding on the waves; in season you can watch the fishing boats motoring from buoy to buoy, winching up the traps.

The descent to the base of Smokey Mountain is considerably steeper than the climb up the other side. The 366-meter drop is accomplished in less than 3 kilometers, down a road that is steep and serpentine, carved into the bare-rock side of the mountain. This is definitely not a freewheeling descent. If you can bear to take your eyes off the road, the view of the shoreline to the south is spectacular, with an irregular coast of gravel bluffs lined with the brilliant white fringe of the Atlantic.

From the base of Smokey Mountain the road hugs the shoreline for about 30 kilometers, passing through the tiny villages of Wreck Cove, French River, Skir Dhu, Breton Cove, North Shore, and Indian Brook, where the populations range from ten to thirty-eight. Hills are rolling and wooded, but rarely steep, with the road sometimes dipping down very close to the water, and frequently dropping nearly to sea level when it crosses the many small streams that tumble over rapids and waterfalls into the Atlantic.

A few of the small communities along this stretch have basic services, such as gas stations and general stores. The coast here is rich in lobster, and frequent roadside stands offer lobster and lobster sandwiches for sale, sometimes at lower prices than in other parts of the Maritimes. The general store in Wreck Cove offers fresh lobster in season, at prices well below average—$2.95 per pound when I was there. Accommodations are scarce, although there is a "tourist home" in Breton Cove (but nothing else) and an RV park and grocery with dining room at Indian Brook.

Two miles beyond Indian Brook the Cabot Trail turns inland at the intersection with Hwy. 312. Continuing straight on 312 leads to the ferry across St. Ann's Bay to Englishtown, a shortcut that shaves a few kilometers off the return to Baddeck. The Cabot Trail swings west at the intersection and follows the valley of the tumbling Barachois River. The route is fairly flat, though it climbs gradually through a mostly uninhabited valley lined with modest wooded hills on both sides.

After about 3 kilometers the road curves southwest, away from the Barachois, and begins a gradual climb away from the river. Near the top—and it is not a difficult climb—is a nice view of the valley behind you. Farther on are spruce forests descending from the hills to the boundaries of old farmlands gone to meadow.

A fairly long descent leads to the valley of the North River.

The road, moderately hilly now, follows the North River Valley toward St. Ann's Bay. This broad, lightly populated valley is reminiscent of the Margaree River Valley 48 kilometers to the west. Rolling hills and pastures line the river as it widens and merges with St. Ann's Bay.

For the remainder of the distance along St. Ann's Bay, the road, climbing to about 100 meters above the water but continuing to be only moderately hilly, follows the shoreline closely. The irregular shoreline of the narrow bay gives it a fjordlike look, especially because the water edges up to the base of steep, wooded hills on both shores. The towns of St. Ann's and North Gut St. Ann's have no services. Just before South Gut St. Ann's is a provincial picnic area with fresh water.

South Gut St. Ann's was originally settled in the 1820s by a congregation of Highland Scots under the leadership of Reverend Norman MacLeod. When their ship was threatened by a storm, they took shelter in St. Ann's Bay and were so impressed with the land they found there that they established a permanent colony. Thirty years later MacLeod left with 130 followers to begin another colony in Australia. Aussie descendants of that group still make frequent pilgrimages to St. Ann's to explore their family roots.

Nova Scotia Gaelic College of Arts and Culture, the only Gaelic college in North America, is located in South Gut St. Ann's. It may be the only college in North America that offers bagpipes as part of its regular curriculum. Performances of Scottish dance and music—the Summer Ceilidh—are open to the public every Tuesday, Wednesday, and Thursday evenings during July and August, and through the 7-day Gaelic Mod during the first full week of August.

A short distance beyond the Gaelic College is the intersection with TransCanada 105 and the final leg of the trip. Hwy. 105 can be a relief or not, depending on whether you value wide paved shoulders over fine scenery. The shoulders range from 1 to 2 meters wide and are in excellent condition, making for easy, secure cycling. Most of the 17-kilometer route to Baddeck is relatively flat, with some slight hills. Services, including a motel, restaurant (the Lobster Galley Restaurant, specializing in—what else?—seafood), and bed-and-breakfast inn are clustered near the intersection.

The first exit to Baddeck is at Hwy. 205, a two-lane road with no paved shoulders that provides a quieter ride along the shore of Bras d'Or Lake. When traffic is especially heavy on 105, it makes a good alternative route for the final 8 or 9 kilometers to Baddeck.

·NEWFOUNDLAND·

Bounded on three sides by the North Atlantic and one side by the northern Gulf of St. Lawrence, Atlantic Canada's largest and most remote province is the easternmost point of North America and is so far removed from the rest of the Maritimes that it is often thought of as a kind of distant cousin to those provinces. Such geographic isolation has created a place inhabited by people with a unique culture and heritage, and even a unique version of the English language.

Archaeological evidence shows that as early as 2500 B.C. Dorset Eskimos lived in coastal Newfoundland in the vicinity of present-day Gros Morne National Park. Later came Micmac and Beothuk Indians, the latter a mysterious people who apparently disappeared when their last-known survivor died in 1829. Norse explorers visited and settled the Northern Peninsula of Newfoundland at least 500 years before Christopher Columbus blundered onto the Bahamas and was declared discoverer of America. Other early

European inhabitants included Basque fishermen (who may also have preceded Columbus in the New World), Celtic-speaking Irish, and settlers from England and France. Both England and France claimed Newfoundland for themselves and were quick to fight for its rich fishing grounds. During a 200-year history of struggle, the capital of St. John's was captured and lost three times by the French.

In the Maritimes, where distances between points tend to be relatively short, Newfoundland, with 404,520 square kilometers of area and 17,440 kilometers of coastline, contains more than three times the combined area of Nova Scotia, New Brunswick, and Prince Edward Island. Much of that area, however, is taken up by the province's mainland annex, Labrador. The island of Newfoundland itself is 112,300 square kilometers in area, nearly the size of Nova Scotia and New Brunswick combined. A population of 542,000 (plus 28,741 in Labrador) share a total of only 8,640 kilometers of public highways, including the 704-kilometer length of the TransCanada Highway between Channel-Port-aux-Basques on the southwest coast and the capital city of St. John's on the extreme east coast.

While air transport to Newfoundland is a possibility for cyclists, with Air Canada and Canadian Airline International operating from airports in Stephenville and Deer Lake in the west, Gander in the midsection, and St. John's in the east, most visitors come to the island by car ferry from Nova Scotia. Two commercial routes are available, both from North Sydney, at the northern tip of Cape Breton Island. One is a 5- to 7-hour trip to Channel-Port-aux-Basques ("Channel" is usually dropped in casual usage), in extreme southwest Newfoundland; the other is a 12- to 14-hour trip to the eastern port of Argentia. Both cruises are comfortable, aboard modern vessels 177 meters long and equipped with padded chairs and lounges, berths (for an additional price), and such diversions as live music, movie theaters, cafeterias, wet bars, video games, and vending machines. In 1990, Marine Atlantic charged $14.25 per adult for the trip to Channel-Port-aux-Basques. The cost of transporting a bicycle was an additional $5.30, an automobile, $43.50; and trucks, campers, and RVs were charged according to their size. The rate for the North Sydney to Argentia trip was $38.50 per adult, $10.60 per bicycle, and $93.25 per automobile. Reservations are required and must be picked up at least one and a half hours before departing.

Weather

Newfoundland's climate, while similar to the rest of Maritime Canada, is obviously affected by its northern latitudes and will generally be somewhat cooler than provinces to the south. Average summer temperature is about 70 degrees F during the day, and 55 degrees F during the night. Annual rainfall is about 104 centimeters, plus another 300 centimeters of snow. Fog is common in coastal areas, especially on the east coast where the cold Arctic Current merges with the warm Gulf Stream. Winds can be a problem, especially along open coastal areas and in the uplands where treeless, tundralike terrain offers little protection.

Language

Except for the French-speaking residents of the Port Au Port Peninsula north of Channel-Port-aux-Basques, most Newfoundlanders speak English as their primary language. The various dialects, however, are probably the most unusual versions of English you'll hear in North America. They include musical blends of Irish and west-country English, with something like Finnish or Swedish thrown in. In some towns along the west coast, the dialect has a lovely, Australianlike lilt. The common greeting throughout the province is "Good-day," pronounced in a rush, with a decidedly Australian accent. *H*'s are often dropped, in the Cockney manner. Conversation between locals is guttural and fluid and can be difficult for outsiders to understand, especially when sprinkled with phrases and expressions unique to the province, such as "good morrow to you," and "don't get in a hobble about it." I noticed, however, that the rapid-fire, slurred speech Newfies fling at one another is often slowed somewhat and enunciated more clearly for visitors. Residents, incidentally, pronounce Newfoundland as new-fund-LAND, to rhyme with "understand."

Traffic Laws

The maximum speed limit on TransCanada 1 is 90 kilometers per hour. On other paved roads, it is 80 kilometers per hour, and on gravel roads, 60 kilometers per hour. Limits in urban areas are posted.

Miscellaneous

Newfoundland clocks operate in their own time zone, Newfoundland Standard Time, which is 30 minutes ahead of the Atlantic Standard Time used throughout the eastern Maritime Provinces.

Because of the expense of transportation from the mainland, prices for many goods are higher in Newfoundland than elsewhere in eastern Canada. Canned goods, dairy products, gasoline, photographic film, and other imported supplies are especially high-priced. On a positive note, local produce and especially local seafood are competitively priced or downright cheap.

For reasons that escape me, drivers in Newfoundland like to warn cyclists of their presence by waiting until they're 30 meters away, then honking their car horns. My impression is that their intentions are good and they don't realize the gesture is unnecessary and irritating. You get used to it. The practice is so prevalent that weeks later on Prince Edward Island, when an approaching vehicle sounded its horn, John Klepetka said wryly, "Must be a Newfie." It was.

For Further Information

For general information about travel in Newfoundland, contact the Department of Development, Tourism Branch, P.O. Box 8730, St. John's, NF, Canada A1B 4K2; phone 1-800-563-6353 or 709/576-2830.

For more information about Gros Morne National Park, write to P.O. Box 130, Rocky Harbour, NF, Canada A0K 4N0; or phone 709/458-2066.

For information about entry permits to the Avalon Wilderness Preserve, write to the Government of Newfoundland, Department of Environment and Lands, Parks Division, P.O. Box 8700, St. John's, NF, Canada A1B 4J6; or phone 902/576-2431.

For ferry information and reservations, contact Marine Atlantic at P.O. Box 250, North Sydney, NS, Canada B2A 3M3; phone 1-800-341-7981 (from the continental United States, except Maine), 1-800-432-7344 (Maine), 1-800-565-9411 (Ontario and Québec), 1-800-565-9470 (New Brunswick, Nova Scotia, Prince Edward Island), 1-800-563-7701 (Newfoundland and Labrador).

3

Gros Morne National Park

Begin/End: Wiltondale to River of Ponds Provincial Park, and side trips
Roads: Hwy. 430, Hwy. 431
Accommodations: Campgrounds, motels
Length: 214.4 kilometers (134 miles)
Difficulty: Easy to difficult

From the deck of the ferry between North Sydney, Nova Scotia, and Port-aux-Basques, Newfoundland, the first glimpse of Newfoundland is a memorable one. In the fog of a June evening, watching the strange, barren, rocky coastline come gradually into view, I thought it looked like nothing so much as the surface of the moon. From about a kilometer offshore there seemed to be nothing growing along the shoreline or on the stark, sharp-angled range of low mountains behind it. Only closer, as the huge ferry swung into the harbor, did I see that the ground was covered with low, brushy shrubs and stunted trees. The wind on this unprotected corner of Newfoundland is too fierce to allow trees to grow much above the height of a man, the soil too thin to give root to them even if the wind allowed it. In the town itself, small, functional houses perch on steep banks around the port, and bizarre equipment seems poised as if to begin excavating the lunar surface.

Cyclists planning to cross from Nova Scotia with only their bicycles should be warned that the distances from Port-aux-Basque to almost anyplace else in the province are great and discouraging. From Port-aux-Basques to Gros Morne are 288 kilometers of two-lane highway, most of it without paved shoulders, through some difficult but eerily beautiful terrain. It varies from the minimalist lunar landscape of the port area and the southern end of the Long Range Mountains, to dense forests of spruce and fir in the interior, to the tundralike bogs of the coastal fringe of the Northern Peninsula. The steep-sided mountain pass the highway enters just north of Port-aux-Basques at the base of Table Mountain is famous for funnelling winds up to 192 kilometers per hour—a potentially hazardous condition for cyclists, though winds of that speed are rare. Surprisingly, considering the ruggedness of the surrounding mountain range, those first miles are relatively flat.

Travelers driving an automobile to Gros Morne National Park from Port-aux-Basques can make good time on TransCanada 1 to the town of Deer Lake, then turn west on Route 430 toward the national park. Along the way are a half dozen provincial parks and campgrounds, some stretches of beautiful country, and an interesting detour into Corner Brook, the largest city in western Newfoundland.

At the little city of Deer Lake, (pop. 5,500) turn north on Hwy. 430, the only paved highway in the entire 320-kilometer Northern Peninsula. Hwy. 430 is also known as the Viking Trail, in reference to a 1,000-year-old Viking settlement discovered at L'Anse aux Meadows at the northern tip of the Northern Peninsula. It is possible—even likely—that Leif Eriksson and his Vikings explored the entire west coast of the island.

From Deer Lake, expect a 22.4-kilometer ride along two-lane highway in fair to good shape, with a paved shoulder about a third to a half meter wide. The terrain

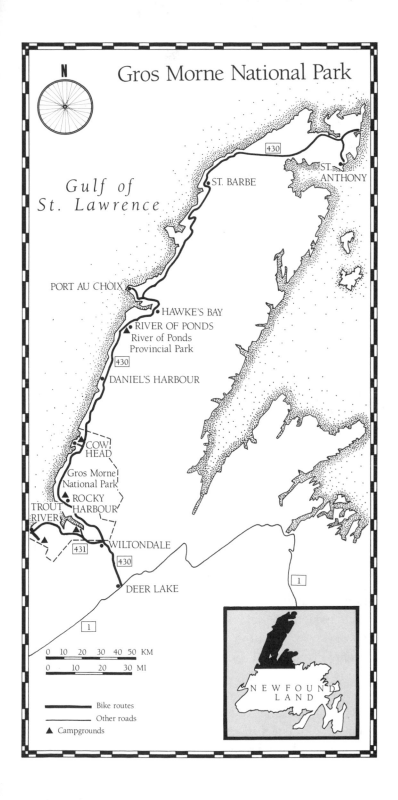

Gros Morne National Park

N

Gulf of
St. Lawrence

430

ST. BARBE

ST. ANTHONY

PORT AU CHOIX

HAWKE'S BAY

RIVER OF PONDS
River of Ponds
Provincial Park

430

DANIEL'S HARBOUR

COW HEAD

Gros Morne
National Park

ROCKY HARBOUR

TROUT RIVER

431

WILTONDALE

430

DEER LAKE

1

0 10 20 30 40 50 KM

0   10   20   30 MI

——— Bike routes
——— Other roads
▲ Campgrounds

NEWFOUND
LAND

here is hilly, with fairly long, fairly steep slopes much of the way. The Long Range Mountains rise in distant ranks to the northeast.

WILTONDALE TO TROUT RIVER— 53 KILOMETERS (33 MILES)

Wiltondale, at the southern entrance to Gros Morne National Park, is a crossroads village with a gas station, craft shop, and the Wiltondale Pioneer Village, a reconstruction of an early twentieth-century lumbering community. At the intersection, go west to Hwy. 431 (locally known as Bonne Bay Road). The first 10.7 kilometers of highway—a narrow two-lane with broken shoulders—parallels the southern boundary of the national park through a narrow valley with high wooded slopes and along the shore of an attractive, cliff-lined pond. About 6 kilometers of the trip are virtually flat road along the pond's shore, with great views of sharp, conical peaks scattered along the valley. Right before the park entrance the road crosses the Lomond River, a sport-fishing headquarters with a grocery store and lodge and unofficial (but well-used) campsites along the river near the bridge.

Shortly after the river, the road enters the park and begins climbing gradually away from the river valley. Long views of mountain peaks ahead reveal exposed rock on treeless peaks frequently lost in clouds. Two and a half kilometers from the park entrance is the turnoff north toward Lomond Campground. A 4-kilometer ride leads to the campground, on the shore of the East Arm of Bonne Bay. The camp has twenty-five sites, hot showers, and flush toilets, and is open from mid-June until mid-October.

West of the Lomond Campground turnoff, Hwy. 431 begins a series of fairly strenuous ascents, most less than 2 kilometers in length, that taken together add up to a major climb. From the peak, the descent is a world-class drop of 5.4 kilometers that includes several extremely steep pitches, slowed only by a few slight curves. During the descent the road leaves the national park, then reaches sea level finally in the town of Glenburnie, where there are several grocery stores and gas stations scattered among houses spread out on hillsides along the fjord-like South Arm of Bonne Bay. The hillsides where the houses perch are so steep that small wooden platforms have been erected to create enough flat space to park cars or build garages. The road through Glenburnie is in rough shape—broken and imperfectly patched—and rolls over tightly bunched though mercifully short hills.

Eight kilometers along the coast, and passing through the overlapping villages of Birchy Head, Winterhouse Brook, and Shoal Brook, scattered stores are supplemented by a seafood restaurant and hospitality home that look out over a stunning view of mountains rising above the far shore of the bay. Those mountains are at the heart of the national park and can be seen in intimate detail during the Hwy. 430 leg of the trip through Gros Morne.

After the intersection with the road to Woody Point, Hwy. 431 climbs a steep 2-kilometer ascent with views of impressive peaks ahead. Snow in the shaded passes near the peak never completely melts and gives rise to several sizable riversheds. Near the top of the ascent you enter the national park again and one of the loveliest and strangest places in eastern Canada. Called the Tablelands, it is a region of stark, tan-colored mountains that were forced out of the ocean 500 million years ago by the pressure of continental collisions. Below the first peak the road descends into a valley with the Tablelands rising on the left and the more usual dark-colored, granite peaks of the region on the right. The valley is mostly barren and flat and looks in some ways like the American Southwest.

A steep climb takes the road out of the valley, into rolling hills that continue to be barren except for light, patchy covers of vegetation. From the hilltops you can see glimpses of the Gulf of St. Lawrence far in the distance. Two trailheads here lead to the Green Gardens area of the park, where extensive meadows are elevated along a rugged, rocky stretch of coastline. Three primitive campgrounds are spaced along the bluff, 3 to 6 kilometers by trail from Hwy. 431.

After several kilometers of gradual ascents, a 3-kilometer descent on Hwy. 431 winds through barren hills littered with scrabble rock, past gorges cut by rivers that had their origin in the snow-filled passes at the mountaintop. The road here is in fair condition, with occasional patches and uneven shoulders that vary in width from a few centimeters to over half a meter wide. The descent is gradual, dropping a short distance, flattening out, dropping again as it winds slowly through the hills. Near the town of Trout River, at the boundary of the national park, the road enters wooded country.

On the highway, I met a pair of teenagers keeping swarms of blackflies at bay with alder switches. They were hitchhiking the 80 kilometers from their homes in Trout River to Deer Lake to attend a Saturday night party, the only recreation they could find on a summer weekend in rural Newfoundland. It would be a relief, they said, to graduate from high school and join the army so they could see the world, or at least the rest of Canada. As with 17-year-olds everywhere, their primary objective was to leave home, where their only options were to become commercial fishermen like their fathers ("I already had enough of that, thanks," one said, referring to the summers and weekends he had spent working, since the age of about 12, on his father's boat) or try to land one of the coveted government jobs in the national park. Better to join the military, get free tickets away, and a pension.

Trout River nestles at the base of the mountains and, except for its ocean beach, could be mistaken for a sleepy Montana ranching town. Small box houses, complete with corrals and wooden fences, crowd the street. A restaurant and tiny grocery are the only services.

About one and a half kilometers beyond town, following the course of the Trout River to the end of the road, you enter the national park again at a picnic area on the shore of Trout River Pond. A playground, kitchen shelter, and water pump (the water must be boiled) look out over a great view of mountain peaks rising beyond the pond. A dirt road continues around the pond to the opposite shore, where a campground with primitive sites and pit toilets is located.

WILTONDALE TO ROCKY HARBOUR— 40 KILOMETERS (25 MILES)

Although I've listed **Wiltondale** as the starting points for both Gros Morne trips, the decision was based only on its convenient location. The town does not make an ideal starting place, primarily because it is so small and offers no readily apparent spot to leave a vehicle. Unfortunately, the national park's information pavilion, administrative offices, and the first campground are located at Rocky Harbour, approximately midway through the park on Route 430, 37.6 kilometers from Wiltondale.

An alternative plan, for those traveling by automobile, is to drive the first leg of the trip, setting up camp in the Rocky Harbour area, and bicycling north from there. It means driving through some of the most spectacular sights in the park (maybe not such a bad idea, considering the size of the hills), but allows you to base camp in secure national park campgrounds with their hot showers and kitchen shelters, or to rent housekeeping cottages or motel rooms in Rocky Harbour, and begin serious cycling from there.

From Wiltondale, Hwy. 430 is in good condition, with a paved shoulder about a third to a half meter wide. It begins climbing immediately after entering the park, winding back and forth as it makes its way up the first mountain. The steep climbs are all equipped

with passing lanes that give cyclists a little more security. Gros Morne never suffers the traffic problems
typical of most national parks, but in summer enough
tourists visit to create some nuisance traffic. The ascents offer some good views of valleys with lakes nestled in them, all tucked away in deep passes below.
Most of the slopes are forested in those relatively protected, inland portions of the park.

For scenic beauty and tough riding this section of
Gros Morne rivals western Cape Breton Highlands National Park. Three or 4 kilometers of ascent—steep
climbs alternating with stretches of flat road—lead to
the top of Southeast Hills and the highest point on the
route. From here, expect several difficult ascents and
descents of 1.5 to 4 kilometers in length. The mountains in this section of the park are distinctive, with
wooded slopes beneath bald, rounded but still fairly
rugged tops. Much of the route follows passes and
hanging valleys, so that even at relatively high elevations there are always rounded mountains looming
overhead in several directions.

Fifteen kilometers from the park entrance, Hwy.
430 descends to the shore of the East Arm of Bonne
Bay. Looking more like an inland lake than a saltwater
fjord, East Arm is nestled at the base of impressive
mountains along most of its length. Hwy. 430 remains
mostly flat for the next 9.6 kilometers as it follows the
shore of the bay.

At Deer Arm of Bonne Bay, an ascent of a kilometer
and a half is followed by a descent of equal length, then
by rolling hills with climbs up to a mile long as the road
cuts across the base of the Norris Point Peninsula. About
one and a half kilometers after losing sight of Deer Arm
is a large visitors' center, with natural history displays,
restrooms, and an information desk. Two and a half kilometers farther is Rocky Harbour, the administrative and
commercial center of the park.

The town of **Rocky Harbour**, spread out along the
shore of its well-named bay, offers most services, includ-

ing restaurants, motels, a post office, and modest grocery stores. Several boat tours and excursions are available in town. The wharf at the end of the main street is a good place to purchase locally caught cod and other seafood— we bought freshly caught and filleted cod at $1.25 per pound, about one-third the going supermarket price in Newfoundland.

About one kilometer beyond the turnoff to Rocky Harbour is Berry Hill Campground, the largest in the park. Open from mid-June until mid-October, it has 156 campsites, hot showers, flush toilets, a kitchen shelter, and access to three interesting trail systems. Right before the campground, on a slight promontory overlooking Hwy. 430, is a community recreation center with an indoor swimming pool.

ROCKY HARBOUR TO RIVER OF PONDS PROVINCIAL PARK—122 KILOMETERS (76 MILES)

The northern portion of Gros Morne National Park has plenty of spectacular scenery, but to see the most impressive landforms up close it is usually necessary to leave the coast-hugging road and hike to it. Once out of the park on the Viking Trail (Hwy. 430) and beyond the reach of the Long Range Mountains, the road follows the Northern Peninsula coastline closely for almost 240 kilometers and is virtually flat the entire distance. Backed by the prevailing southwest wind off the Gulf of St. Lawrence, you can maintain an average speed of 32 kilometers per hour for hour after hour; a 160-kilometer ride is as easy here as along almost any stretch of highway in eastern North America.

Naturally, the winds that make the trip north delightful can be an absolute curse if you're traveling south. On the return trip they will be dead-on into your face the entire distance or (and maybe worse) will be coming at you from

45-degrees off straight ahead. Be prepared for a grueling ride: winds of 40 or 50 kilometers per hour are common, and there is little protection from them. In a few places the road curves inland enough to create crosswinds that can be tricky regardless of which way you're traveling.

If you don't like the idea of returning to the park on a bicycle, your only alternatives are to spot a vehicle someplace on the peninsula or to arrange a bus ride back with Viking Express bus line. One-way fare from St. Anthony, at the tip of the peninsula, to Rocky Harbour in Gros Morne National Park, was $37 in 1990. The catch is that the driver will only load a bicycle in the baggage compartment if it won't interfere with the bus line's parcel delivery service. To discuss details, call Viking Express at the Corner Brook office at 709/634-4710.

From Berry Hill Campground north the road is in good condition, with half-meter-wide paved shoulders, and alternates flat stretches with slight rolling hills. One kilometer after the campground is the turnoff to Lobster Cove Head, where a lighthouse built early in the century has been restored and converted into a museum. A trail from the lighthouse leads to the shore and tidal pools filled with marine life.

Traffic through the northern portion of the park is usually light, even during summer. The road follows the coast closely, often riding the crest of short bluffs directly above it. To the east the North Range Mountains appear smokey in the distance—not as spectacular as the peaks to the south, but impressive nonetheless.

Green Point Campground offers eighteen primitive sites on the shore, and is open from mid-May to mid-October.

Four kilometers beyond Green Point, the road leaves the national park briefly and enters the tiny community of Sallys Cove, then reenters the park just south of the trailhead to the best-known and probably most spectacular natural feature in the park, Western Brook Pond. From the road, the mountain range appears to have been notched where Western Brook exits the pond. The largest of several flooded, glaciated valleys in the park, Western Brook Pond is a narrow, deep lake with sheer canyon sides nearly 600 meters (2,000 feet) high. A 4-kilometer hiking trail leads from the parking area at Hwy. 430 to a landing at the outlet of the pond, where a commercial excursion company offers boat tours the length of the pond and back. Tours are available, for a fee, from the first of June through the end of September.

Western Brook Day-Use Area is located at the mouth of Western Brook, a few kilometers north of the Western Brook Pond trailhead. Picnic tables, a picnic shelter, and outdoor toilets are located nearby at Broom Point.

The road leaves the park just beyond Western Brook and enters the town of St. Pauls, on St. Pauls Inlet, a broad, sprawling bay frequented by harbor seals and other marine wildlife. The town offers only a few services, including a gas station/restaurant combination (lacking, sadly, an "Eat Here and Get Gas" sign).

North of St. Pauls the road turns inland but remains mostly flat or slightly rolling. The town of **Cow Head** has a hospitality home, small museum, and the Shallow Bay Motel, with a restaurant and lounge. The explorer Jacques Cartier anchored in Cow Cove to ride out a storm during his exploration of the western shore of Newfoundland in 1534.

Just north of Cow Head is the final section of Gros Morne National Park. On the shore of Shallow Bay is the second-largest campground in the park, with hot showers, flush toilets, and a swimming beach. The campground is open from mid-June to mid-October.

From the northern boundary of the national park, the Viking Trail follows the coast of the Gulf of St. Lawrence closely and continues to be a mostly flat route through strange and lovely terrain. Icebergs are a familiar sight along this coastline, even in summer. Small towns dot the coast, but they offer very few services. Restaurants seem to come and go with the seasons and are often opened in partnership with other businesses, such as craft shops and tiny grocery stores.

A few kilometers up the coast, the Arches Provincial Park is a picnic area built on the shore beside limestone formations that have been eroded into a pair of arches by the action of waves and weather.

Daniel's Harbour is a small mining community, with a motel and restaurant.

Gros Morne National Park, with the outlet of

After Daniel's Harbour, the landscape is barren and heaped with tailings from the mines, and little grows here except the grotesque, stunted trees known by Newfoundlanders as tuckamores.

River of Ponds, with a few housekeeping cottages and a tiny convenience store, is typical of many small towns along the west coast. Life is not easy in northern Newfoundland, and the difficulties are reflected in the

Western Brook Pond visible in the background.

homes: small, no-nonsense, ranch-style houses stripped of everything unessential. Boxlike, they are stuck along not-very-precise streets or on bare hillsides. Little attention is given to such superfluities as yards and flower gardens. In these fishing and lumbering communities hardly any effort is made to capture the tourist trade.

Adjacent to the community, **River of Ponds Provincial Park** has forty campsites and a day-use area, and is located on the shore of River of Ponds itself, one of the province's finest trout and salmon rivers. Virtually every river and lake in the region is acclaimed for its sport-fishing for brook trout and Atlantic salmon.

The village of **Hawke's Bay** supports a motel and restaurant, Maynard's Motor Inn, and Valhalla Lodge Bed-and-Breakfast. Just north of it is an interesting side trip to **Port au Choix**, on a slightly narrower paved road without shoulders. Following some moderate rolling hills are a couple of long, steep slopes after the fishing community of Port Saunders (where there are stores, restaurants, and a small hospital). Port au Choix National Historic Park is an archaeological site at the burial grounds of primitive hunter-gatherers known as the Maritime Archaic People, who lived in the area from 2000 to 1000 B.C. Nearby are the sites of Eskimo communities established after the disappearance of the Archaic villages. In Port au Choix itself is the Sea Echo Motel, with a lounge and restaurant.

Although I ended my tour of the Viking Trail at Port au Choix, local residents assured me that good cycling exists for the remaining 229 kilometers to St. Anthony, at the end of the Northern Peninsula. The route continues mostly flat and follows the coastline closely to the village of Eddie's Cove, then cuts inland across the northern tip of the peninsula to St. Anthony. Along the way are a number of villages, including Plum Point, which offers most services. The port village of **St. Barbe** is the terminal for the ferry to the Labrador mainland. Cyclists find few opportunities in nearly roadless Labrador, although a recently paved road now connects villages along a 65-kilometer strip of coastline in its extreme southeast corner. The ferry operates two or three trips per day on a first-come, first-served basis, May through December.

L'Anse aux Meadows National Historic Site is reached by following Hwy. 436 north of Hwy. 430, shortly before the town of St. Anthony. Located on the site of the only known Viking colony in North America, it consists of several reconstructed sod houses and a visitors' center. Archaeological evidence and carbon dating

The coastline of the Northern Peninsula, in western Newfoundland.

of relics suggest the settlement was inhabited between the years A.D. 860 and 1060.

Located at the end of Hwy. 430, on the northeast tip of the Northern Peninsula, **St. Anthony** is the largest community on the peninsula and is equipped with a shopping mall, restaurants, motels, and most services.

4

Avalon Peninsula

Begin/End: St. John's
Roads: TransCanada Hwy. 1, Hwy. 90, Hwy. 10
Accommodations: Campgrounds, some bed-and-breakfast inns, and motels
Length: 300 kilometers (186 miles)
Difficulty: Easy to fairly difficult

Newfoundland is so full of contrasts that it is never difficult to find unusual and varied country, regardless of where you travel in the province. Still, when I set out in search of a cycling destination that differed from mountainous Gros Morne National Park, I was hardly prepared for the landscape of the southern and eastern portions of the Avalon Peninsula. It is a place of uncommon, stark beauty, a flatlands of such enormous dimensions that under some circumstances it must be unbearably harsh and lonely. Strange rock formations and eerily uniform boulders lay scattered over fields of lichen and moss; ponds and small lakes are scattered everywhere across the savannahlike plains, but they rest at various levels—sometimes a meter or a meter and a half higher than a neighboring pond 6 meters away. Caribou can be seen grazing far across open plains. Moose inhabit lowlands and forests in such numbers they are a traffic hazard. The place is eminently exotic.

The Avalon Peninsula is a large H-shaped wing dangling to the east of the bulk of Newfoundland and is itself composed of four sizable peninsulas. The largest of these, at the southeast corner of the peninsula, is circled by Hwys. 90 and 10 (and connected by a short section of TransCanada 1) and is easily reached from St. John's to the north or from the Argentia ferry terminal to the west. At the heart of the loop is the 868-square-kilometer Avalon Wilderness Reserve, home to Newfoundland's largest caribou herd. Illegal hunting had reduced the herd to fewer than 100 animals before the establishment of the reserve in 1964. Today, after 25 years of protection and management, about 5,500 caribou live on the peninsula. Accessible only by hiking trail and canoe—and by a strictly enforced permit system—the wilderness area also supports approximately 3,500 moose, as well as healthy populations of lynx, fox, otter, beaver, hare, weasel, mink, willow ptarmigan, and ruffed grouse.

Travelers coming to Newfoundland via the Nova Scotia ferry have the option of taking the 5- to 7-hour ferry route to Channel-Port-aux-Basque and motoring (or pedaling if they have the time and energy) the 848 kilometers to the Avalon Peninsula. More convenient is to take the 12- to 14-hour ferry trip from North Sydney, Nova Scotia, to Argentia, on the west coast of the Avalon Peninsula. A third alternative is to fly to St. John's airport and bicycle from there south to the loop.

Unseasoned seafarers should be warned that the ferry ride from North Sydney to Argentia can seem exceedingly long, especially when seas are high. The boat is equipped with high-backed, padded lounge chairs and booths that are comfortable for playing cards, reading, or watching video movies but are patently unsuitable for sleeping. If you can afford the extra $85.00 for a four-berth cabin (or $26.50 for a single berth), it can make the trip much more enjoyable. By the end of the cruise, passengers are sleeping on the deck, beneath tables, curled

between armrests in chairs and anywhere else they can find a flat spot out of the main flow of pedestrian traffic. Be sure also to pack a lot of food. Although the cafeteria meals on board are not priced much higher than at mainland restaurants, servings are small and quality is unremarkable. If you're prone to seasickness, keeping a full stomach is one way to avoid nausea.

ST. JOHN'S TO HWY. 90 INTERSECTION—44.8 KILOMETERS (28 MILES)

For the sake of convenience, I've described the route beginning and ending in St. John's, although it is not necessary to visit the capital city in order to bike the loop. A counterclockwise circuit of the loop has two advantages. It increases the probability of tailwinds across the southern portion of the peninsula, where vast open spaces can be swept by substantial winds, and it leaves the most scenic portions of the trip for last.

St. John's (pop. 155,500) is one of several cities in Canada that advertises itself as the oldest community in North America. Although it is likely it was first visited by Basque fishermen or Viking explorers, the first written evidence of Europeans visiting the harbor at St. John's came in 1497, when John Cabot took refuge there and christened it "New founde land." An English merchant followed and constructed the first building on the shore of the harbor in 1528. Later still, in 1583, Sir Humphrey Gilbert claimed the entire island for England. In subsequent conflicts between the British, Dutch, and French, all of whom recognized the strategic importance of the city and the potential wealth of the Atlantic fishing grounds it commanded, ownership changed hands several times and various fortifications grew up on hills around the harbor.

Perched on hillsides sloping down to the docks of the deep, natural harbor, the inner city of St. John's today is a dense cluster of colorful buildings and homes lining narrow, somewhat erratic streets. The historic inner city is surrounded by a metropolitan sprawl of suburbs and shopping centers that extends for several kilometers to the north and east. Cyclists leaving the city are faced with most of the usual problems associated with urban travel.

The TransCanada Highway originates in St. John's, then proceeds for 7,776 kilometers to its western terminus in Vancouver, British Columbia. From the city and through its eastern suburbs, the highway is a divided four-lane that opens up to include paved shoulders one meter wide. Terrain is moderately uneven, although no hills are large enough to be troublesome. Traffic can be very heavy, especially in summer, and might motivate some riders to take the less populated but more scenic route along the coast of Conception Bay on Hwy. 60.

Butter Pot Provincial Park, located about 29 kilometers southwest of St. John's, has 149 camping sites and such amenities as an interpretation center, amphitheater, swimming beach, and hiking trails. Because of its proximity to St. John's, the park is quite popular and will often be filled to capacity on summer weekends.

Immediately after the provincial park, Hwy. 1 shrinks to a two-lane without paved shoulder. The 16-kilometer trip from here to the turnoff on Hwy. 90 can be unpleasant due to heavy car and truck traffic, so it is best, if possible, to travel that section early in the morning.

HWY. 90 INTERSECTION TO HOLYROOD POND PROVINCIAL PARK—75 KILOMETERS (46.7 MILES)

The intersection of Hwy. 90 and Hwy. 1 is well marked and is serviced by a gas station and small restaurant.

Hwy. 90, a two-lane secondary road without paved shoulders, offers immediate relief from the traffic of the TransCanada Highway. It passes at first through terrain that is wooded and gently rolling, with numerous ponds nestled among the spruces in the low spots. Here, as elsewhere in the poorly drained soil of Newfoundland, the ponds are at various levels, sometimes perched virtually on hilltops while other ponds only 100 meters away may be 3 or 6 meters lower.

This portion of the peninsula is on the fringe of the St. John's resort area and is developed with clusters of cottages, trailer parks, and stores, especially around the shores of the larger ponds and lakes. Weekend traffic will be fairly heavy along the first leg of the loop.

A little over 9 kilometers south of the intersection is a picnic site, Father Duffy's Well Provincial Park, named for a locally famous priest of the mid-nineteenth century whose parish duties required him to frequently pass this way on foot. During one of his treks he discovered the spring and afterward often used it as a resting place. Later, local residents came to believe the water was blessed.

About one and a half kilometers beyond Father Duffy's well is Salmonier Nature Park, a self-guided preserve administered by the provincial government. On display in sizable enclosures and spread out along a 2-kilometer trail are about thirty species of native mammals and birds, including moose, caribou, and lynx. An entrance fee of 50 cents is collected at a kiosk beside the parking area.

The road continues to wind around hills and ponds, and through rolling hills wooded mostly with spruce. Houses soon become more scattered and diminish in frequency. The road varies from good to fair condition, with some sections of bumpy pavement apparently caused by frost heaves in winter.

A gradual descent of one and a half kilometers leads to the valley of the Salmonier River. This popular salmon stream passes through the town of **Salmonier**, where there is a grocery store and service station, then empties into the Salmonier Arm of St. Mary's Bay. The road follows the eastern shore of Salmonier Arm for nearly 16 kilometers, climbing and dropping gradually on slowly rolling hills along the inlet. The landscape here can best be described as gentle: low, rounded hills topped with sparse growths of spruce. Houses crowd both sides of the inlet.

At the intersection with Hwy. 94, Hwy. 90 turns east and inland, climbing a long hill and leaving most of the development behind. From here expect a gradual ascent, never steep and sometimes flat, but enough of a climb to reach a fairly high elevation. Forests of spruce and fir give way to more open country, with hills rolling away in the distance toward the interior. Low ranges of spruce thickets are scattered across tundralike hillsides— a preview of the bleak and sparse country to come.

At the towns of Gulch and Riverhead, the road returns to the coast, running along the shore of St. Mary's Harbour. This end of the peninsula is much less utilized as a resort area, yet, paradoxically, is far more attractive than the relatively crowded country to the north. Riverhead has a small grocery store but no other services.

The fishing community of **St. Mary's** is in the heart of Newfoundland's Irish region, and natives speak a dialect definitely tinged with Emerald Isle brogue. The town is spread out along the bay, much of it on a bluff about 45 meters above the water, and looks out on a pleasant view of the water and the rocky, lightly inhabited shoreline across it. Services include a grocery, post office, and gas station, but no lodging is available.

The terrain after St. Mary's becomes increasingly more interesting. Low, rolling hills are barren of anything but low vegetation and are frequently used to pasture sheep. Hills are low and gradual, although occasional steep pitches lead down to shallow river bottoms, then climb up the other side.

About 3 kilometers south of St. Mary's is Point La Haye Natural Scenic Attraction, a beach and picnic area situated beside a warm-water lagoon along the coast of St. Mary's Bay. It was the site of a community of Basque fishermen who settled there in the early sixteenth century.

After Point La Haye, the road winds along a rolling bluff above the coast, past fenced pastures that end at the bluff, and passes through fairly bunched hills in the village of Gaskiers.

HOLYROOD POND PROVINCIAL PARK TO LA MANCHE PROVINCIAL PARK— 135.5 KILOMETERS (84.2 MILES)

Holyrood Pond Provincial Park is located on the slope of a steep hill leading down to the shore of Holyrood Pond, a 19-kilometer-long saltwater estuary. The park is small, equipped with only 15 primitive sites and a small number of picnic tables and vault-type toilets.

Beyond the park, Hwy. 90 follows the shore of the pond south along the top of a steep bluff. The pond is often obscured by fog in summer. From the road, situated high enough to look out over the top of the fog, it is like looking down on cloudbanks from an airplane.

The village of **St. Vincents** has a restaurant, grocery, and post office, all located on the bluff above Holyrood Pond. The road is the largest piece of flat terrain in the village, forcing many of the houses to be built almost to the end of the road. The coastline of the Atlantic here, beyond English Cape, is notable for deep water very close to shore. During summer those depths attract large numbers of whales that can often be seen cruising surprisingly close to shore. After St. Vincents the road number changes without fanfare to Hwy. 10 and winds gradually down to sea level and a causeway at the mouth of the pond. Prominent signs warn that during storms this stretch of low highway may be washed out by surf that breaks over the dunes and a seawall along the shore. A bridge crosses the narrow outlet of the pond.

The town of St. Stephens, with a grocery store but

no other services, begins on the far side of the pond, after a winding, fairly steep climb away from the water. A hairpin turn near the top of the bluff offers a good view of the ocean and the valley of the Peter's River.

At the outskirts of the towns of St. Stephens and Peter's River begins a long stretch of barren flatlands. A road sign at the beginning of it warns that caribou may be in the roadway for the next 20 kilometers. It's not an idle warning. This area, though well south of the boundary of the Avalon Wilderness Reserve, is the favored summer range of much of the Avalon caribou herd. The animals migrate north to rutting grounds within the reserve in late August and early September, but often return to the Peter's River area in winter. When I passed through in late June, large numbers of scattered caribou were visible a half kilometer to a kilometer away. According to a local ranger, by the end of July and into August the 200- to 600-pound animals often stray close enough to the road to create traffic hazards. Although large, caribou are not aggressive and probably never create a problem for cyclists except when they run inadvertently onto the highway. For better viewing of wildlife in the expansive, barren flatlands around Peter's River, consider carrying a pair of compact binoculars.

The barrens are ideal habitat for caribou, who depend on a diet of lichen, mushrooms, and tender plants. The country here is so desolate and flat that it's tempting to compare it to Australia's Outback or Africa's Seringhetti Plains, though of course the scale is not nearly as grand as in those famous flatlands. Still, as far as you can see in every direction, the terrain is flat, scattered with patches of low-lying arctic vegetation and large numbers of jumbled stones and boulders, known as "erratics," that were dropped by receding glaciers 10,000 years ago. Only at close range does the terrain prove to be rich in vegetation. Because the road is newly paved (it remained gravel until 1986) and raised on a bed of stones, it's possible to look out over the land and see thousands of tiny ponds and bogs nestled in hollows on the plains. Slow-moving streams connect many of the ponds, filtering gradually into small rivers that wind toward the coast.

After the intersection with St. Shotts Road, a paved two-lane that dead-ends 13.6 kilometers south at the village of St. Shotts, distant views of the ocean open up to the east and south.

A winding descent along a fairly steep bluff leads to the town of **Trepassey**, which is situated at the outlet of

Sheep pastures sloping to the coast of Newfoundland's Avalon Peninsula.

several rivers flowing into Trepassey Harbour. The Welsh name of the town translates to "the dead," or "dead souls," presumably in reference to a Welsh settlement that collapsed there in the 1620s. With a population of 1,460, Trepassey today is the largest community on the southern peninsula and is best known for being the departure point for Amelia Earhart's celebrated transatlantic flight in 1928. Services include grocery stores and restaurants and the Trepassey Motel and Tourist Home, which has a dining room and lounge. But if the government-owned fish plant that employs up to half the population closes in 1991 or 1992, as employees have been warned it might, some of those services are likely to close as well.

A steep but short climb out of the valley leads to more savannahlike terrain east of Trepassey. Though similar to the flatlands to the west, this portion of the peninsula is hillier, with thickets of spruce in the lowlands and large numbers of erratic boulders scattered elsewhere. Some stretches are so rocky and barren that, as in the Port-aux-Basques region far to the west, they make the landscape seem moonlike.

The villages of Biscay Bay and Portugal Cove South offer no services. At Portugal Cove South the road cuts northeast, away from the coast, and enters the last long stretch of Avalon barrens. From here the route follows a shallow river valley for several kilometers, with rocky canyons, waterfalls, and rapids visible. Elsewhere, although less flat than before, the barrens remain enormously flat and open, with batches of vegetation showing among the rocks and the large numbers of randomly sown ponds. Although the habitat appears similar to that in the Peter's River region, caribou are seldom spotted in this area. That may be partly due to the increased number of fishing shacks erected by local residents as weekend retreats. Most of them are tiny, very basic structures built on blocks beside the abundant ponds. Local residents admit the ponds, once filled with native brook trout and landlocked salmon, have been overfished and produce mostly small fish now. The road continues to be in excellent condition on its raised bed; shoulders are soft gravel. Traffic is extremely light.

Forty kilometers east of Trepassey is a gravel road south to **Chance Cove Provincial Park**. The narrow road is almost 6.5 kilometers long and is so rough—with large, sharp stones imbedded in it—that skinny tires are unlikely to survive the ride. It might be worth a walk, however, since it is the only campground in this corner of the peninsula and is located on a wonderfully remote and interesting beach. The road passes through lowland clumps of spruce draped in the moss known locally as "old man's beard." Passing through dense growth here, we rounded a corner and surprised an adult moose crossing the road 9 meters ahead of me. The moose herd, numbering more than 100,000 throughout the island, is descended entirely from four animals introduced early in the 1900s.

The campground is loosely arranged around a large parking area where some campers simply stake out a campsite on the perimeter. Better sites are located under the trees on the low bluff above, where there is a view of the ocean. The campground is equipped with picnic tables and outhouses, but the tea-colored water available from a hand pump must be boiled before it can be used for cooking or drinking. There is no fee for camping. Whales and seals are often seen in the waters of Chance Cove, a short walk down from the campground. Chance Cove, incidentally, is just one of the dozens of colorful place names in Newfoundland. A few minutes with a map uncovers such gems as Blow Me Down, Heart's Desire, Ireland's Eye, Tickle Harbour, Mistaken Point, Too Good Arm, and Come by Chance.

Hwy. 10 east of the campground continues to pass through pond-strewn barrens but after a few kilometers begins a long climb up to more heavily forested terrain. It remains mostly flat, but a range of low mountains is visible inland, and the spruce-filled lowland areas are becoming larger and more predominant.

Cappahayden is a fishing village located on a bluff above the coast. Its only services are a gas station and tiny grocery. From here the road shifts gradually north and follows fairly close to the coastline. Hills at first are gently rolling, with some fairly long ascents but few steep ones. Forests of spruce begin to predominate.

The eastern coast of the peninsula is dotted with small fishing villages, most offering grocery stores and gas stations and many having some historical significance worth investigating. Renews, for instance, was visited by the Pilgrim ship *Mayflower* in 1620, when the English vessel stopped there for supplies on its journey bringing settlers to the New World. Farther up the coast, Aquaforte was the site of an eighteenth-century clash between the French fleet and English soldiers. According to legend, French sailors grounded their ships near the town and buried a treasure on the beach before escaping on foot across the peninsula to Placentia. Just north of Aquaforte, an English colony was established at Ferryland, only to be destroyed by Dutch invaders in 1763.

Commercial fishing is the primary source of income along this irregular coastline and remains today a difficult and dangerous business. Wool sweaters knitted in the villages and popular today with tourists were traditionally constructed with distinctive designs that varied from village to village. The designs on the sweaters served to identify the home towns of fishermen who occasionally drowned and washed up on the beaches.

In the vicinity of the village of Fermeuse, about 26 kilometers from Chance Cove Campground, the terrain becomes much hillier, crossed by rivers that have cut deep, rocky gorges through the valleys, and is predominantly forested with spruce. The inlets along the coast are deep and steep sided, with outcroppings of rock dropping straight into the ocean. Descents into the towns at the bases of those inlets (and the ascents out of them) become steeper and longer.

Ferryland, the largest town along this section of coast, offers all services, including bed-and-breakfasts and restaurants (the Downs Inn is highly recommended). Again, as on the west shore, this area is within easy vacation range of St. John's residents and is popular with resorters and tourists.

Just beyond Ferryland and the town of Calvert, the terrain changes dramatically. A low range of mountains rises to the west, and the road follows the coast high along an irregular bluff. Ascents and descents continue to grow in intensity and frequency. Especially where the road slices across the bases of peninsulas, hilly terrain creates ascents as long as one and a half kilometers, with some pitches quite steep. At the top and bottom of each small peninsula is an inlet and town, usually accompanied by the characteristic steep drop to sea level.

By the town of Cape Broyle the terrain can be considered mountainous. Though it does not match Gros Morne in magnitude or difficulty, frequent outcroppings of rock and the rounded, barren tops of some of the peaks are reminiscent of the national park. The road negotiates the higher slopes by taking long switchbacks up and down them.

LA MANCHE PROVINCIAL PARK TO ST. JOHN'S—44 KILOMETERS (27.5 MILES)

La Manche Provincial Park is a large, well-equipped campground located on the La Manche River, near its mouth at the site of the abandoned town of La Manche. The Witless Bay Islands Ecological Reserve is a bird sanctuary on nearby offshore islands and is home to such seabirds as puffins, kittiwakes, petrals, razorbills, and murres. Guided boat tours originate from Witless Bay, about 10 kilometers north of the campground.

The route north of La Manche continues to be hilly, with bare-topped mountains inland, and rocky shoreline sometimes visible along the coast.

Twenty-one kilometers north of the provincial park

is the intersection with gravel-and-pavement Hwy. 13, which runs west to TransCanada 1 and will be a good shortcut back to the highway once it is fully paved.

From Witless Bay the region becomes much more developed with houses scattered along the road and communities blending one into another. Services expand to include convenience stores and supermarkets. A final 8-kilometer stretch of undeveloped and lightly rolling country north of Bay Bulls gives way to the outskirts of suburban St. John's. About 6.5 kilometers of suburbs and busy highway precede the city limits of St. John's.

ST. JOHN'S TO ARGENTIA FERRY TERMINAL—131 KILOMETERS (81.9 MILES)

As mentioned above, the ride along TransCanada 1 from St. John's to the ferry terminal in Argentia can be a tiresome one, especially after the paved shoulders end at Butter Pot Provincial Park. As always, of course, you can beat much of the traffic by traveling early in the morning and during the week. The 51-kilometer stretch from Butter Pot Provincial Park to the turnoff on Hwy. 100 is the most difficult, but traffic does ease somewhat after each intersection along the route.

Hwy. 100 to Argentia is a wide two-lane with busted shoulders. Most of the 45 kilometers from the intersection to the ferry terminal is through undeveloped country, where long wooded hills alternate with sparse plains dotted with ponds. About midway on the route is Fitzgerald's Pond Provincial Park, with twenty-four unserviced sites, drinking water, picnic tables, and vault-type toilets.

After following the valley of the North East River, Hwy. 100 passes over some sizable hills near Dunville and Freshwater, before ending at the enormous and in-

Car ferries like this make daily trips between Newfoundland and Nova Scotia.

congruous U.S. Naval Base in Argentia. Just outside the town, Castle Hill National Historic Park is located on the site of an eighteenth-century French garrison from which French soldiers made frequent forays against the English fort at St. John's. The ruins of the fort are perched on a large hill with a commanding view of huge Placentia Bay.

· PRINCE EDWARD · ISLAND

In the real world there may be no ideal bicycling destinations, but some people would argue that Prince Edward Island comes as near to it as you can reasonably expect to get. First, it is an island, so it is automatically buffered from many of the traffic and population problems typical of so many mainland areas. Second, it is enveloped in an atmosphere that is nearly perfect for bicycling. From the moment you step off the ferries at Wood Islands or Borden, it's apparent that this is a place where the pace of life is better suited for bicycles and secondary roads than automobiles and superhighways. Highways are busy in the vicinity of Charlottetown (capital of the province and largest city, with a population of 15,800) and in the tourist snarl in the Cavendish area, but elsewhere traffic is light to moderate. More important, local drivers yield the way to cyclists (without resenting it) and often wave as they pass, genuinely pleased to see visitors to their province.

Still, one misconception needs to be addressed. While the island's reputation as a world-class cycling destination is well founded, it is not a reputation based entirely on a lack of hills. The coastal regions of the island, where many of the most interesting cycling routes are located, tend to be flat or lightly rolling, but most of the interior of the island is surprisingly hilly. Hills tend to be long and steep, though seldom exceeding one kilometer in length or 4 percent in gradient. The highest point of the island is near the town of Springton, east of Charlottetown, where a hilltop reaches 152 meters above sea level. None of the climbs compare to those in Cape Breton National Park or on the Gaspé Peninsula, but don't come to P.E.I. looking for nothing but easy, flatland riding.

It's difficult to characterize any one province in simple terms, but P.E.I. is the least rugged, the most gentle, perhaps the quietest, and certainly the greenest of the eastern provinces. Much of the island has been cultivated or turned into pasturage in the 270 years since it was first settled by Europeans, giving the landscape a pastoral appearance that brings to mind old agricultural regions of Europe, particularly Ireland. Irish settlers who came to the island in large numbers in the eighteenth and nineteenth centuries were comfortable in the familiar climate and surroundings, and joined large numbers of English, Scottish, and United Empire Loyalists who had already established homes there. Today's residents of the island are proud of their Irish and Scottish heritage and won't hesitate to recall it at the slightest provocation.

P.E.I. is the smallest Canadian province and is compact enough to be easily explored on bicycle. By way of comparison, it is somewhat larger than New York's Long Island, but with only 2 percent of its inhabitants. The population of 128,000 and the 3,725 kilometers of paved highways and secondary roads combine to give it the highest ratio of road kilometers to population of any province in Canada.

Weather

The climate of P.E.I. is determined to a large degree by its island status. In winter it can be cold, but during summer temperatures are pleasant and moderate, with daytime highs averaging about 75 degrees F, although days of 90 degrees F are not uncommon. Temperatures are noticeably cooler near the coast, and evenings are often cool enough for sweaters or light jackets, even during the height of summer. Winds are generally light, though strong winds along the coast are fairly common. Weather can be hotter than in coastal regions such as those along the Bay of Fundy, but will certainly be milder than in the interior regions of the larger provinces. Rainfall averages a little over 7.6 centimeters per month in June and increases slightly in July and August, reaching about 10 centimeters in October.

Transportation

Charlottetown Airport is served by Air Canada, Canadian Airlines International, Air Nova, and Inter-Canadian, and connects with major cities throughout the Maritimes and the eastern United States.

Ferry service to the mainland is provided by Marine Atlantic between Cape Tormentine, New Brunswick, and Borden, P.E.I. (a 45-minute crossing). To the east, Northumberland Ferries Ltd. crosses between Caribou, Nova Scotia, and Wood Islands, P.E.I. (a 75-minute crossing). Schedules vary, but in summer ferries depart at roughly one-hour intervals from 6:00 A.M. to late evening. Reservations are requested. For exact schedules and reservations, contact Marine Atlantic at the address and phone number listed at the end of this introduction.

Bus service on the island is provided year-round by Island Transit (phone 902/892-6167).

Language

English is spoken almost exclusively, except in some portions of Prince County on the west end of the island, where pockets of Acadians still speak French. The accent of the English speakers is musical and lilting, reminiscent of Irish and Scottish roots, but is easily understood by Anglophiles "from away."

Traffic Laws

Speed limits on island roads vary from 40 to 60 kilometers per hour in urban areas, to 80 kilometers per hour on most provincial highways and 90 kilometers per hour on TransCanada 1 and a few sections of other major highways.

Cycling Laws

Cyclists must obey the same traffic laws as motorists. The only specific bicycling law mentioned in the P.E.I. Visitors Guide is that all bikes must be equipped with an audible bell. While that might be a good idea, especially for urban riding, nobody I talked to on the island—including the owner of the island's largest bicycle shop—had heard of the "law" or knew anyone who obeyed it.

Miscellaneous

Keep in mind that Prince Edward Island's tourist season does not really get under way until late June. Although that has advantages for the early-season cyclist, many of the national and provincial campgrounds do not open until then, limiting the choices for lodging. On the plus side, motel and hotel prices will be somewhat lower before and after the tourist rush, and bed-and-breakfast inns will seldom be filled.

For More Information

For general information about Prince Edward Island, contact the Visitors Services, P.O. Box 940, Charlottetown, P.E.I., Canada C1A 7M5; phone 1-800-565-7421 (from the Maritimes), 1-800-565-0267 (from the rest of North America).

For more information about Prince Edward Island National Park, write P.E.I. National Park, District Superintendent, Environment Canada, Canadian Parks Service, P.O. Box 487, Charlottetown, P.E.I., Canada C1A 7L1.

Ferry schedules and reservations are available from Marine Atlantic at 100 Cameron Street Cape, Moncton, NB, Canada E1C 5Y6; phone 902/858-3753. Contact Northumberland Ferries Ltd. at P.O. Box 634, Charlottetown, P.E.I., Canada C1A 7L3; phone 902/566–3838.

5

Blue Heron Drive

Begin/End: Charlottetown or ferry terminal at Borden
Roads: Blue Heron Drive, Hwys. 1, 19, 6, 104, and connectors
Accommodations: Motels, bed-and-breakfast inns, provincial and national parks
Length: 191.7 kilometers (119.8 miles)
Difficulty: Easy to moderately easy

BORDEN TO CHARLOTTETOWN— 80.8 KILOMETERS (50.5 MILES)

Charlottetown, the business and political capital of P.E.I., is an excellent starting point for any number of cycle tours of the province. Not only does the city support a large variety of accommodations and services, but it is accessed by numerous roads and highways that radiate outward like spokes, all leading to interesting destinations and combining into a variety of trips. Gordon MacQueen, owner of MacQueen's Bike Shop (430 Queen Street, Charlottetown,

P.E.I., Canada C1A 4E8; phone 902/892-9843), promotes a number of short trips from the city. Others are described and mapped in *Cycling the Islands: P.E.I. and the Magdalen Islands* by P.E.I. resident Campbell Webster (Breakwater Press, St. John's, Newfoundland).

From a practical standpoint, however, cyclists arriving on the island by ferry from New Brunswick will want to begin and end their trip at the terminal in the town of **Borden** (as those arriving from Nova Scotia will want to begin at the terminal in Wood Islands). There is little advantage in traveling clockwise as opposed to counterclockwise except that prevailing south and southwest winds can make the counterclockwise tour a bit easier along the southern coast.

From the ferry dock in Borden, go east on Trans-Canada 1 for about 3 kilometers to the intersection with Hwy. 10 and take a right onto the Blue Heron Drive. The first leg, 11 kilometers on a two-lane secondary road to the junction with Hwy. 1 at Tryon, is through country you'll soon recognize as typical of rural P.E.I.: rolling hills of meadows and woodlots, their striking colors representing what island author Ian MacQuarrie calls in his book *The Bonshaw Hills* the "thirteen shades of green." You may also notice the absence of billboards on P.E.I. In their place, small, tasteful signs erected by the provincial government point toward accommodations, parks, restaurants, tourist attractions, and other services.

Cape Traverse was named by French settlers who originally used it as the embarkation point for crossings to the mainland. Until the early 1900s, a treacherous crossing across the ice in hand-drawn sled-boats was the only way, in winter, to transport mail and passengers between the island and the mainland. There is an exhibit and monument to that ferry service beside the road in the village.

At Tryon, take the left fork at the intersection with 116, then take an immediate right onto TransCanada 1. This busiest of island highways is a surprisingly pleasant ride. The surface is in good condition, the highway is lined with paved shoulders almost 2 meters wide, and traffic is heavy

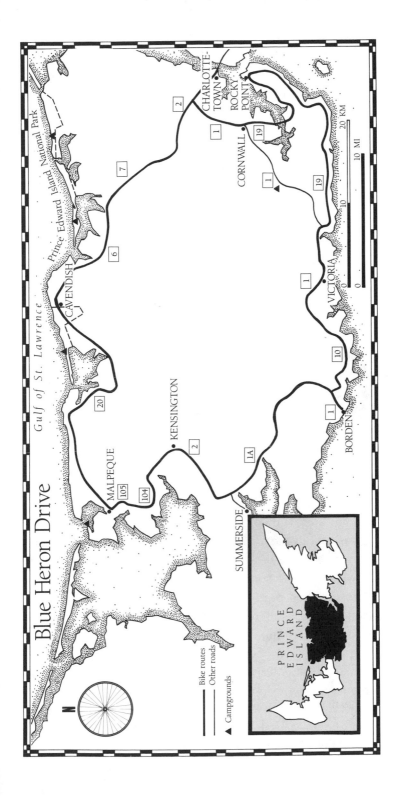

Blue Heron Drive

only during weekends. It offers long views of farmlands and river valleys and progresses from here to Charlottetown over long rolling hills. It is, in fact, a good alternative to the more circuitous and less traveled roads of the rest of the Blue Heron Drive. If you're in a hurry, you can do worse than to proceed directly to Charlottetown on Hwy. 1.

After several kilometers, the highway drops south from the interior farmlands to the coast at the village of **Victoria**, where there are several bed-and-breakfast inns, the Orient Hotel, Victoria Village Inn, and the Lobsterland Restaurant. The Victoria Playhouse offers excellent regional theater—both comedy and drama—evenings from July 1 to Labor Day. Just across Victoria Harbour is Victoria Provincial Park, with picnic grounds, swimming beach, showers, flush toilets, and changing house (no camping).

Almost 5 kilometers out of Victoria, at the village of DeSable, take a right turn onto Hwy. 19 to stay on the Blue Heron Drive (all such intersections are well marked; simply follow the distinctive Blue Heron markers). Hwy. 19 is a wide two-lane without paved shoulders, but it is in good condition and lightly traveled. Much of the route from here to Charlottetown is along flat, coastal terrain with spectacular views of the Northumberland Strait and the coasts of New Brunswick and Nova Scotia beyond it.

A bumpy gravel lane leads a few hundred meters off Hwy. 19 to Argyle Shore Provincial Park, a day-use picnic area with outhouses and no water, on a short, grassy bluff above the water. A short climb takes you down to a fine beach, expansive and interesting during low tide, and a good view of the characteristic red-clay bluffs of this portion of the coast. The redness of the soil is the result of its high iron content. During the summer, large numbers of blue heron can be seen stalking fish in tidal pools here.

A small grocery and cottages are the only services in the town of Argyle Shore, 2.4 kilometers beyond the provincial picnic park. From here the road continues to be flat, just above sea level, through lightly inhabited farm country. Long fields and meadows of brilliant green slope gently down to the bluffs above the beach. Some of the old farm-houses, with their high, four-sided gables, have elaborate Victorian touches. Portions of the road are in poor condition, with patches and crumbling edges.

Beyond Canoe Cove and Rice Point (no services at either village), the coastline bends eastward and Hwy. 19 circles a peninsula bounded by the Northumberland Strait on the south and the broad West River on the north. Just beyond Nine Mile Creek, a paved road left is a shortcut to New Dominion and shaves nearly 16 kilometers off the ride to Charlottetown. The ride around the peninsula is pleasant, however, and fairly flat, and includes the opportunity to stop at Fort Amherst National Historic Park at **Rocky Point**, site of Port La Joye, the first white settlement on the island. It was established by the French in 1720 and was captured by the British in 1758. Picnic facilities and a museum are located there, and nearby is a reconstructed Micmac village portraying the life of the island's original settlers.

The town of Rocky Point has a restaurant and a view of Charlottetown across Charlottetown Harbour. Legend has it that the shore here is haunted by the ghost of a woman drowned during a storm 200 years ago. Witnesses say she staggers from the water, dressed in white and draped in seaweed, crying "Samuel, Samuel," the name of her lost husband.

From Rocky Point the road passes through hillier terrain, with some hills bunched tightly, though none are especially high or long. Small prosperous farms are interspersed with newer houses, occasional bed-and-breakfast inns, and a private campground. Some patches of spruce and fir break up the otherwise open, rolling landscape.

After New Dominion (no services), Hwy. 19 turns north and crosses a causeway over the West River. From here to Cornwall and the intersection with TransCanada 1, the road passes through rolling hills with green pastures and meadows—and grazing cows and sheep—and views of the river beyond. Development increases near the intersection with Hwy. 1.

Beaches at low tide along Prince Edward Island's south shore.

Cornwall has most services and can be considered the beginning of suburban Charlottetown. From here to the city, Hwy. 1 is a busy two-lane (changing to four lanes where the heaviest development begins), with a one-and-a-half-kilometer paved shoulder for most of its length. The surface is in fair condition, but may be broken and patched in places. Just across the North River concentrations of fast-food restaurants, auto dealerships, and other trappings of civilization begin. Traffic can be very heavy, especially during traditional rush hours and on summer weekends.

CHARLOTTETOWN TO CAVENDISH —38.9 KILOMETERS (24.3 MILES)

Charlottetown, with all services, has much to offer visitors. It seems a larger city than its population of 15,800 would suggest, although that may be a relative matter since the second-largest city on P.E.I., Summerside, has a population of only 8,000, and the majority of the island's communities are very small.

The downtown region of Charlottetown is centered

on Province House, headquarters of the provincial legislature and the site of an agreement reached in 1864 that first united the Maritime Provinces into the Confederation of Canada. Other points of interest include the Confederation Centre of the Arts and Saint Dunstan's Basilica. Downtown businesses offer a variety of gift and craft shops, galleries, an excellent store selling used books, and a great selection of restaurants, with cuisine ranging from Irish to Chinese to traditional P.E.I. seafood. I came away dazed with pleasure after meals at the Claddagh Room, on Sydney Street, and at the Queen Street Café. At least two bike shops thrive in the city. MacQueens, on Queen Street, is the best equipped for repairs and is the area headquarters for P.E.I. cycling information.

If you weren't aware of it before visiting P.E.I., you certainly can't leave the island without knowing it is the setting for a series of novels written by L. M. Montgomery. The first of the novels, *Anne of Green Gables*, was published in 1908, has since been translated into thirty-six languages and made into at least three movies, and is one of the world's best-known books for young adults. Tourist publications and commercial enterprises of almost every variety—in Charlottetown there are even "Green Gables" convenience stores—capitalize rather shamelessly on the popularity of the books. In Cavendish, the island's primary tourist destination, "Anne" gift shops and museums appear with dreary regularity. Lucy Maud Montgomery grew up and lived most of her life in that coastal region of the island and would no doubt abhor the theme parks and tourist shops that have sprung up there to cash in on her fame.

She would probably be pleased, on the other hand, with the musical adaptation of her novel performed at the Confederation Centre for the Arts in Charlottetown. The presentation is splendid, professional in every regard, and a fine centerpiece to an evening in the capital city. One measure of the show's quality is its staying power: since 1965 it has been a virtual sellout every performance during the annual Charlottetown Festival from June to September. It and the other musicals during the festival are well worth seeing, but be sure to get tickets in advance. For information, contact Festival Ticketworks, P.O. Box 848, Charlottetown, P.E.I., Canada C1A 7L9; phone 1-800-565-0278 or 902/566-1267.

The section of the Blue Heron Drive between Charlottetown and Cavendish includes some of the best and worst that P.E.I. has to offer. The worst is that most of the 700,000 tourists who come to the island each summer seem to head directly to Cavendish, drawn like pilgrims to a religious shrine. On a more positive note, this portion of the island is beautiful, filled with long rolling hills and wooded valleys, with farmhouses so meticulously maintained and painted you might think they receive a stipend from the tourist council. The architecture is not quite as striking as in southern Nova Scotia, but the high gables, ornate trim, and imaginative paint jobs make the houses very interesting. They are often set in spectacular surroundings, among brilliant green fields dotted with rolled bales of hay, bordered by lush growths of lupines and enormous, perfectly manicured lawns. Many of those houses have been converted to bed-and-breakfast inns—so many, in fact, that there is probably never any shortage of lodging in this most popular region of the island. The more heavily traveled roads are often lined, in season, with vegetable stands offering strawberries and other island produce for sale.

To continue on the Blue Heron Drive north of Charlottetown, follow Brackley Point Road out of the city, past the airport, until it turns into Hwy. 15. During the peak of the tourist season, however, that two-lane highway can be extremely busy, so it may be a better idea to leave town via Hwy. 2. Eight kilometers after the intersection of Hwys. 2 and 1, turn right at the town of Milton on Hwy. 7, a two-lane secondary road that gets little traffic. It passes through rolling farm country for about 11 kilometers before joining the Blue Heron Drive at Hwy. 6. At this point you have a choice of going left to Cavendish and the remainder of the loop, or right on a side trip to **Prince Edward Island National Park**.

The national park extends in a narrow strip along 40 kilometers of sand dunes and beaches and can be entered via several access roads. The Rustico and Stanhope campgrounds are both reached by taking the right turn at the intersection of Hwys. 6 and 7, then after 3 kilometers turning left at Brackley Beach on Hwy. 15 and entering the park. The well-paved Gulf Shore Parkway runs the entire length of this portion of the national park, making an excellent bike ride and forming the heart of a number of possible day trips and assorted loops using secondary roads in the area. The coastal ride on the parkway is flat, separated from the beach by a low, rounded dune, with Rustico Bay and Covehead Bay on the inside, where a large population of blue heron can be observed close-up hunting small fish and other prey in the tidal shallows near shore. At any point along the route you can get off the road and walk over the dune to some of the finest, least crowded sand beaches in the Maritimes.

The three national park campgrounds vary in size, popularity, and services available. Rustico Island Campground, located 5 kilometers west of Brackley Beach, has a large number of unserviced campsites, flush toilets, access to the beach, and three kitchen shelters. It's open from June 19 through September 4 and is generally less crowded than the other campgrounds.

Stanhope Campground, 8 kilometers east of Brackley Beach, has serviced and unserviced sites, flush toilets, hot showers, and a camper's store. Facilities are open from June 16 through September 3.

Cavendish Campground, which is separated by water from the other campgrounds and can only be reached by circling back around Rustico Bay and continuing along Hwy. 6 to the town of Cavendish, is the largest and most popular of the campgrounds in the national park, largely because it is located near the heart of the theme parks and other tourist attractions in Cavendish. It is often full during summer weekends, and because reservations are not accepted, the best hope of getting a site is to arrive early in the day. Serviced and unserviced sites are available, as are flush toilets, hot showers, kitchen shelters, and a laundromat. Several hiking trails radiate from the campground (including the Homestead Trail, 13 kilometers long and open to hikers and bicyclists), as does a fine coastal bike ride along the campground's own section of the Gulf Shore Parkway.

Hwy. 6 leading to Cavendish is a busy road during the tourist season, and when I was there in the summer of 1990, was under extensive construction for resurfacing. It passes through a number of interesting villages, many of them offering basic services plus gift shops, galleries, and outstanding seafood restaurants. One P.E.I. tradition worth investigating is the prolific lobster suppers put on as fundraisers by various churches, such as Saint Ann's Church on Hwy. 224 between Hunter River and Stanley Bridge (meals are served daily except Sunday from 4:00 to 9:00 P.M. from the third Monday in June to the last Saturday in September). Similar lobster suppers are available at restaurants, churches, and even Lions Clubs in most sizable communities.

Towns like Rusticoville and North Rustico along Hwy. 6 have a scattering of services, including groceries and restaurants (Fisherman's Wharf Lobster Suppers in North Rustico is especially popular). Bed-and-breakfast inns continue to be abundant.

CAVENDISH TO BORDEN—72 KILOMETERS (45 MILES)

Cavendish is a sprawling, busy-as-a-beehive concentration of theme parks, minimalls, Anne of Green Gables museums and gift shops, and enormous RV parks. A few good restaurants and pubs redeem it somewhat (try Thirsty's, Cavendish Arms Pub, and Gilligan's Landing), but in general the heavy traffic, lack of paved shoulders, and carnival atmosphere are not conducive to good cycling.

Quintessential P.E.I. countryside begins again a short

distance beyond the concentration of development near the entrance to the national park campground in Cavendish. Hwy. 6 out of Cavendish is in fair condition, with occasional patches and cracks, and traffic is moderate to fairly heavy.

The town of Stanley Bridge, 8 kilometers from Cavendish, has a motel, grocery, and craft shops, as well as a natural history museum and marine aquarium. Because the road cuts across the base of several points of land here, glimpses of New London Bay are possible only at the inlets and from the tops of hills. From those elevations—modest as they are—you can see inland across kilometers of farm country, with geometric pastures and fields lined with thickets of spruce, and fading away in mist and distance.

The village of New London, birthplace of L. M. Montgomery, has several restaurants (including the New London Wharf Restaurant and New London Lions Lobster Suppers), as well as a tourist home and rental cottage. Staying on Hwy. 6 here leads directly to Kensington but leaves the Blue Heron Drive. Take the right turn in New London on Hwy. 20 to stay on the Blue Heron and continue through farmlands with unobstructed views of the Southwest River Valley and New London Bay. The road is in fair condition—narrow, often broken, and imperfectly patched—but the long views and rural atmosphere make it a worthwhile leg of the Blue Heron Drive.

French River has housekeeping cottages and limited services including a small grocery store off the main road in town. The country here is gorgeous, with long, rolling hills—some fairly high—and attractive houses. Views of the hills and fields reveal varied patterns and colors. One long stretch of rolling hills is a little more difficult than most of the route, but most ascents are minor and actually quite welcome because of the views of ocean and farmlands they afford. I met more cyclists here than on any other portion of the island.

Darnley has a restaurant and store. Bed-and-breakfast inns and housekeeping cottages continue to be scattered all along the coastline. Darnley Basin has one of the most varied and interesting shorelines on the island. Be aware that the old wooden bridge crossing the inlet of the basin is very rough and potentially damaging to skinny tires.

At **Malpeque** take a right to Cabot Provincial Park, where there are serviced and unserviced campsites, flush toilets, hot showers, a kitchen shelter, and an ocean beach. The campground is open June 16 through September 3. Nearby Malpeque Bay is world-famed for its Malpeque oysters. They can be sampled in Malpeque at Cabot's Reach Restaurant—six on the half shell for $5.95.

Continue south from Malpeque on Hwy. 105, then take a right on Hwy. 104. Again, signs marking the Blue Heron Drive are conspicuous and make it difficult to miss a turn. The route from here to Kensington is through more farmlands, though farms are smaller and less active than those to the north. Hwy. 104 is in only fair condition, with frequent patches and chuck holes.

Kensington is a quiet farming community with paved shoulders, tree-lined streets, and most services. On the outskirts of the town, turn right on Hwy. 2 to stay on the Blue Heron Drive. For the next 6 to 8 kilometers the highway can be fairly busy with local and truck traffic, and it is lined with paved shoulders about a meter to a meter and a half wide. Road conditions vary from good to poor, with some sections bumpy and patched, through flat and nondescript potato fields and abandoned farms. You'll smell the unmistakable odor of stale french fries before passing the Cavendish Farms potato plant, where a significant percentage of P.E.I.'s potato crop is frozen and packaged before distribution to the rest of Canada.

At the town of Traveler's Rest, turn south on Hwy. 1A at a confusing intersection, then continue on this highway after another strange intersection near Wilmot. The paved shoulders in this area are in sorry shape, broken and poorly patched, and some sections of the road's surface are rough as a washboard. Follow the signs for the Blue Heron Drive and stay on Hwy. 1A.

About 3 kilometers southwest on Hwy. 11 is the

city of **Summerside**, P.E.I.'s second-largest community and home to many attractive bed-and-breakfast inns, hotels, restaurants, and shops. Other attractions include fiddling contests, a dinner theater, harness racing, and the P.E.I. Sports Hall of Fame.

For the remainder of the distance to Central Bedeque, the terrain is flat, mostly hay and potato fields, and broken only by a view of the broad Wilmot River

Coastal dunes and farmlands are a common sight along the north shore of Prince Edward Island.

Valley. At Central Bedeque, where the limited services include a grocery, go west on Hwy. 10 to remain on the Blue Heron Drive. Down the road are Bedeque, where the Village Store has a good luncheon bar, and the turnoff to the picnic area and beach at Chelton Provincial Park (located 4 kilometers off Hwy. 10).

The final leg of Hwy. 10, to the intersection with Hwy. 1 and the short drive to Borden, continues through lightly rolling farm country. The final kilometer and a half of Hwy. 1 descends a gradual slope into Borden and affords a good view of the Northumberland Strait and New Brunswick beyond it.

6

Kings Byway Drive

Begin/End: Wood Islands Ferry
Terminal
Roads: Hwys. 1, 2, 16, 3, 4, 17, 18,
and connectors
Accommodations: Motels, bed-
and-breakfasts, provincial campgrounds
Length: 322.7 kilometers (201.7
miles)
Difficulty: Moderately easy to
moderately difficult

With the capital city and most of the population located
in the center of crescent-shaped Prince Edward Island,
the two ends become progressively less populated. The
eastern third of the island, the region roughly encom-
passed by Kings County, is more remote and rural than
the busy Charlottetown and Cavendish regions, though
it contains a number of small, vital communities. The
island's most extensive woodlands and a sizable lumbering industry are found there, as are some of the most
active fishing villages. Farms are perhaps less prosperous on the whole than in Queens and Prince counties—
abandoned farmhouses and overgrown fields are more

common here than elsewhere on the island—but they contribute nonetheless to a fine country atmosphere.

WOOD ISLANDS TO CHARLOTTETOWN— 60.6 KILOMETERS (37.9 MILES)

The view of P.E.I. from the Northumberland Ferry after departing from Nova Scotia is a fine introduction to the province. Flat green meadows ending abruptly at the red bluffs along the coast can mislead an eager cyclist into believing the entire province is as flat and inviting as this section of shoreline.

On shore at **Wood Islands Ferry Terminal** is a small cafeteria and a visitors' information center. TransCanada 1 begins on the island here, and is a wide two-lane with a nicely paved shoulder along most of its length. When the ferries unload, expect a short-lived surge of traffic heading west toward Charlottetown; otherwise Hwy. 1 here is a lonely and neglected stretch of road, perfect for cycling.

The flat coastal region around Wood Islands gives way somewhat to hillier terrain as Hwy. 1 cuts inland to the west. Hills are never difficult, although a few are long enough to be somewhat imposing, and some stretches of short, bunched hills can be a nuisance. The terrain is largely rolling hills, with abandoned and semiactive farms alternating. Meadows and pastures are often separated by narrow strips of vegetation or woodlots. The Northumberland Strait can be seen occasionally from the tops of the hills.

About 19 kilometers from Wood Islands, a long descent down to the town of Pinette and Pinette Harbour leads to Pinette Provincial Park, a picnic area and beach without camping facilities. Lobster and other shellfish are available for sale on the wharf in Pinette. Four kilometers

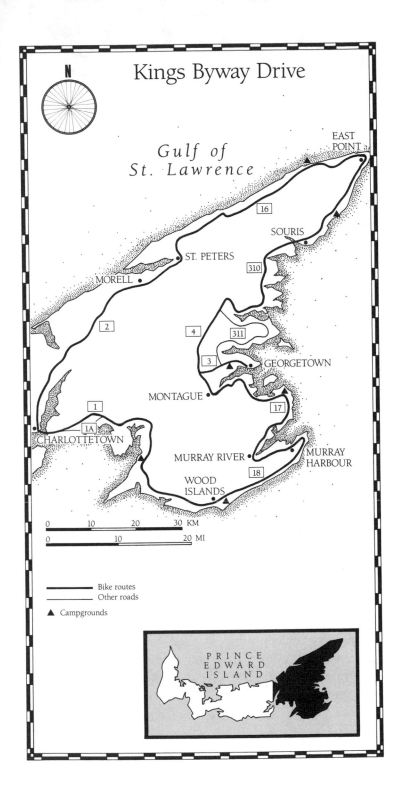

Kings Byway Drive

N

Gulf of St. Lawrence

EAST POINT

16

SOURIS

ST. PETERS

310

MORELL

2

4

311

3

GEORGETOWN

MONTAGUE

17

1

1A

CHARLOTTETOWN

MURRAY RIVER

18

MURRAY HARBOUR

WOOD ISLANDS

| 0 | 10 | 20 | 30 KM |

| 0 | 10 | 20 MI |

——— Bike routes
——— Other roads

▲ Campgrounds

PRINCE EDWARD ISLAND

Active and semi-active farms dot the interior of eastern P.E.I.

farther is the turnoff to Lord Selkirk Provincial Park, with primitive and serviced sites, flush toilets, hot showers, a kitchen shelter, laundromat, and great clam digging on the beach. The park is open June 29 through September 4.

Just south of the park, Hwy. 209, a paved secondary road, leads 11 kilometers out to the end of Point Prim and the oldest lighthouse on the island. Built in 1846, the lighthouse is still in operation.

Some of the largest hills in this stretch are between the provincial parks and the town of Cherry Valley. Again, none of them are back breakers, but expect to work a little on several. Traffic increases noticeably as you approach Charlottetown.

Eldon, just north of the provincial park, has a restaurant offering lobster suppers, as well as a grocery, motel, and cottages. Many of the other towns along this stretch, though too small to support restaurants or lodging, have craft shops and historical sites (such as Orwell Corner, a restored post office, store, and farmhouse from the late 1800s in the village of Orwell). Occasional bed-and-breakfast inns and small groceries offer the only services.

At Cherry Valley, Hwy. 3 turns east and cuts almost straight across the county to the Brudenell River and Montague area. This is a convenient route for a smaller loop back to Wood Islands and makes a pleasant 2- or 3-day trip. Hwy. 3 is a broad two-lane, with wide paved shoulders along most of its length, through rolling hills and farm country. Traffic is normally light to moderate.

If you're traveling the entire Kings Byway circuit, you have a choice right after Cherry Valley of turning west off Hwy. 1 onto 1A and taking the coastal route to Charlottetown, or staying with the heavier traffic and paved shoulders of Hwy. 1. The larger highway offers the more direct route and the security of paved shoulders, but Hwy. 1A is the more scenic ride of the two. Near the end of 1A, Tea Hill Provincial Park offers picnic grounds and a beach, but no camping.

Just after the intersection of Hwys. 1A and 1 begin the outskirts of **Charlottetown** and, a short distance farther, the causeway over the mouth of the East (also known as the Hillsborough) River. From here expect heavy traffic and plenty of commercial development, although it's difficult for anyone who has cycled in major North American cities to think of this largest of P.E.I.'s cities as much more than a large town. For a description of Charlottetown's features and services, see "Blue Heron Drive," Chapter 5.

CHARLOTTETOWN TO ST. PETERS— 52.8 KILOMETERS (33 MILES)

To bypass as much of the city as possible, take Riverside Drive north at the first intersection after the river. Riverside winds along the river, past Queen Elizabeth Hospital and Hillsborough Park, and joins Hwy. 2 (labeled as St. Peter's Road within the city) in the suburb known as Sherwood. At the intersection take Hwy. 2 north. The busy road's four lanes and intermittent paved shoulders within the city shrink finally to two wide lanes with wide paved shoulders in good condition. Development dwindles gradually, replaced by farm country dotted with sub-divisions.

By the town of Marshfield, 6.4 kilometers from the East River Causeway, the country is all farmlands, with some scattered houses and interesting old farms, and lightly rolling terrain of long, low hills. The Hillsborough River is visible to the east—broad and tidally influenced, filling a wide and lush valley. The paved shoulder here is almost two and a half meters wide and in good condition. Marshfield has no services, but about 5 kilometers beyond it is a bed-and-breakfast inn.

Right after the village of Dunstaffnage (where there is a restaurant and lounge, but no other services), the Kings Byway Drive turns left on Hwy. 6 to make a loop to the village of Corran Ban and the Stanhope portion of Prince Edward Island National Park. Hwy. 6 and the return loop on Hwy. 219 are two-lane secondary roads in disrepair. The poor road conditions and unremarkable terrain on this side loop of the drive can be by-passed entirely by staying on Hwy. 2 and continuing north.

At this point, Hwy. 2 loses its paved shoulders and is itself in rough condition with cracks, potholes, and patches. Traffic from here north is light, however, so the inconvenience of the road's condition is somewhat balanced out.

The towns of Tracadie and Tracadie Cross have no services and overlook country that is largely forested, scattered with the small meadows and hay fields of a few active farms. The Hillsborough River in this area remains wide and slow, with saltwater marshes lining both shores. Hwy. 2 through the stretch is in fair condition: patched and rough in places with occasional serious chuckholes.

In the vicinity of Mt. Stewart, where there is a gas station and a small grocery, the highway is in very poor condition, with the edges so crumbled in places that it's necessary to ride in the center of the lane.

By St. Andrews, road conditions are much improved, with sections of new surface and slightly wider lanes (though no paved shoulders). Rolling hills in this area give a good view of the wide, shallow valley of the Hillsborough River and its marshes. Compared to the busy areas around Charlottetown and Cavendish, this portion of the island—and indeed, most of Kings County—is quiet and sparsely inhabited. The many tiny communities along the route are marked as "dots" on island maps, but have no services and few houses.

Morell, 35 kilometers from Charlottetown, is the largest community along this stretch of Hwy. 2 and has a gas station, bakery, grocery, restaurants, pharmacy, bank, and a couple of bed-and-breakfast inns. It's home, also, to Morell Legion Lobster and Salmon Suppers. Farms surrounding Morell are larger and more active, with large fields sloping gently down toward the shore of St. Peters Bay. The route continues to be mostly flat, with some long but gentle hills.

ST. PETERS TO SOURIS— 78.1 KILOMETERS (48.8 MILES)

A municipal park and campground are located on the shore of St. Peters Bay shortly before the town of **St. Peters**. St. Peters was settled in the early 1700s by a party of shipwrecked French sailors and for a time was the commercial fishing headquarters of the island. The town today is small and quiet, with a grocery and gas station, and is modestly busy in summer with resort trade. Be sure to check out Wilma's Bake Shop across the road from the grocery, located at the end of a short driveway between buildings—the hand-lettered sign is easy to miss. Wilma's baked goods, sandwiches, and hot lunch of the day are reasonably priced and made with a grandmother's touch.

After St. Peters, Hwy. 2 turns southeast and cuts

across the base of the large eastern peninsula of the island. This alternate route to the south coast misses the rugged, isolated shoreline around East Point and the long, hilly return along the shore to Souris.

To continue on the Kings Byway north of St. Peters, take Hwy. 16 left (north) at the only intersection in town, and climb a fairly steep hill out of town. The road on this leg of the circuit is in fair shape, without paved shoulders, and is an average-sized two-lane that receives little traffic. The ride from here is parallel to the north coast of the island, but generally runs about one and a half kilometers inland so that views of the water are infrequent. The terrain is moderately hilly, with some long but not especially steep climbs. Except for scattered, not-very-prosperous farms, most of the countryside is thick with tag alders and underbrush and second-growth forests.

As before, few of the small towns along the way offer services. Use caution at Naufrage, near the lighthouse at Shipwreck Point, where the bridge over the Naufrage River is paved with rough, loose planks so treacherous a bicycle should probably be walked over it. From here to the end of the island at East Point the country is remote and lightly inhabited. A few small farms are scattered along the route, but more of them are abandoned than active, and the forests of spruce and tag alder have begun creeping in to reclaim them. Some of the deserted farm buildings are beautiful, with high arched gables, weathered-gray shingled sides, and walls that are slinking gradually into the earth. The road conditions seem to match the terrain here—rugged and patched—making for slow going much of the way.

After Rock Barra the road improves slightly, and the terrain opens up into more meadows and fields allowing frequent views of the ocean as the road approaches closer to the shore. Most of the active farms are modest in size and appearance and are obviously operated by fishermen who leave their boats and lobster traps stored in the yards during the off-season.

Campbells Cove Provincial Park is a modest campground with about a dozen unserviced sites located on a low bluff above the beach. A kitchen shelter, flush toilets, and hot showers are available. The park is open June 29 through September 4.

Six and a half kilometers east of Campbells Cove is a turnoff toward the coast that circles to North Lake Harbour and the town of North Lake. Services at North Lake include a restaurant, motel, and tourist home. The harbor is a busy commercial fishing center and is popular for its sport-fishing, with anglers chartering boats in August to early October to go out after giant bluefin tuna in the Gulf of St. Lawrence. In 1979 a world's record tuna weighing 1,496 pounds (680 kilograms) was caught offshore here.

This portion of the coast is fringed with low, grass-spotted sand dunes, and short, abrupt bluffs. Cow pastures often back right up to the bluffs and dunes and are fenced to prevent cattle from floundering in the sand. The road continues fairly flat to the cape at East Point.

Not surprisingly, wind can be a nuisance in this flat, open portion of the province. I noticed—and it is probably not an unusual phenomenon—that the prevailing west winds switched around to the east as I approached the tip of the island, swirling considerably as they struck the protruding headland.

The road to the East Point lighthouse and the easternmost point on the island is 2 kilometers long, paved, and ends at a small parking area next to the lighthouse. Built in 1867, this is one of the three remaining manned lighthouses on the island. Guided tours (available for a small fee) and a gift shop are open to the public. Local legend has it that the pirate Captain Kidd left buried treasure somewhere in the vicinity of this point, which was known then by its Micmac name Kespemenagek—"the end of the island."

From East Point to Souris the character of the land and the road changes markedly. This protected southern coastline is apparently a much more desirable place to live than the desolate northern coast. Especially after the town of South Lake, the road is in good condition, freshly surfaced, and wider than before. While not densely populated, the coastline is scattered with attractive, Cape Cod–style houses. Terrain is open and hilly, and when in season huge fields of lupines are in blossom.

Kingsboro is a small community with a great view of the ocean and an unbelievable abundance of lupines in the fields around it. Houses and yards are attractive and well maintained, and the landscape is largely open and scenic. Long rolling hills lead away down the coast, and the road, which has been flat so much of the Kings Byway, begins to roller-coaster up and down fairly sizable slopes. Basin Head Road at the bottom of a long slope leads to the beach and the Basin Head Fisheries Museum, which commemorates the island's history of commercial fishing.

Red Point Provincial Park is off Hwy. 16 just west of Basin Head Road. It is a small park, with only twenty-four unserviced and twelve serviced sites, but offers a kitchen shelter, flush toilets, and hot showers. The park is open June 16 to September 10.

In the 9.6 kilometers between the provincial park and Souris, the largest community on this portion of the coast, the hills continue to grow in size and length. Most are not terribly steep but are long enough to be fairly difficult. From their tops are long views of the Northumberland Strait and, inland, rolling meadows dotted with farmhouses and small woodlots. The road drops steeply at intervals, wherever a stream or river has carved a valley down to the coast.

SOURIS TO BRUDENELL RIVER PROVINCIAL PARK—
48 KILOMETERS (30 MILES)

Souris is a moderately large town and offers most services, including bed-and-breakfast inns, motels, restaurants (for seafood try the Bluefin Restaurant, for lunch and snacks try Bye the Sea Coffee and Tea), and grocery stores. Perched on a hilltop, it offers good views of the coast. Originally a French settlement, it earned its name—French for "mouse" and pronounced "surrey"—after a plague of field mice overran it early in the eighteenth century. Today it is a fish-processing center and the point of departure for the car ferry to Cap-aux-Meules in the Magdalen Islands.

Hwy. 16 ends at Souris and becomes Hwy. 2 as it crosses a long causeway and bridge over the mouth of the Souris River. Paved shoulders about a meter wide last about 4 kilometers, to the town of Rollo Bay, where there is a motel, restaurant, and grocery. After the town, the paved shoulders disappear and the land flattens somewhat.

At Rollo Bay West, take a left on Hwy. 310 to remain on the Kings Byway. This 22-kilometer loop off the main highway passes through a number of small villages, and up and over rolling farmlands adjacent to several deep bays. The road is in fair condition, with busted edges and asphalt patches. Hills are short and rolling for the most part and are parceled with farmers' fields and pastures. Other than a country inn in Bay Fortune, none of the villages along Hwy. 310 offer services, although there are signs advertising several bed-and-breakfast inns located on connecting roads down by the coast in the vicinity of Spry Cove. Still, the route is scenic and relaxing, along a road that receives little traffic.

At the intersection with Hwy. 4 in Dundas, turn south toward Brudenell River Provincial Park. This section of Hwy. 4 does not have paved shoulders but is a wide two-lane in good condition. It passes through open farm country and low rolling hills.

Just past Bridgetown, where there is a convenience store but no other services, the Kings Byway continues on another side loop, this one following Hwy. 311, a narrow two-lane that skirts the coast through mostly un-inhabited country. I took the loop and found it so unre-markable that I resolved not to take it the next time, but to stay on Hwy. 4 with its more direct route to the state park on the Brudenell River. A few short stretches of the side trip offer views of Boughton Bay and Cardigan Bay, but much of the ride is through crowded, second-growth woods or past halfhearted farms in poor repair. The town of Cardigan, where Hwy. 311 intersects Hwy. 321 to Bru-denell River Provincial Park, is a pleasant community with a grocery, restaurant, and gas station.

BRUDENELL RIVER PROVINCIAL PARK TO WOOD ISLANDS FERRY TERMINAL—83.2 KILOMETERS (52 MILES)

Whether you take the Hwy. 311 loop or remain on Hwy. 4, the last few kilometers to Brudenell River Provincial Park are through rolling farmland of pastures and potato fields. The park is on Hwy. 3, about 3 kilometers east of Hwy. 4. It is one of the largest provincial parks on the island and offers an 18-hole golf course, tennis, lawn bowling, a sailboat and canoe marina, beach, and horse-back riding. The park also contains a motel, dining room, laundromat, and kitchen shelter. Serviced and unserviced campsites, flush toilets, and hot showers are available be-tween May 19 and October 9.

Six and a half kilometers east of the campground, at the end of Hwy. 3, is the town of **Georgetown**, a busy fishing port, with all services. It's the home of the King's Playhouse, one of three outstanding regional theaters on P.E.I.

Back at the intersection of Hwys. 3 and 4, at the town of Pooles Corner, there is a motel and restaurant. On the opposite corner, the elaborate provincial visitors' center has restrooms and drinking water and is a good place to take a break. The visitors' center also has interesting displays describing the history and commerce of Kings County.

Hwy. 4 south of Pooles Corner is a wide, fairly busy two-lane with a paved shoulder in poor condition. It passes over a few fairly sizable hills, through fields of hay, clover, and strawberries. Fields are separated by fencerows, some made with ornamental turnposts painted in bright colors—a tradition on this part of the island.

Montague is a fairly large town, with all services and a relatively heavy concentration of traffic. A combination fishing and farming community, it is the commercial headquarters for the eastern section of the county.

Because P.E.I. is crossed by so many roads, it's possible to plan extremely flexible touring schedules. If you find yourself running short of time or energy, you can almost always find a convenient shortcut such as the one south of the Montague River, where Hwy. 315 cuts straight south to the Wood Islands ferry terminal. To continue around the remainder of the Kings Byway Drive, take Hwy. 17 east for a 75-kilometer loop around the irregular coastline of the southeast end of the island.

Hwy. 17 is a two-lane secondary road in good condition and appears to be only lightly traveled. Out of Montague it passes over bunched, rolling hills, none particularly high, on a bluff overlooking the lower Montague River. This is wooded terrain, with farmers' fields—including a few small fields of tobacco—hewn out of stands of hardwoods and spruce. Houses are small and humble, and many old farmhouses in various stages of disrepair sit now on inactive farmland.

At Lower Montague, a gravel road proceeds east

about one and a half kilometers to the St. Andrews Point lighthouse. Hwy. 17 turns south and inland here, and passes through several kilometers of rolling, forested country before approaching the coast again at the mouth of the Sturgeon River.

Gaspereaux is a small fishing village with a bed-and-breakfast inn but no other apparent services. A left here onto Hwy. 347 leads to Panmure Island Provincial Park, with serviced and unserviced campsites, flush toilets, showers, a laundromat, and one of the finest white-sand beaches on the island. The park is open June 29 to September 4. Continue out to Panmure Island for other beaches and the lighthouse.

A small general store about one and a half kilometers south of Gaspereaux is the last opportunity to purchase provisions until Murray River, 19 kilometers south. The route along the coast of Murray Harbour is quiet, mostly flat, through inactive farm country and woodlots. The harbor is most visible at Seal Cove, where a sizable herd of seals is often seen basking on sandbars or rocks, or bobbing in the waves. A private campground is located on the shore of the cove.

Murray River has a grocery store, gift shops, a take-out restaurant, and Terrace Heights, a full-menu restaurant apparently open only in the evenings. Take Hwy. 18 out of town to stay on the Kings Byway, past side roads to a private tent and trailer park, and the picnic area and beach at Fantasyland Provincial Park (no camping). In that vicinity also are a bed-and-breakfast inn and housekeeping cottages.

Eight kilometers east of Murray River, **Murray Harbour** is a fishing village built around a classic Maritime wharf piled high with lobster traps in season and lined with the colorful, no-nonsense boats of the fishermen. Services include a motel, grocery, crafts, and gifts, and Brehaut's Restaurant (take-out or eat-in), where you can get excellent sandwiches and seafood and for dessert the best (guaranteed) butterscotch pie you've ever eaten.

Hwy. 18 loops around the end of Murray Head and

Cape Bear, then turns west and follows the long straight coast of the Northumberland Strait to Wood Islands. This stretch of virtually flat road offers perhaps the easiest ride on the island, assuming headwinds aren't a problem. It also offers good views of the strait, with Nova Scotia visible beyond it, and the chance to see the locally famous Northumberland Ghost Ship. Like a similar apparition reported along the Acadian coast of northwest New Brunswick, the ship is said to be a fully rigged sailing vessel that appears to be burning. Some witnesses claim to have seen sailors climbing the rigging to escape the flames.

The towns of Guernsey Cove, White Sands, High Bank, and Little Sands are nothing more than concentrations of farms, without services except at Little Sands where a fine bed-and-breakfast inn is situated on the bluff above the beach. Farms along here are owned mostly by fishermen, to judge by the lobster pots and fishing trawlers stored behind the houses, and are seldom actively farmed. Fields and meadows reveal, however, the old division of property on the island, with the farms laid out long and narrow so that as many as possible could come in contact with the shore. Fields 180 meters wide, separated by fencerows and lines of trees, descend in various shades of green and yellow to the sheer red bluff at the coast. Some of the old, ornate farmhouses have been recently restored to something like their original condition.

Located about 8 kilometers from Wood Islands ferry landing, Bayberry Cliff Inn offers virtually the only lodging along this portion of the Northumberland Strait shore. Owned by Nancy and Don Perkins, the inn is composed of two buildings, formerly barns, that have been renovated and expanded into eight bedrooms decorated in a variety of eccentric motifs, including at least one with walls and ceiling painted with Nancy's murals of coastal landscape and wildlife. The buildings are perched on the edge of a cliff 12 meters above the beach. During low tide the beach offers excellent swimming, though it's a good idea to scout the area from above first, to make sure the jellyfish aren't in. Breakfast is the best I've eaten at any bed-and-breakfast.

Northumberland Provincial Park, located just under 3 kilometers east of the Wood Islands ferry terminal, has primitive and serviced sites, a laundromat, kitchen shelter, and a good clam-digging beach. It's open June 16 through September 10. Seals are often seen bobbing in the waves offshore from this portion of the beach, and whales can sometimes be spotted spouting in the distance as they migrate through the Northumberland Strait. Swimming here is somewhat limited by the large numbers of stinging jellyfish, although their population is cyclical and observant swimmers can enjoy themselves if they take a few minutes to locate stretches of beach clear of the pests.

NEW
· BRUNSWICK ·

Travelers crossing by land from the United States to Prince Edward Island, Nova Scotia, and Newfoundland must travel across New Brunswick, a 72,481-square kilometer (27,985-square-mile) province home to 700,000 Canadians. As a result, the province has sometimes been considered a place to be traveled through, rather than a destination in its own right. Yet, parts of New Brunswick's interior and coastline—and it has 2,160 kilometers of ocean shore—are as spectacular as any places in Atlantic Canada, and have the added attraction of being relatively unknown.

The capital of New Brunswick is Fredericton, located at the approximate center of the province on the broad Saint John River. Both Fredericton and the unofficial commercial capital of Saint John, located southwest of Fundy National Park on the Fundy coast, are served by large modern airports and offer all services, including fine accommodations, restaurants, and good bicycle shops.

Bicyclists seem to be welcomed in New Brunswick. It and Québec have the most native bikers of any of the eastern provinces, and drivers therefore are accustomed to seeing them and don't often panic or hit their horns. That's not to say the roads are cluttered with rows of wind-drafting cyclists. In my two days on Grand Manan Island, for instance, I met only one cyclist, and he was a resident of the island biking to work on his battered Peugeot.

Weather

The trips described in this chapter are located along the coast of the Bay of Fundy and are subject to some special weather concerns. Because the Bay of Fundy is continuously flushed with water from the North Atlantic, it remains cold in summer, helping to moderate temperatures in its coastal regions. Summer highs are consistently 5 to 10 degrees cooler than the highs in Fredericton and other interior portions of the province, or even in the interior of Fundy National Park itself. The cool afternoon and evening breezes that are common along the coast do not reach to the interior, so that in the space of just a few kilometers average summer temperatures vary considerably. Fog forms frequently over the bay and along the coast as warm, moist land air settles over the cold water. The fog most often appears with a rising tide, settling over land in late evening or early morning. In July, expect dense fog along the coast nearly half the time.

Also expect about half the days of summer to be overcast. It rains often on the coast—with total precipitation for the year averaging about one and a half meters in Fundy National Park—so rain gear is requisite. Some local pessimists say you should expect rain and thunderstorms 2 or 3 days out of 5.

Language

First-time visitors are often surprised to learn that not all New Brunswick citizens speak English. In fact, about 35 percent of all residents of New Brunswick are Acadian French, and French is spoken predominately in large sections of the northern and eastern portions of the province, especially along the Acadian Peninsula northeast of the city of Bathurst, and in western regions near the Québec border. The two trips described in chapters 7 and 8 are in English-speaking New Brunswick, although it's not unusual to hear both languages spoken in crowds anywhere in the province.

Traffic Laws

The speed limit on most provincial highways is 80 kilometers per hour. The speed limit in urban districts, unless otherwise posted, is 50 kilometers per hour.

Cycling Laws

Cyclists in New Brunswick must obey the same traffic laws that apply to motorists, and are especially reminded to ride on the right side of roads, signal direction changes, and stop for traffic lights and stop signs.

For More Information

Tourist information centers operated by the provincial government are located at major entry points in New Brunswick, including Edmundston, Woodstock, St. Stephen, Aulac, Campobello, and Campbellton. All offer free reservation service to make advance reservations with motels, hotels, farm vacation hosts, bed-and-breakfast inns, and campgrounds throughout the province.

For general information about New Brunswick, contact Tourism New Brunswick, P.O. Box 12345, Fredericton, NB, Canada E3B 5C3; phone 1-800-561-0123 (from the United States or Canada, except New Brunswick), 1-800-442-4442 (from New Brunswick).

For more details about Fundy National Park, write Fundy National Park, Box 40, Alma, NB, Canada E0A 1B0; or phone 506/887-2000.

For an excellent overview of Fundy National Park features, history, and natural history, see *A Guide to Fundy National Park* by Michael Burzynski (Douglas and McIntyre, Vancouver, 1985). It is available for sale at park information kiosks.

For additional information about Grand Manan Island, write Tourism Grand Manan, P.O. Box 193, North Head, Grand Manan, NB, Canada E0G 2M0.

7

Fundy National Park

Begin/End: Headquarters Campground, Fundy National Park
Roads: Hwy. 114, Hwy. 915, Point Wolfe Road
Accommodations: Campgrounds, housekeeping cottages, motels, bed-and-breakfast inns
Length: 96 kilometers (60 miles)
Difficulty: Moderately easy to moderately difficult

Established in 1948, and at 206 square kilometers somewhat smaller than many of Canada's national parks, Fundy National Park is located on one of the most remote stretches of New Brunswick's otherwise well-discovered Fundy Coast. Much of the Fundy shore, which in New Brunswick represents the entire southern coastline of the province, is popular among tourists and offers some outstanding cycling (see Chapter 8, "Grand Manan Island and the Quoddy Loop"). The park at Fundy is remarkable, however, not only for spectacular scenery, diverse landscapes, and interesting cycling, but also because it manages to sustain a sense of remoteness uncommon along the Fundy coast, while being located only about an hour's drive by automobile from the city of Moncton and

2 hours' drive from the province's two largest cities, Fredericton and Saint John.

That the park is not more popular can be traced to simple geography: the coastline northeast of Saint John is too rugged for roads, making Hwy. 114, a humble, circuitous blacktop in frequent need of repair, the only route to Fundy and one that no doubt discourages large numbers of motorists from visiting. Though an extended bike trip from Saint John is certainly possible, I would not be enthusiastic about it, partly because of that same narrow road, with its rough surface and many hills, and partly because much of the route from the city is through nondescript country where towns are scarce and campgrounds and other accommodations are few and far between. The national park itself, however, makes any difficulties in reaching it well worthwhile.

There is no convenient loop to be made within Fundy National Park, unfortunately, although it is possible to make a rather unremarkable 224-kilometer ride from the park north to Moncton, returning back on TransCanada 2 to Hwy. 114 and to the park. More interesting is to cycle across the park, then set up camp at Headquarters Campground, near the northeastern boundary, and use it as a base for 1- or 2-day trips. Besides having the advantage of being *below* the steepest hills and near the shore of the Bay of Fundy, the Headquarters area is close to the town of Alma, the only real community on that part of the Fundy coastline and a worthwhile place to go nosing around.

TRIP A: PARK ENTRANCE TO HEADQUARTERS CAMPGROUND— 20 KILOMETERS (12.5 MILES)

Just inside the western boundary of the park, an information center has plenty of material on Fundy, including

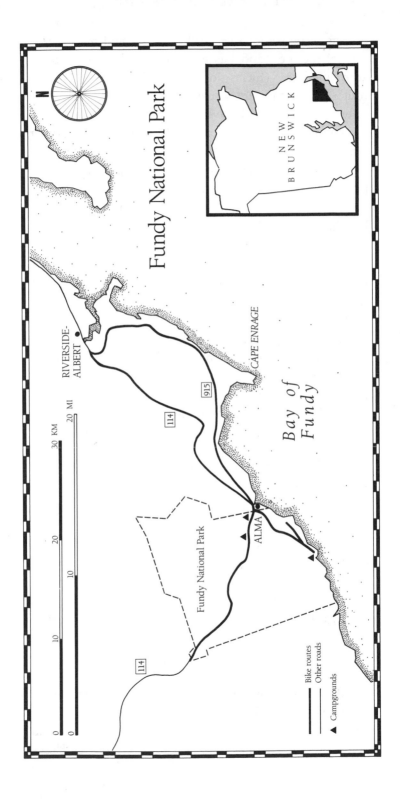

Fundy National Park

dozens of books for sale on the history and natural history of the area, and has a parking lot large enough to accommodate vehicles for extended periods. Touring routes in the park are somewhat limited simply because only one paved road traverses it. That road, Hwy. 114, is well maintained in the park and is wider and smoother than the same road outside the national park service's jurisdiction. Shoulders are gravel and narrow, but the paved lanes are wide enough to give cyclists some security. Traffic can be quite heavy on summer weekends, but the nature of the route keeps vehicles moving at sane speeds.

From the northern entrance of the park are 20 kilometers of interesting though not particularly spectacular riding over some hills (including a few tough ones) and past a number of small lakes and ponds. Geologically, the Fundy Park region is an extension of the Appalachian Mountains and is rugged enough and inaccessible enough to remain an island of wildernesslike terrain containing fine examples of the Maritime Acadian Highlands—and some of the most beautiful undeveloped country in New Brunswick. Terrain is uneven, with lots of steep hills and quick turns through the densely forested interior of the park. The final descent to the coast is especially hairraising on the downside and backbreaking on the upside. Watch the hairpin curves partway down. On a happier note, if you happen to be following the route in the morning, you're likely to see incredible banks of fog covering the entire surface of Chignecto Bay from New Brunswick to the dark hills of Nova Scotia. Currents of air often cause the fog to move inland, pouring over the top of a rock headland just beyond the eastern edge of the park; it flows over like snow drifting over a mountain peak.

At the bottom of the steep descent toward the coast, **Headquarters Campground** is the administrative center of the park and is located near many of the park's broad variety of features and services. The 600 campsites (and an additional 100 in overflow campgrounds) at Headquarters Campground and the park's other two main campgrounds, 53 housekeeping cottages, and 20 motel units offer plenty of accommodations (park rangers say they *never* run out of campsites, although the housekeeping cottages and motels do fill up; reservations are suggested). The park's three primary campgrounds are equipped with fireplaces, hot showers, dump stations, and hookups for RVs. Several areas along the park's 13-kilometer shoreline have been developed to provide good views and easy access to the beaches.

During the tourist season, from June to October, park naturalists lead free guided beachwalks and evening programs to explain the natural history of the park and the Fundy coast. A children's program is provided during July and August.

A nine-hole golf course is located near Headquarters, with a clubhouse and restaurant (appropriately named the Clubhouse Restaurant) which serves light lunches and full-course dinners, with local cuisine the specialty. Nearby are three tennis courts, a putting green, and a lawn bowling green. Rental equipment is available at a pro shop. A heated saltwater swimming pool is open from late June to early September.

An elaborate 120-kilometer trail system opens the backcountry to hikers and leads to fourteen remote campsites located on or near some of the waterfalls, vistas, and deserted homesteads that dot the interior of the park. Two of those trails are open to mountain bikers: the trail to Lac Marven Campground, which originates at the end of Point Wolfe Road; and Black Hole Trail, reached off Forty-Five Road (off Hwy. 114) on the far western border of the park, which leads 5 kilometers to a warden station overlooking the rapids and falls of the Upper Salmon River.

From Headquarters Campground it is only a half-kilometer jaunt downhill to **Alma**, where supplies and services are available. Expect to pay considerably more for groceries in small towns like Alma, where supply routes are difficult and lengthy. Mysteriously, however, in the summer of 1990 gasoline was a penny per liter less in Alma than in the capital city of Fredericton, and the cost of many services—like the town laundromat, equipped with machines that still used one quarter at a time—was comparable to other Canadian towns and villages.

The best thing about Alma is that it is a genuine New Brunswick fishing village, free of pretensions and seemingly unconcerned about making a killing off the tourist trade. Local residents earn their livings honestly (fishing and lumbering, mostly) and apparently have not been willing to throw away four or five generations of experience on the sea or in the woods to start hawking postcards and plastic lobsters. Visitors are just uncommon enough to be treated with courtesy. The town's two small grocery stores, coffee shop, restaurant/inn (the Parkland Hotel, locally famous for "Kentucky Style Chicken"), and other businesses seem oriented more toward local trade than the potentially lucrative tourist market about a kilometer away in the park. That makes those businesses, of course, great places to spend your money.

A memorable (and easy to prepare) dinner idea is to purchase fresh lobster in Alma and return to the campground to cook it. When I visited, largish, precooked lobsters were available at a reasonable price from a house at the east edge of the downtown district (look for prominent, handmade signs). Pedal back to camp, add garlic to a few tablespoons of melted butter, and start cracking. The preboiled lobsters are excellent cold, or buy your lobster live and boil it yourself.

On the subject of food, the most famous local delicacy is a dried seaweed called dulse which is eaten as a snack and is often distributed free to patrons of bars and restaurants. It is usually very inexpensive and can be purchased at roadside stands or grocery stores in many parts of New Brunswick, but especially along the southern coast. Locals who have a taste for dulse chew it and then wash it down with beer, but it seems to be a taste that must be acquired; to me, it was about as pleasant as chewing very salty dried fish skins. In the spring, young fiddlehead ferns are harvested and served boiled. Flavored with butter and salt and pepper, they taste similar to artichokes. Here and elsewhere in the Maritimes, local seafood is excellent. Besides lobster, such shellfish as scallops, clams, crab, mussels, and oysters are abundant and often reasonably priced, although prices in well-traveled tourist areas are often escalated to meet demand.

No trip to the Maritime Provinces is complete without at least one lobster dinner.

Though the food is delicious and the landscape lovely, the famous tides of Fundy are the central focus of the park. Widely recognized as the highest in the world, Fundy's tides rise twice a day to as much as 16 meters above the low-water mark. That figure is somewhat misleading, since the average figure is more like 9 meters—about the height of a three-story building. One popular misconception is that the tides arrive dangerously fast, accompanied by a wall of rising water that can sweep an unsuspecting beachcomber off his or her feet. On the contrary, the tides require 6 hours and 13 minutes to rise or fall completely, a pace so slow it is difficult to notice unless you keep your eyes on a stake, stone, or other mark to gauge the water's progress.

Tides are the result of water pulled or pushed by the gravitational attraction of the moon and sun, and they will therefore vary according to season and time of month. During the full and new moons, when the earth, the moon, and the sun are aligned, the gravitational forces reach their greatest power and cause the highest, or "spring," tides. "Neap" tides are the lowest in the cycle, when the moon and sun are at right angles to the earth and unable to exert as much pull. The shape of the Bay of Fundy causes North Atlantic water to flood into it during high tide, creating a wave known as a "seiche" that rises progressively higher as it reaches toward the upper ends of the bay.

The best place to view tidal effects in Fundy Park is at the Alma beach, right below the Headquarters Campground area of the park. An interpretation center across the road from the beach and a self-guided boardwalk explain much about the tides and the marine life of the beach area.

TRIP B: POINT WOLFE ROAD AND RETURN— 9.6 KILOMETERS (6 MILES)

Within the park a short but pleasant trip is possible on Point Wolfe Road, which runs southwest from the Head-quarters area about 5 kilometers to the mouth of the Point Wolfe River. The road is moderately hilly (with a couple of hills slightly worse than moderate) and is perhaps better suited to all-terrain bikes than skinny-tire road bikes, although the surface is good enough for medium-paced road touring. The road is a paved two-lane, but the pavement is rough and in only fair condition, and there are no paved shoulders at all.

Except during the busiest summer weekends, Point Wolfe Road is not heavily used, especially during the week and early in the morning. For most of its length, it passes through wooded hills spotted with small meadows and is paralleled by small, tumbling creeks. At the Point Wolfe River is the site of an old lumber mill and a covered bridge over the final tumbling rapids where the river empties into an estuary at its mouth. A campground and picnic area are located here, as are the beginning of several hiking trails. A number of interesting hiking trails originate as well off Point Wolfe Road, including the trail to Dickson Falls and the coastal trail that loops through Mathews Head to Herring Cove and Herring Cove Road, so it's a good idea to carry a lock and chain should you decide to do some exploring on foot.

Side trips are possible on Herring Cove Road, where extremely steep hills lead up and over the coastal range of hills 3 kilometers to Herring Cove on the Fundy shore. The trail to Lac Marven Campground, which originates at the very end of Point Wolfe Road, is open to mountain bikers.

TRIP C: ALMA TO RIVERSIDE-ALBERT LOOP— 65.6 KILOMETERS (41 MILES)

This 1- or 2-day trip originates at Fundy National Park and the town of Alma and travels northeast on Hwy. 915 along the Fundy Coast to the town of Riverside-Albert, then loops back to Fundy on Hwy. 114.

Just north of Alma turn right at the intersection with Hwy. 915 and be prepared for a series of fairly long and steep hills. Once you've made it past the first 3 kilometers, the route flattens considerably.

Hwy. 915 is a moderately rough paved road, without shoulders, and passes through attractive country wooded with spruces, firs, poplars, and hardwoods. The road is often in disrepair and has been patched rather haphazardly, making for slow progress in places. Scattered farms are found along the route, but it is obvious that farming is a difficult occupation in this part of New Brunswick. Most farms appear to be inactive, and some are deserted.

Following 3 kilometers of sizable hills, the road flattens and is maintained in better condition. It is not a busy automobile route. On a Sunday in June I counted an average of only one automobile for every 6 kilometers of road. Likewise, it is not a heavily inhabited region, so be prepared for a moderately easy ride in fairly undeveloped country.

After 8 kilometers the road descends to just above sea level, opening onto a view of expansive saltwater marshes leading down to the Fundy shore. Especially on rising tides, when the water cools warm, moist air, dramatic banks of fog often cover the water like a thick and puffy quilt. When the tide is out, it's not unusual for a kilometer or more of wet, exposed ocean bottom to be visible, though if the fog is in you won't see the ocean at all. On a clear day the view is magnificent. The route

Rugged coastline near Alma, on the outskirts of Fundy National Park.

remains flat and easy, through wide marshes dotted with tidal pools and crossed by undulating tidally influenced streams.

Only a few houses line the road in the vicinity of the mostly nonexistent town of Waterside, where there is a church and cemetery and little else, but they're quaint, well-maintained houses with Victorian flourishes and a touch of Cape Cod atmosphere. A long sandy beach is said to be found at Waterside, but its location is not marked from the road and I could find no public site.

Sixteen kilometers along Hwy. 915 is a possible side trip to Cape Enrage. The road to the cape is partly gravel, partly paved, but the pavement is in such poor condition that it is a road definitely not suitable for skinny tires. All-terrain cyclists will have no difficulty with it, however, and might find it an interesting detour. About a kilometer off Hwy. 915 is a private campground that would do in a pinch (though you'd be camping in an open field). The entire road is approximately 6 kilometers long, with several very steep hills spiked with hairpin curves. Near the end of the road is a fine public beach nestled in a cove between spectacular heads of rock.

Cape Enrage itself is crowned with a lighthouse and is a 60-meter-high cliff of sloughing sandstone. During high tide the surf blasts against the base of the cliffs in a manner that undoubtedly inspired its name. The road leads to the top of the cliff, but the unfenced access is sure to give you a dose of vertigo. When the fog is in (most mornings in summer), the place seems gothic and haunted.

Back on Hwy. 915, the road climbs another long saddle of highlands, then descends again nearly to sea level. Lightly rolling hills follow in a region that is mostly uninhabited. The road continues to be in decent condition, surfaced with rough-pebble pavement.

At about the 29-kilometer mark is another possible side trip on Mary's Point Road, a well-maintained gravel road that loops toward the ocean for several kilometers before rejoining 915. This route, again suitable only for all-terrain bikes, during low tides offers good views of expansive mud flats, and during high tides is quite close to the shore. Broad marshes make it an important resting area for migratory birds, which has led to its being set aside as a sanctuary, part of the **Shepody National Wildlife Area. Mary's Point Shorebird Preserve** was established specifically as a preserve for migrating sandpipers and other shorebirds that in July and August pass through the area in large numbers on their way from nesting regions near the Arctic to winter feeding grounds in South America. Hiking trails lead to the shoreline, offering views of the more than one million shorebirds that stop here each year. Birders will want to time their visit with the highest tides, when the birds are forced to congregate along the upper beach (tide schedules are available free of charge at the administration building near Headquarters Campground in the park). Other marshes and floodings in the area are managed for wildfowl.

At the eastern intersection of Mary's Point Road and Hwy. 915 is a bed-and-breakfast inn, Florentine Manor, the first of several in the vicinity of Harvey and Riverside-Albert (another is Cailswick Babbling Brook Bed-and-Breakfast). The road here is elevated above an enormous saltwater marsh, parts of which have been diked and drained to create cattle pasturage.

Riverside-Albert is a small, widely scattered village with most services, including general stores (Grandpa's General Store at the intersection of Hwys. 915 and 114 has farm supplies and groceries and is a Sears catalog sales merchant), a restaurant, a bank, a hospital, and several bed-and-breakfasts. About one and a half kilometers east of town on Hwy. 114 is Broadleaf Farms, a bed-and-breakfast offering farm vacations that provide the opportunity (for a fee) to help attend the farm's 400 head of cattle, 75 horses, and 560 hectares of hayfields and other crops. The farm also maintains a basic campground (with showers and laundry) in the field beside the house.

The return loop to Fundy National Park is along Hwy. 114, a busier and better-maintained highway than neglected Hwy. 915. In this leg it has two wide lanes, without paved shoulders, and is moderately busy, with truck traffic minimal and local drivers relatively slow and considerate of cyclists. Much of the route passes through lowlands and marshes within the Shepody National Wildlife Area. Hills are modest and gently graded. Scenery is lovely: meadows and salt marshes to the south; rolling, wooded hills to the north. Only occasional glimpses of the Bay of Fundy are possible.

The terrain becomes more rugged within a few kilometers of Alma, culminating in a 3-kilometer, gradual ascent to the highlands above the town. Descent is equally gradual, except for the final few steep hills on the outskirts of the town.

8

Grand Manan Island and the Quoddy Loop

Begin/End: St. Stephen to Saint John

Roads: TransCanada 1 and connectors

Accommodations: Motels, bed-and-breakfast inns, provincial and private campgrounds

Length: 357.1 kilometers (223.2 miles)

Difficulty: Easy to moderately easy

I admit I'm afflicted with a romantic streak wide as a four-lane highway, but even seasoned cynics have to agree that there is something wonderfully exotic about bicycling on islands. The reasons may be as practical as they are sentimental, however, since islands (at least small ones) are often free of major traffic problems and offer the kind of idyllic cycling many of us dream of. On islands cut off from the frenzies of mainstream North America, the pace of life can be more reminiscent of the nineteenth than the late twentieth century.

Grand Manan and the other islands described in this chapter, and their connecting loop of highways (including some major highways) in southeastern New Brunswick, combine to make a varied and interesting tour that is remarkably accessible to U.S. cyclists. Perhaps more remarkable is that the region does not seem to suffer from excessive tourism. Most of the small villages are, for lack of a better term, authentic; that is, the routines of daily living there go on pretty much the way they would if there were no visitors. Commercial fishing is the primary means of livelihood in the coastal regions, and with the exception of a few communities, there is little of that self-consciousness that results from residents becoming aware of the marketability of their quaint and unusual life-styles.

Although the so-called Quoddy Loop is a convenient tour of the southwestern corner of coastal New Brunswick, the highlight of the region, Grand Manan Island, is not actually part of that loop. For that reason, this chapter is laid out as a lineal trip from St. Stephen, on the Maine border, to Saint John, 106 kilometers east along the coast of the Bay of Fundy. The Quoddy Loop—dropping down on county roads and taking ferries to Deer and Campobello islands, then returning to St. Stephen inside the Maine border—is treated as a side trip, as is the literal side trip by ferry to Grand Manan. The remaining ride along Hwy. 1 to Saint John is then offered as an optional trip.

TRIP A: QUODDY LOOP, 217 KILOMETERS (135.6 MILES)

This famous circle-drive around Passamaquoddy Bay ("The Place of Pollock"), in extreme southwest New Brunswick, follows coastal roads, jumps from peninsulas to islands, and includes a stretch of U.S. highway in Maine.

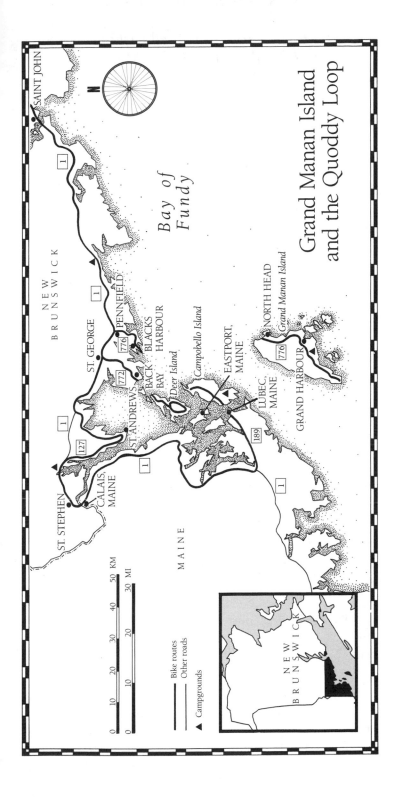

Grand Manan Island
and the Quoddy Loop

St. Stephen to Campobello Island—
112.2 Kilometers (70.1 Miles)

The logical starting point for travelers from the United States or points west in Canada is **St. Stephen**, a busy border town and one of the primary points of entry from the United States. Located across the St. Croix River from its sister city **Calais, Maine**, St. Stephen was settled in the late eighteenth century by British Loyalists. It has since distinguished itself as the home of one of the world's first chocolate bars, created in 1906 by the Ganong Candy Factory, which is still a major employer in the community. Relations between St. Stephens and Calais have traditionally been so good that during the War of 1812, when the cities' mother countries were at war, St. Stephen loaned Calais a supply of gunpowder so the U.S. community could celebrate the Fourth of July holiday.

TransCanada 1 east of St. Stephen is a wide, very busy highway, with paved shoulders about 2 to 3 meters wide along most of its length. Two lanes break occasionally into a divided four-lane. Hills are generally gradual and not very high, though some are long enough and large enough to demand a workout. The route is the major artery leading from the United States to the Maritimes, so traffic tends to be heavy and moves along at speeds well in excess of the speed limit (100 kilometers per hour). For a cyclist, the wide shoulders and great scenery make it somewhat easier to overlook the traffic. Keep in mind that traffic is less of a problem during the week and early and late in the season.

Eight kilometers east of St. Stephen is Oak Bay Provincial Park, with primitive and developed sites, a saltwater beach, and showers.

A few kilometers east of the provincial park, Hwy. 127 turns south in a loop around a peninsula at the mouth of the St. Croix River, and forms a worthwhile side trip of about 34 kilometers (round-trip) to the town of St. Andrews. The ride south on Hwy. 127 along the lower

St. Croix is scenic and interesting, with the two-lane road (no shoulders) staying close to the river over moderately hilly, partially wooded terrain. Old, well-established farms alternate with squared woodlots of hardwoods. Along the way the road rises to a low bluff offering a good view of tiny Dochet's Island, where Samuel de Champlain and Sieur de Monts spent their first winter in America in 1604, before moving across the Bay of Fundy to establish the Port Royal settlement in Nova Scotia the following year.

St. Andrews, with a permanent population of 1,600, is among the busiest resort towns in New Brunswick, and since the nineteenth century has been patronized by well-off tourists from both the United States and Canada. It is one of the few places along the Fundy coast of the province where you will see concentrations of pleasure boats—impressive sailing craft and motor yachts anchored in the sheltered water just offshore. The downtown district is quaint but touristy, with interesting shops housed in old clapboard buildings that overdo slightly a nautical decorating scheme. It's said that more than half the town's buildings are over 100 years old, which becomes most apparent on the tree-lined residential neighborhoods that rise away from the waterfront and downtown area. Many bed-and-breakfast inns and resort cottages are available, as well as most other services. The most famous accommodations are at the Algonquin Hotel, an enormous, 100-year-old establishment with rooms and restaurant. If you have an interest in marine life, check out the Fisheries Biological Station and the Huntsman Marine Laboratory with their aquariums and displays of various fish and marine flora.

The return to Hwy. 1 is on Hwy. 127 along the east shore of the peninsula. When I traveled to St. Andrews the east leg of Hwy. 127 was closed due to road construction, but it is said to be a pleasant ride through country as attractive as the western drive. Eight kilometers north of St. Andrews, at the town of Chamcook, is the Atlantic Salmon Centre with an interpretation area and museum celebrating the life history of the salmon and its role in the economy and history of the Maritimes. Return to

Hwy. 1, where heavy traffic can be expected to continue, especially on summer weekends.

Sixteen kilometers from the intersection of Hwy. 127 and Hwy. 1 is the town of **St. George** (pop. 1,500), with most services and an impressive view of the gorge of the Magaguadavic River. Take the Hwy. 772 exit toward Back Bay and the ferry to Deer Island. The 14-kilometer trip is along a wide two-lane road in good shape, over rolling hills. Some of the hills are tightly rolling and therefore a nuisance, but much of the route is over moderately hilly terrain and unremarkable wooded landscape broken by occasional houses.

Back Bay is a small but busy fishing village on a rocky harbor and has no apparent services. About a kilometer and a half beyond Back Bay, near the village of Letete, is the landing for the free ferry to Deer Island. Two ferries make the 20-minute crossing, one on the half hour, the other on the hour, and pass between rocky points and islands through the Letete Passage to the northern tip of Deer Island.

Deer Island, with a permanent population of about 900, is a 12.8-kilometer by 5.6-kilometer island at the center of the West Isles archipelago across the mouth of Passamaquoddy Bay. Hwy. 772 traverses the island north to south and makes a circuit around the lower half. It is a quiet, paved road ideal for bicycling and makes the island highly accessible. Lodging and other services are relatively scarce, though there are bed-and-breakfast inns at Fairhaven, Lambertville, **Lord's Cove**, and Lambert's Cove, as well as take-out restaurants and small groceries in most of those small communities. For much of its length, the island is fairly low and flat, although Daddy Good's Mountain is high enough to provide a view of most of the Passamaquoddy region.

At Northern Harbor, the deep bay on the island's west shore, is a lobster pound—said to be the largest in the world—where lobsters are raised for commercial sale. Farming of lobster and Atlantic salmon, and more conventional fishing for herring and other ocean fish, are the primary sources of income for island inhabitants.

At the extreme south end of the island is Deer Island Point Park, a small private campground with an excellent view across the half-kilometer Western Passage to the town of Eastport, Maine. In that narrow channel, visible during each changing of the tide, is "The Old Sow," thought to be the second-largest tidal whirlpool in the world. The whirlpool, which becomes most powerful about 3 hours before high tide, is large enough to spin a sizable barge in slow circles, but does not present a hazard to the ferries that depart the island here for Eastport and Campobello Island. Observers on shore often watch seals, whales, and porpoises traveling through the narrow channel.

Ferries leave the southern point of Deer Island for Campobello Island every hour and a half most days from the last weekend in June to Labor Day. Keep in mind that the last ferry leaves at 6:15 in July and August, and at 4:40 in June and September, and the schedule is variable, affected by weather and perhaps whim. Price varies from $2 to $3 per bicycle and rider (depending on who's taking tickets, apparently) or $10 for an automobile and driver and $2 for each additional passenger.

The ferry to **Eastport, Maine**, leaves Deer Island from the same dock every hour between 9:00 A.M. and 7:00 P.M. between mid-June and mid-September. Prices are slightly lower than those for the Campobello ferry.

A short ferry ride leads to Campobello Island, Franklin D. Roosevelt's vacation home. The 1,300 residents of the island support themselves by commercial fishing and catering to the tourists attracted to the island and the national park that has grown up around the Roosevelt property. Better known and more developed than Deer Island, it still remains a quiet, slow-paced destination and offers fine bicycling on Hwy. 774, which runs from the north to south ends of the island, and on several short side trips off it.

FDR's summer home is now at the center of the 1,040-hectare Roosevelt Campobello International Park at the southern end of the island, a national park administered by a commission of both Canadian and U.S. members. Much of the park is a nature preserve crossed by hiking trails and dotted with picnic areas. Activities include tours of the Roosevelt Cottage, an orientation film, and displays of Roosevelt memorabilia. No overnight accommodations or campgrounds are available on the site. The park is open 7 days a week, from late May through mid-October, and there is no entry fee.

Not far from the FDR park, **Herring Cove Provincial Park** is equipped with a large campground that has primitive and serviced sites, a saltwater beach that is one and a half kilometers long, a nine-hole golf course, and showers. Freshwater swimming is possible in Lake Glensevern, adjacent to the park.

Other facilities on the island include the Island Club Lodge in Welshpool (room and dining) and a number of bed-and-breakfast inns and housekeeping cottages, a motel (in Welshpool), several restaurants and take-outs, groceries, and fish markets. Most services are available in the communities of **Wilson's Beach**, near the north end, and **Welshpool**, located near the provincial park and Roosevelt Park in the southcentral portion of the island.

Campobello Island to Calais, Maine— 104.8 Kilometers (65.5 Miles)

The FDR International Bridge connects Campobello Island at its southwest tip with **Lubec, Maine**. From Lubec, the Quoddy Loop can be completed by riding about 25 kilometers west on Hwy. 189 to Hwy. 1, then turning north and continuing 80 kilometers to Calais, Maine, and the border crossing into St. Stephens. Nearly 48 kilometers can be shaved off the U.S. leg of the trip by returning to Deer Island by ferry, and taking the short ferry crossing to Eastport, Maine. From there, Hwy. 190 proceeds approximately 14 kilometers to Hwy. 1. It is another 43 kilometers on Hwy. 1 to Calais and the end of the Quoddy Loop.

TRIP B: GRAND MANAN ISLAND— 62 KILOMETERS (38.8 MILES)

The short section of TransCanada 1 from St. George to the turnoff to Blacks Harbour and the ferry landing to Grand Manan Island is most remarkable for passing along the southern tip of Lake Utopia, home of a semimythological creature witnesses claim resembles the Loch Ness Monster or "Champ," the resident sea serpent of New York's Lake Champlain. According to *Mysterious America*, by Loren Coleman (Faber and Faber, Winchester, Massachusetts, 1983), one of the more recent sightings of the Lake Utopia monster was in July 1982, when a man named Sherman Hatt saw a creature he later described as "like a submarine coming out of the water with spray on both sides. It was about ten feet long and put me in mind of the back of a whale."

At **Pennfield**, 5 kilometers east of St. George, take the Hwy. 776 exit south toward Blacks Harbour. Within a short distance of the intersection are a gas station and small grocery, but otherwise no services are available until you reach Blacks Harbour, about 10 kilometers south. Hwy. 776 is a two-lane in good condition, without shoulders, and passes through rolling hills, woodlots, and farm country.

Blacks Harbour is a fishing village of 1,200 residents and is dominated by Connors Brothers sardine factory, said to be the largest sardine cannery in the world, and in continuous operation since 1855. Services in Blacks Harbour include guest rooms, a convenience store, grocery, and post office. Cool ocean air—tainted by the unmistakable but not unpleasant odor of the sardine plant—gives Blacks Harbour an atmosphere that can be a relief after the hot ride down from Hwy. 1.

Two kilometers beyond Blacks Harbour, in a picturesque bay lined with rocky points and islands, is the ferry landing for the Grand Manan Ferry Service. Misted by fog, as the coast often is, the black rocks and spruces that sprout from the islands and points make the area seem untamed and exotic.

During the tourist season, the ferries to the island can be crowded, so it is wise to arrive well before scheduled departure times. No reservations are accepted. The schedule varies by season, but from June 25 to September 4, two ferries operate, leaving Blacks Harbour at approximate 2-hour intervals, starting at 7:30 A.M. and ending at 6:15 P.M. Fares are collected only on the return trip from Grand Manan and cost $6 per adult, plus $2 for bicycles. Automobiles are charged $18.

Grand Manan Island, with a population of just over 2,500, is the largest of the Fundy Isles, measuring about 32 kilometers long and up to 14 kilometers wide. Although well settled, at least along the low east side of the island, with several communities and a fairly broad range of services, it is not a particularly busy tourist destination. On summer weekends the ferries will be filled, but many of the passengers are residents or relatives of residents. Bicycle tourists are uncommon enough to be a curiosity, a remarkable fact considering the proximity of the island to the United States. In spite of the efforts of the Grand Manan Tourism Association and the obvious need for tourist dollars, there seems to be an ambivalence toward tourism. Residents are friendly and curious about mainlanders, but they admit to a reluctance to see the island change and fear large numbers of visitors will bring such changes. You don't have to be on the island long—just long enough to recognize the slow, relaxed pace, the quiet, everyone's habit of waving as you pass on the road—to begin to share those concerns.

The ferry dock on Grand Manan is at the town of **North Head**, the largest community on the island, where there are a number of bed-and-breakfast inns (I stayed at a beauty—the Compass Rose—in a corner bedroom look-

The harbor at North Head, Grand Manan Island.

ing over the harbor), restaurants, a motel, bakery, grocery, and drug store, and various gift and craft shops. Accommodations, in spite of the several inns, are limited, so it is a good idea to call ahead for reservations.

Grand Manan is surrounded by nutrient-rich waters that attract a large variety of marine life, including whales, seals, and porpoises. Commercial fishing is an important source of income for many island residents, as evidenced by the large number of stationary pens set up along the shore to trap sardines, herring, and other salable fish. An 80-year-old fisherman, still not retired, said that even that sedate inshore fishery is not without its hazards: he once discovered a 7.5-meter-long great white shark in one of his pens. He watched helplessly (from a safe distance) as the shark destroyed the nets, shredding them entirely before it managed to escape.

The island and its surrounding islands are also home to approximately 250 species of birds, a diversity that attracted famed naturalist John James Audubon to Grand Manan in 1831. Puffins and other rare species are sometimes seen in the immediate area or on excursion boats that explore the surrounding rocky islands. Whale cruises and other excursions can be chartered from North Head, Seal Cove, and Ingalls Head Village.

One of the island's most famous inhabitants was the American novelist Willa Cather, who spent some of her late years in a cabin in Whale Cove near North Head. With a view of the open ocean beyond the window of her study, and the harsh, jagged rock of that craggy shoreline, she claimed to feel right at home, perhaps seeing an unexpected connection between the sea and the rolling plains of her Nebraska homeland. She wrote several novels in the cabin and used it for the setting of her short story "Before Breakfast."

Geologically, Grand Manan is divided dramatically by major epochs in the earth's history. The remote western side, where the high elevations and irregular terrain prevent road construction, is lined with a 91-meter-high cliff along the entire length of the island, formed from volcanic upheavals 16 million years ago. To the east, beyond a geologic fault, the island slopes down nearly to sea level and is characterized by sedimentary rock 6 billion years old. At Red Point (beyond the old gravel pit south of Anchorage Park Campground) an exposed cliff clearly shows the two rocks, one the young rock of the American mainland, the other the ancient land mass that originated in Europe.

The long, sloping, generally flat eastern quarter of the island creates excellent, easy-paced cycling along most of the 17-kilometer paved road that traverses the island north to south. A network of over 67 kilometers of trails and footpaths meanders across the island—especially along the top of the cliffs on the rugged west shore— creating the potential for some interesting if challenging mountain biking. "Heritage Trails and Footpaths," a booklet published by Tourism Grand Manan and available for a nominal fee in several stores on the island, provides good descriptions and clear maps of each of those trails.

From the ferry landing in North Head, Hwy. 776 passes through the town as a wide two-lane with paved shoulders averaging about one meter wide. Outside of town, development dwindles quickly and the paved shoulders shrink to nothing. The route is virtually flat at first, following the coastline closely and about 6 meters above the high-water mark, with a low fringe of bushes and small trees between the beach and the road. During much of the ride, good views are possible of the water, the beach, and the many off-shore islands and islets along the coast. Houses are scattered but are generally well maintained and interesting.

Castalia, the first small community south of North Head, has a convenience store, postal outlet, printmaker's shop, and Morse Code Cottages. Dark Harbour Road cuts west from here and crosses the width of the island to the only western community, Dark Harbour, the center of the island's dulse industry. Dark Harbour is aptly named, since sunshine never reaches it until late morning, when the sun finally rises over the high hills east of the harbor. Dulse seaweed is harvested from the ocean and left to dry on a rock breakwater in the town. From there it is packaged and exported to the mainland.

Immediately beyond Castalia Picnic Area is a spit of land with ocean on one side and a salt marsh and lagoon known as Castalia Marsh on the other. There are picnic tables and restrooms here (but no drinking water), and a good beach on the ocean side.

Woodwards Cove has a bed-and-breakfast inn, a grocery, and laundromat. It is difficult to separate this village from nearby Grand Harbour since it blends with the larger town. The Thoroughfare Road to the left in the village proper leads to the shore, where at low tide it's possible to walk across a narrow channel to Ross Island, site of the first settlement on Grand Manan—built in 1784 by a group of Loyalists who left the United States after the American Revolution.

In **Grand Harbour**, the Grand Manan Museum houses naturalist Allan Mose's collection of hundreds of mounted birds indigenous to the island, as well as a geo-logical display and historical and marine artifacts. There are more services in this town than in Woodwards Cove, including cottages, bed-and-breakfasts (try Grand Harbour Inn), a seafood restaurant and take-out, gift shops, and groceries.

Just south of the village, Ingalls Head Road, a paved two-lane, leads a little over 3 kilometers to Ingalls Head and the landing for the free ferry to White Head Island. The ferry leaves every 1½ or 2 hours starting at 6:15 A.M. and ending at 5:00 P.M. most days (except Sundays, when it leaves at 10:30 A.M., 1:30 P.M. and 4:30 P.M.) for a 20-minute crossing to White Head Island, where a rough paved road leads to fine sandy beaches and a lighthouse. The wharf at Ingalls Head is crowded with fishing boats, including some of the finest-looking, best-maintained, and most colorful boats I saw anywhere in the Maritimes.

After Grand Harbour the road cuts inland for several kilometers. Terrain here is low rolling hills, with one or two fairly long hills forested with mixed spruces and hardwoods. Houses are sparse and scattered.

Anchorage Provincial Park, located 13 kilometers from North Head at about the midpoint of the island, offers primitive camping in a central open area not far from the shore and adjacent to a large wildlife preserve. Long Pond Beach is a lengthy, sandy beach with good swimming. Trails lead from the campground south to Red Point and north beyond Long Pond and Big Pond to Ox Head.

From the campground it is a fairly easy ride into Seal Cove, although hills here become somewhat larger and fairly steep, especially on the long descent into town. Before the descent, the hilltop affords views of the interior of the island, where the terrain appears to be mostly wooded and quite rugged.

Seal Cove, like other communities on the island, has a paved shoulder within the village limits. Services are limited but include Abiding Place Guest Home, Amble Inn Cottages, two bed-and-breakfasts (Bagley's and Chez Annette), a post office, and a grocery store. At the bottom of the hill, in the heart of the village, a bridge crosses the narrow outlet of a river, where fishing boats and the wharf are located. A left-hand turn near the bottom of the hill leads to Red Point and interesting exposed cliffs.

Outside Seal Cove, the road is slightly rougher and passes through lowlands of woods and tag alders. It eventually comes out along the coast again, where scattered houses and housekeeping cottages are in evidence. Where the road follows along the water's edge, there are good views of fishing boats at work, numerous islands, and the long rocky coastline. At Deep Cove, the beach is said to be the best on the island, with broad stretches of clean sand and good swimming.

The pavement stops about one and a half kilometers before the end of the road at Southwest Head, and the remaining gravel road is too steep and rough to be recommended for skinny-tire bikes. At the bottom of the first hill after the pavement ends, turn left on a trail to Southern Head Beach, where other trails lead left to a row of granite boulders known as "The Flock of Sheep," or go right along the coast to the top of the cliffs at Southwest Head.

At the end of the gravel road, 31 kilometers from North Head, Southwest Head is a headland on a high cliff looking out across the Grand Manan Channel toward the coast of Maine. To the south is Machias Seal Island, a nesting ground for puffins, auks, terns, razorbills, and other seabirds. Whales and seals can often be seen from the headlands. The lighthouse at Southwest Head is a modern automated beacon and transmitter, and not particularly attractive.

When you leave Grand Manan, it's a good idea to arrive at the ferry landing early in the morning, to allow time to buy your ticket and get in line. In the summer, when large numbers of residents and visitors may want to go to the mainland, be prepared to wait at least 2 hours for passage, although cyclists are sometimes allowed to jump ahead of motorists.

Back on the mainland, an alternative route to Hwy. 1

from Blacks Harbour is on Hwy. 778 along the east shore of the peninsula. Although it winds along an irregular coast and over many more hills, it is definitely the more scenic of the two roads to Blacks Harbour. It offers spectacular views of the ocean and the rocky shoreline—with dramatic high-level marks easily visible 4 to 6 meters above the low-tide water level—and passes through alternating woodlots and scattered farms. In some places the tightly bunched hills and sharp S-curves are as abrupt as an amusement-park ride and would be tiresome except for the good views and the light traffic.

TRIP C: PENNFIELD TO SAINT JOHN—78 KILOMETERS (48.8 MILES)

From Pennfield, at the turnoff to Blacks Harbour and Grand Manan Island, TransCanada 1 continues east along the coast of Fundy to Saint John. The shoulder remains about 1.5 to 2.5 meters wide and in good condition for most of the distance, and the road itself is busy and wide. Terrain flattens considerably, with scattered farmlands opening the view to the coast.

New River Beach Provincial Park, located just south of Hwy. 1 on the Fundy shore near the community of New River Beach, has primitive and developed sites, showers, and picnic grounds.

Services tend to be scattered along the route, but are concentrated in small communities like Lepreau, where there are groceries and restaurants. From Lepreau the paved shoulders shrink to about half a meter to a meter wide. After Musquash the highway expands to four divided lanes with one-meter-wide shoulders. There are some hills, but most of them are relatively low and long, and the going is easy the remaining 24 kilometers to Saint John.

Saint John, with a population of 76,380, is the largest city in New Brunswick. If you're a fan of shopping malls and franchise food, check out Market Square at the center of the city, and the Skywalk—a network of above-street, covered overpasses—that connects dozens of downtown shops, malls, restaurants, hotels, and even the public library. If you're after a more culturally authentic experience, head for the side streets around the center of the city, and poke around in gift shops, galleries, and seafood restaurants. A bicycle shop, Eastern Sports Ltd., is located on West Morland Road. Although the Reversing Falls—where the Fundy tides literally reverse the direction of the falls at the mouth of the Saint John River—are hyped generously by the tourist bureaus, they really are an amazing natural phenomenon well worth viewing.

·QUÉBEC·

Extending from the St. Lawrence lowlands in the south to beyond the sixtieth parallel in the north—only 440 kilometers from the Arctic Circle—Québec is Canada's largest province and encompasses an area twice the size of Texas and seven times the size of the British Isles. Most of its 1,553,637 square kilometers (579,000 square miles) are covered by vast undeveloped forests and tundra. The majority of the province's 6,500,000 inhabitants live in the agricultural regions along both shores of the St. Lawrence River and in the two major cities of Montreal and Québec.

Founded as a territory of France by Jacques Cartier in 1534, the province has a long history of separation from English-speaking North America. Following the French and English War, the king of France yielded control of all of Canada, including French-speaking Québec, to the British crown. Shortly afterward, Canada was divided into two provinces, the English-speaking Upper Canada (what is now Ontario) and the French-speaking Lower Canada (now Québec and the Maritimes). Québec has remained spiritually if not politically independent from the rest of Canada ever since and has often in the past two centuries entertained the idea of breaking away as a separate nation. And while a majority (so far) of Québec residents oppose an independent government for Québec, the vast majority support cultural independence.

Those cultural differences with neighboring Canada have given the province a reputation as the most "foreign" of the provinces, a reputation that tends to intimidate inexperienced travelers. Stories circulating about unfriendly attitudes toward outsiders, especially Americans, seem to be unfounded. In fact, during my own travels I found the people of Québec to be the most courteous and friendly of any I met in eastern Canada. Instead of animosity toward Americans, I witnessed only curiosity and a healthy-minded willingness to discuss issues.

Weather

Climate varies somewhat between the two areas of Québec described in the following tours, but in general expect temperate weather, with hot summers and cool, moderate autumns and springs. Temperatures in the Gaspé Peninsula average about 5 degrees cooler than in the Charlevoix and Québec City regions, but are likely to be less harsh than in those Maritime Provinces facing the North Atlantic.

Language

Naturally, language differences can be a handicap for travelers in Québec, where 83 percent of the residents speak primarily French. Road signs are printed entirely in French, but most use easily recognized universal symbols. Although it is often possible to find someone in a public place who speaks passably good English, there are times when you will be left to your own devices. Travelers' tales are true in this regard: it will put you in good graces to make at least some effort to communicate in French before you run off shouting in English for help. With the aid of a basic book like the Berlitz guide, *French for Travellers*, and a few hours practice with rudimentary phrases, you should be equipped well enough for standard situations. In spite of 2 years of lackadaisical effort in high school French classes (many years ago), I found myself unable to understand anything but the simplest words and expressions. Nonetheless, it was not difficult—and in fact was a great deal of fun—to make my way across the province able to say almost nothing except, "bonjour," "au revoir," "pardon," "excusez-moi, s'il vous plaît," and "merci." If the conversation showed promise of proceeding further, I could dazzle them with, "Excusez-moi, je ne parle pas français. Parlez-vous anglais?" ("Excuse me, but I don't speak French. Do you speak English?"). At the very least, my efforts would initiate laughter, and mirth, as everyone knows, is one of the universal languages.

Traffic Laws

The maximum speed limit is 100 kilometers per hour on major highways and is posted on lesser highways. Bicyclists must obey the same traffic laws as motorists.

Miscellaneous

Because of language difficulties and (at least in the remote sections of Gaspé) a relative scarcity of tourists, travelers checks are sometimes difficult to cash in Québec. You'll have your best luck cashing them at banks in metropolitan areas, but in smaller communities they may be refused. Likewise, foreign currency creates difficulty in some areas. Generally, it's best to carry Canadian cash.

For Further Information

For general information, write Tourisme Québec, P.O. Box 20,000, Québec, Canada G1K 7X2; or phone 1-800-443-7000 (from the eastern United States), 1-800-361-6490 (from Ontario and Maritimes), 1-800-361-5405 (from Québec), or 514/873-2015 (from elsewhere).

For tourist information about the Gaspé region, write Association touristique de la Gaspésie, 357 Route de la Mer, Ste.-Flavie, Québec, Canada G0J 2L0; or phone 418/775-2223.

For more details about Gaspé's Forillon National Park, write Canadian Parks Service, Forillon District, 146 Gaspé Boulevard, Gaspé, Québec, Canada G0C 1R0; or phone 418/368-5505.

Tourism staff members are usually bilingual.

9

Gaspé Peninsula

Begin/End: Percé to Gaspé, and loops around Forillon Park and Gaspé Peninsula
Roads: Hwys. 132, 198, 197
Accommodations: Campgrounds, hotels and motels, bed-and-breakfast inns
Length: 447.2 kilometers (279.5 miles)
Difficulty: Moderate to difficult

TRIP A: PERCÉ TO GASPÉ— 72.8 KILOMETERS (45.5 MILES)

The Gaspé—derived from "gespeg," the Micmac word for "land's end"—is a large peninsula protruding far into the Gulf of the St. Lawrence. A popular vacation destination for native Québecers, it seems to be largely undiscovered by visitors from the United States. Though a few of the more popular coastal regions of the peninsula can be crowded, much of the interior is a remote wilderness area that is rarely visited. From a cyclist's perspective, the only shortcoming to the region is its lack of campgrounds. Except for the several excellent public campgrounds in Forillon National Park, at the eastern tip of the peninsula, only private RV parks are found along most of the route. Motels and tourist cabins are available in most of the larger communities.

The heart of the peninsula's tourist region is on the south and east shores of Gaspé, along the Baie des Chaleurs ("Bay of Warmth," named by Jacques Cartier when he saw it during a sweltering July day in 1534), and especially in the vicinity of the little seaside resort of **Percé**. Named for enormous "Pierced Rock," which dominates its harbor, Percé is one of those towns so dependent on tourism for its economic survival that it is always in danger of descending into gaudiness and trivia. It has its share of gift shops—you can buy photographs, paintings, and diminutive sculptures of Percé Rock in a hundred variations, at any of dozens of shops—and is top-heavy with hotels and seafood take-outs, yet the place is surrounded by terrain so lovely it is far from being spoiled. Views of the town from the ocean and from the top of Mont Ste.-Anne behind the town are simply beautiful. It is one of those rare communities that seems somehow a compliment to the landscape rather than an insult to it.

With only 200 year-round residents, Percé is surprisingly busy during summer and offers all services. In spite of the large number of hotels and motels (I recommend the Hotel la Normandie—nice ocean-front balconies and an excellent dining room), accommodations can be scarce during the busiest weekends. Camping is available at a large RV park near the center of the town. Most of the tourist activity takes place along the boardwalk-lined beach and the wide wharf looking out at Percé Rock, where shops, galleries, and restaurants are clustered in an open mall and along the beach.

The rock that gave the town its name is an enormous block of limestone, 470 meters long and 88 meters high, located just offshore. Wave action over the centuries bored through the rock in two places, creating two

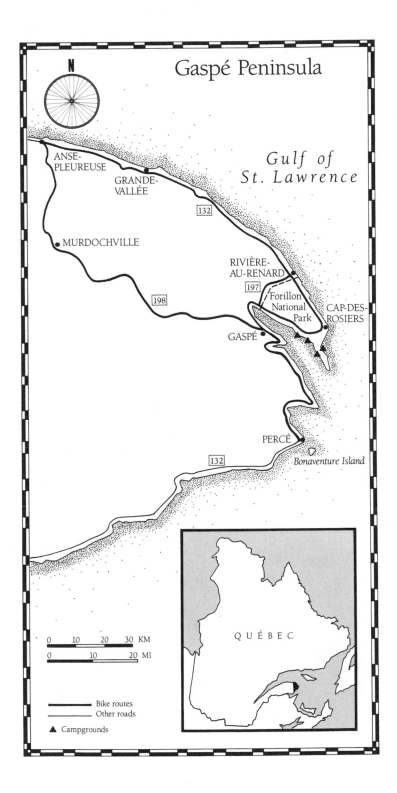

N

Gaspé Peninsula

Gulf of
St. Lawrence

ANSE-
PLEUREUSE

GRANDE-
VALLÉE

132

MURDOCHVILLE

RIVIÈRE-
AU-RENARD

197

Forillon
National
Park

CAP-DES-
ROSIERS

198

GASPÉ

PERCÉ

132

Bonaventure Island

0   10   20   30 KM

0   10   20 MI

QUÉBEC

——— Bike routes
——— Other roads

▲ Campgrounds

arched openings, the outer of which collapsed in the middle of the nineteenth century. Excellent views of the rock are possible from almost anywhere in town, but especially along the beach and wharf, or from any of the several excursion boats that cruise past it on the way to Bonaventure Island about 3 kilometers offshore. During low tide a narrow strip of beach can be walked to the near edge of the rock.

Percé Rock, on the east coast of the Gaspé Peninsula.

Perhaps the most memorable view of Percé, the rock, and the island is from the top of Mont Ste.-Anne, a very high, wooded peak that rises over the back of the community. It can be reached on foot via a one-and-one-half hour walk, but it is far easier to book an excursion to the top with Denis Harbour's Excursion Panoramiques. Denis, a bilingual resident of Percé, is friendly, energetic, and knowledgeable about local history, culture, and ge-

ology and provides an entertaining and informative 2-hour tour of the entire Percé area. Contact him in Percé at 418/782-5054.

Bonaventure Island is a 4-square-kilometer provincial park maintained as a seabird sanctuary. During the summer, tour boats offer frequent daily excursions to the island from the Percé wharf. A typical excursion takes you on a 45-minute tour around the rugged, rocky coast of the island, then drops you off at a small service area (gift shop and snack bar) located near the remnants of a fishing village displaced when the island was purchased by the provincial government in 1971. Trails from the service area lead across the island to cliffs used as nesting areas by a variety of seabirds, including a colony of 50,000 gannets. Return to the mainland at your leisure on the next boat.

Leaving Percé and heading north on Hwy. 132 toward the city of Gaspé, be prepared for some major ascents and descents. Directly out of town is the first long hill, a 2.7-kilometer climb with a very steep gradient. Here, as elsewhere on most of the major hills on the Gaspé, a passing lane opens for uphill traffic, giving some relief to cyclists. Most of the tight bends likewise open somewhat with a paved shoulder up to 2 meters wide. In some stretches the paved shoulders continue on the hilly straightaways.

The first leg of the ride, over the rocky, mountainous terrain just north of Percé, is through dramatic cuts and canyon walls. Like the Long Range Mountains in Newfoundland, this range of rugged terrain is an extension of the Appalachian Mountains. One of the more spectacular peaks, a jagged, sheer-faced cliff looking over the water, is known as Le Pic de L'Aurore—"The Peak of the Dawn"—because it is the first rock to be lit with the rosy light of sunrise each day.

After about 9 kilometers of continuous climbs and descents, the road slopes down to sea level at Percé Coin-du-Banc, one of several "suburbs" of Percé. Coin-du-Banc is remarkable for lovely sand beaches on both shores of a one-and-a-half-kilometer natural sandbar that extends in an arching line around the coast. Also remarkable is Auberge du Coin du Banc, a unique restaurant/inn found on the shore at the bottom of the hill. Watch especially for the goats on the roof of the barnlike structure next to the restaurant (the goats climb a ladder to the roof and seem to enjoy looking out over the ocean). The restaurant offers excellent and moderately expensive French cuisine in an extremely casual atmosphere. Perspiring cyclists need not feel underdressed. Several of the dining rooms seem to share space with the living quarters of the owner's family; silverware and dishes are eclectic assortments of old, random but lovely odds and ends; the walls are covered with an abundance of oddball gadgets and gewgaws, including numerous Irish souvenirs, reminders that the French-speaking family that runs the place are descended from Irish fishermen who settled on Bonaventure Island.

After the restaurant, the route continues flat along the coast, then cuts inland a short distance. Houses and small businesses are scattered for much of the way, though they never crowd the stretch. The terrain inland has softened considerably from the impressive, mountainous landscape inland from Percé, and is predominantly wooded over low hills. From anywhere along the coast you can look back and see Percé Rock and the cliffs along the coast. In places the road climbs slightly and travels near the edge of a bluff 9 to 12 meters above the water, through grasslands and pasturage cleared of most trees.

Percé Belle-Anse is a tiny fishing community with a natural harbor and barely active fish plant. It offers no travelers' services, though the next fishing village, Saint-Georges-de-Malbaie, has a restaurant, store, service station, and motel. The coast here is lined with low but spectacular carved and sculpted cliffs. The road climbs slightly, but without major hills, and offers a view of the long, rugged mountains of the Forillon Peninsula across Baie de Gaspé. The mountains are visible in outline, like jagged paper cutouts.

The villages of Fort-Prével and Douglastown have

motels, restaurants, and small grocery stores. Auberge Fort-Prével is especially noteworthy, because of its large size and elegant appearance, and because it fronts an enormous, nearly vertical cliff that drops to the water.

From here expect several kilometers of continuous, fairly long hills that alternate sections of coastal route with the hillier, wooded interior. A provincial picnic area at the mouth of the Sealcove River is a good place to rest but is closed to camping.

The remaining 24 kilometers to Gaspé are through a variety of terrain: flat, coastal lowlands, slightly rolling uplands, and the longer, steeper hills of the wooded interior. Houses are scattered along much of the route.

At the intersection of Hwys. 132 and 198, take the left fork on 198 for the most direct route to the town of Gaspé; Hwy. 132 continues around a small peninsula before joining 198 in the town.

TRIP B: GASPÉ TO FORILLON NATIONAL PARK LOOP— 107.7 KILOMETERS (67.3 MILES)

With a population of 16,000, **Gaspé** is a thriving little city at the base of Baie de Gaspé. It is the largest community on the peninsula and after the quaintness of Percé can seem unpolished and blatantly commercial. All services are available in the downtown district and, to a lesser degree, in the commercial areas leading out of town. Among the highlights of the community are several excellent restaurants and bed-and-breakfast inns, interesting galleries and shops, and the Gaspésie Museum with exhibits detailing the geography and geology of the peninsula and the history of its native and European inhabitants. The museum also sports a statue and tribute to Jacques Cartier who took shelter from a storm in the bay nearby and claimed possession of New France in 1534.

Gaspé makes a convenient base for two excellent cycle tours. Both are loops, one around Forillon National Park at the very tip of the peninsula, the other a much longer trip that includes a ride through the wild, undeveloped interior of the peninsula.

The Forillon loop follows Hwy. 132 from the downtown district of Gaspé, north along the shore of the bay. In the city, 132 is a busy four-lane highway with paved shoulders one and a half meters wide, diminishing to two lanes near the outskirts. The road follows the bay closely, usually on bluffs and hillsides above it, through fairly dense residential and commercial development, with a view of the base of the Forillon Peninsula across the water.

About 3 kilometers out of Gaspé, development diminishes to scattered houses on rolling, lightly wooded terrain. Most of the route around the bay is relatively flat and offers good views of the bay and the valley around it. When the road reaches the end of the bay and the mouth of the Dartmouth River, it begins a gradual, winding ascent up the north shore of the bay.

At the intersection with Hwy. 197, turn north to cut across the base of the peninsula and skirt the western border of Forillon National Park. This begins a clockwise circuit of the park, the best tactic for dealing with predominant west winds. If you're planning to camp in Forillon, however, it might be more logical to continue east on 132 at this intersection to the South Sector camping areas, since they are much closer than the campgrounds on the north side of the park. Once established at a campground, you can then proceed with clockwise or counterclockwise circuits of the park.

A steep climb on Hwy. 197 takes you away from the bay and most of the development, into an interior region of wooded hills. The ascent flattens considerably after the initial hill and becomes a continuous but not very steep climb through a shallow valley with large wooded hills on both sides. The road itself is in good condition, a two-lane with no shoulders on the flat stretches, that widens to accommodate a passing lane on ascents.

Five and a half kilometers of gradual climbing leads to the top of a saddle of land in the forested, undeveloped interior of the peninsula. From here to the coast is a continuous downhill of nearly 11 kilometers, with pitches of fairly steep descent alternating with long stretches of far more gradual gradient. The hills are more pronounced here than on the uphill slope—both steeper and higher—with the valley sides rising quite high on both sides of the road. Partway down the road parallels a small river flowing through a sheer, steep-sided rock canyon.

Eventually the valley widens and becomes inhabited, with small farms and scattered houses set among hay fields and woodlots. **Rivière-au-Renard**, a fishing village at the intersection of Hwys. 197 and 132, offers most services. Turn right at the intersection in the heart of town and follow Hwy. 132 east toward Forillon. A steep hill immediately after the intersection gives a good view of the town, with its breakwall and man-made harbor and small fish plant.

Once out of town, the road follows a stretch of shoreline that quickly becomes typical of the north shore of Gaspé. Steep, short ascents (most climbs, here at least, will be under one kilometer long) reach a peak, give a good view of the Gulf from bluffs about 100 meters above the water, then drop steeply into valleys and repeat themselves up the other side. It can be a fatiguing stretch, although scenery is attractive and frequent pull-offs in the valleys give good access to excellent beaches. This stretch of shoreline is extremely popular with windsurfers.

About 5.5 kilometers from Rivière-au-Renard is the first boundary of **Forillon National Park**. Just inside the boundary is an information pavilion with restrooms and water. A one-kilometer climb followed by a steep descent with a 10 percent gradient takes you out of the park again and into lightly developed country. This is a typical scenario at Forillon, where numerous small communities exist in pockets of land surrounded by national park.

The next entrance to the park follows 17.6 kilometers of privately owned shoreline. The terrain between the park entrances is interesting and varied, with picturesque wooded hills and meadows sloping down to the road, then dropping off abruptly beyond it at the edge of the bluff above the shore. Scattered along the route are inactive farms and small, modest houses, many of them constructed in the simplest way, yet often painted with very bright colors. The road is in fair condition, with frequent patches and cracks, without paved shoulders.

L'Anse-au-Griffon is a small fishing village with its own breakwalled harbor and fish plant. Services include motels, groceries, a bank, and post office. A long hill climbs to an open bluff above the town. From here views of the ocean are impressive, with wide beaches clearly visible below the bluffs. Most of the distance to the park now is relatively flat, with some rolling hills and a few steep drops and climbs. Houses are more concentrated here as you approach the park boundaries.

The community of **Cap-des-Rosiers** crowds the park boundary with motels, restaurants, housekeeping cottages, ice cream shops, and other services, all squeezed into the final kilometer or two before the commercial-free lands of the national park. If you're impressed by the biggest and best, you might take a few minutes to climb the lighthouse here: measuring 37 meters, it's said to be Canada's highest.

This is the main entrance to Forillon National Park and puts you within easy cycling distance of many of the park's campgrounds and natural attractions. Encompassing an area of 245 square kilometers, the park was created in 1970, becoming the first national park in Québec, and in summer attracts large numbers of tourists.

The park headquarters is right inside the main entrance off Hwy. 132, in the "North Sector." Take the left fork at the first intersection inside the park; it leads to a large and well-equipped interpretation center located 2.3 kilometers from the park entrance. The road to the interpretation center is a paved two-lane in good shape that follows the beach closely and is virtually flat along most of its length. Riprap along the water's edge is designed to prevent heavy surf from washing over the road, and high waves crashing against the stones often throw spray across motorists and cyclists traveling the route. Frequent motorists' pull-offs offer good views of the water and the spectacular high cliffs farther down the shoreline. The beach itself is predominately gravel.

Just beyond the pavilion is an entrance kiosk. Automobiles are charged $4 for a one-day entry permit ($9 for four days, $25 for the season), while cyclists are allowed free entry.

Cap-Bon-Ami is located at the end of the paved road, 6 kilometers from the interpretation center along the north shore of the park. The road here is mostly flat at first along a low plateau next to the water, with impressive slopes coming down almost to the road on the inland side. Des-Rosiers Campground is a large park with 155 sites, half located in the shelter of woods, with well-equipped and comfortable kitchen shelters, flush toilets, and hot showers.

Immediately past the campground the road begins a very steep one-kilometer climb into the woods, past sheer rock cliffs. It peaks, then starts a 15 percent descent that winds tightly around blind curves and ends abruptly in a deadend at a cul-de-sac and parking area at the picnic and camping area at Cap-Bon-Ami. The campground here is small, with 32 primitive sites and a kitchen shelter. From a prominent viewing area, the coastline is incredible, bordered by enormous sheer cliffs that have eroded into strange, columnlike formations that drop nearly straight down to the water. Unfortunately, lovely as it is, the spot is very popular and was the most crowded place I found in the park. Rather than shoulder in to snap obligatory photos, I made a quick escape back to the intersection near the interpretation center, and rejoined Hwy. 132.

This section of the highway cuts across the tip of the peninsula to the "South Sector." It's a wide two-lane in good condition here, with a paved shoulder a half meter to a meter wide that is in only fair shape. The interior of the peninsula is entirely wooded, with high rocky peaks visible above the tree line, especially to the north. The route is moderately hilly, with rolling, rounded hills creating gradual ascents and descents. One or two short descents are quite steep. The road at one point cuts through a narrow pass between high hills and offers views of sheer cliffs and precipices. The final kilometer and a half before the south shore is the hilliest, with an ascent of one kilometer followed by a steep 13 percent grade with a hairpin curve.

At the bottom of the last hill, turn left at the intersection to reach the South Sector area of the park. The road leaves the park briefly and passes through a small village with a few houses but no services, then climbs to the top of a low, fairly flat bluff above the Baie de Gaspé.

A small interpretation center is located inside the park entrance in the South Sector and is followed shortly by Petit-Gaspé Campground. Set among woods of mixed hardwoods and conifers, the campground has 136 primitive and serviced sites, hot showers, kitchen shelters, and drinking water. An amphitheater offers summer lectures on the park's natural history. A nearby recreation center has a heated saltwater swimming pool, wading pool, children's playground, tennis courts, restaurant, convenience store, and launderette.

In the vicinity of the campground, the road winds through tight curves within a spruce forest, then comes out abruptly on the beach, with long views of the rocky shoreline to the east. The road is rough, cobbled in places, with two lanes and no shoulders. A gradual climb takes you to the top of a bluff that follows the coastline, with a fairly steep and partly wooded cliff falling away to the water. The pavement is rough enough to make for slow going on road bikes.

Grande-Grave is a reconstruction of a community established on the shore of the peninsula by early Anglo-Norman fishermen. Exhibits include the community general store, fully stocked with goods typical of turn-of-the-century commerce. Marine life demonstrations are presented on the beach at Grande-Grave on Wednesday and Saturday mornings during the summer. Scuba divers carry marine life specimens to shore and describe—in both French and English—their role in the underwater environment.

The road continues along the coast, rolling, dipping, and rising with the shoreline. It rises at places to about 60 meters above the water, then drops again almost to sea level. At the end of the road is a cul-de-sac with access to a trail to Cap-Gaspé. The trail, about 3 kilometers long, is open to hikers and mountain bikers. It is an easy mountain-bike ride on a wide gravel two-track road, except for one very long, steep hill that will probably have to be walked up by all but the fiercest all-terrain bikers. At the end of the trail, a high vista over the cape gives spectacular views of the ocean and the rugged, jagged rock formations that descend far down to the water. Both pilot and baleen whales are frequently spotted from here. The lighthouse on the cape is not open to the public but is interesting because it is powered by a battery of solar collectors arranged around its base.

Back at the intersection with Hwy. 132, to the east, is the village of Cap-aux-Os, offering such basic services as a grocery, restaurant, post office, and private camp-ground. Privately owned, lightly inhabited country continues for about 6 kilometers.

Just after entering the park again, go into the parking area on the right, which leads to the old Anse-au-Griffon Portage Road. Open to mountain bikes, this trail cuts through remote territory in the interior of the park. Other trails branching out from here are open to mountain bikes as well—about 19 kilometers of biking trails are open altogether and lead through a little-visited portion of the park where sightings of moose, black bear, and other wildlife are common.

Fort Peninsule is a picnic area and tourist pull-off beside the highway. About one and a half kilometers after it is Penouille, a low sandy peninsula sticking into the bay; it is said to harbor the best swimming beaches in the park. It is the site also of a picnic area and an information center with snack bar and restrooms.

One and a half kilometers beyond Penouille the road leaves the park for good. From here to the intersection with Hwy. 197, and the completion of the loop, are 7 kilometers of rolling hills and light development on bluffs above the water.

TRIP C: GASPÉ TO MURDOCHVILLE— 266.7 KILOMETERS (166.7 MILES)

This much larger loop takes an ambitious bite out of the northeast quarter of the Gaspé Peninsula and covers a terrific variety of terrain. As always, direction of travel is a matter of personal preference. The prevailing west winds can make a counterclockwise circuit difficult along the northern coastal route but will be an advantage through the long valleys and semimountainous terrain of the interior. I rode the circuit in a counterclockwise direction (and was lucky with the wind), so it makes sense to describe it that way. In both the coastal and interior legs of the loop there are some major hills to contend with. Allow plenty of time—at least 3 days—to complete the trip.

Gaspé to Grande-Vallée—88.2 Kilometers (55.1 Miles)

Repeat the 27-kilometer trip from the city of **Gaspé** to Hwy. 197 north (see description in TRIP B), then at the intersection of Hwys. 197 and 132 in **Rivière-au-Renard**,

go left (west) along the north coast of the Gaspé Peninsula. From the intersection expect several kilometers of
closely spaced villages, all blending into one another. Although fairly busy, the area is decidedly untouristy and
seems to depend far more on the local fishery for income
than on fickle tourist dollars.

Almost immediately the coast is raw, rugged, and
spectacular. Much of the north shore is lined with massive hills and jagged cliffs similar to those found in
Forillon Park. The first long climb, only a few kilometers beyond the intersection with Hwy. 197, is typical
of what's yet to come: a tough, winding climb of one
and a half kilometers on the side of the mountain away
from the ocean, with a long view of a river valley below. It reaches a peak, then descends immediately to a
village nestled on the shore between the mountains.

That pattern is repeated often during the next 80
kilometers along the north coast. Some of the hills are
back breakers; others are gradual enough to be difficult
but not discouraging.

To L'Anse-à-Valleau, 19 kilometers from Rivière-au-
Renard, the steep hills and deep valleys continue to repeat themselves, with some ascents as long as 3 kilometers. Each climb is rewarded with an unpredictable
view: broad ocean, wooded valley, distant villages with
church steeples rising like spires. The road is a wide two-
lane along the entire route, and a passing lane is added
on most of the larger hills. Wide paved shoulders—up to
3 meters—are irregular and infrequent. Traffic is moderate; most of the tourist traffic that makes its way up from
Québec City seems to funnel across to the south shore
of Gaspé.

L'Anse-à-Valleau, like most of the coastal villages,
has a small store and service station. The highway turns
inland here and for the next 16 kilometers passes through
an uninhabited region of rolling hills and long valleys.
The area is remote and vast enough to give a sense of
the wilderness found in the true interior of Gaspé. Although the scenery is not overpowering, it is pleasant and

attractive, with long views of wooded hills stepping away in ranks. The road is fair to good, with some patches and rough places, and surprisingly flat much of the way. Climbs tend to be gradual for fairly long stretches, then tumble into short, steep hills, some with gradients up to 14 percent. A final 2.5-kilometer descent leads to flats along the shore of a lake. Where the lake's outlet drains into saltwater is a small picnic area on a fine, sandy beach.

The beach and picnic area are immediately followed by a monster climb of a little over a kilometer and a half, up a steep, winding valley away from the coast. From the bluff at the top is a fine, long view of the ocean, then a one-and-a-half-kilometer descent to the village of St.-Yvon. Modest services are available here, including a small motel. The scarcity of accommodations along the coast is baffling, especially since I saw more bicyclists along this route than anywhere in Gaspé, and many of them were tourists equipped for long rides. Without sanctioned campgrounds to rely on, many cyclists simply look for out-of-the-way beaches to spend the night.

Both St. Yvon and its sister village, Cloridorme, are busy fishing communities. The long, lattice-covered tables lined up in fields along the road are called "vigneaux" and are used to air-dry fillets of cod, a method of food preparation that has remained basically unchanged for hundreds of years. The villages, separated by a steep but not very high saddle of land, are crowded right to the shore. Cloridorme offers restaurants and stores but no lodging. Houses cling almost desperately to any flat spot on the hillsides.

A 3-kilometer climb out of Cloridorme leads to yet another spectacular bluff, 91 to 122 meters above the water, with views of the Gulf of St. Lawrence that seem impossibly long. The road is laid like a ribbon for several kilometers along the top edge of the bluff. A motel-hotel is situated at the peak and is followed by a very steep, 19 percent descent to the town of Pointe-à-la-Frégate.

Equipped with a restaurant, motel, and several stores, Pointe-à-la-Frégate is a fishing village like many others along the coast, although its fishermen do not have the advantage of a sheltered harbor and must haul their boats over a sand beach to launch and land them. Houses, as elsewhere along the coast, are humble, blocky, and resolute, with few decorative flourishes except bright colors, especially brilliant red trim. The hills along this portion of the coast are smaller than before, rolling and covered with mostly deciduous trees.

After the town the road follows a bluff about 30 meters above the water, then goes through a section of short but continuous and tiresome rolling hills. Most of the country is uninhabited away from the villages. Eventually the route opens onto a meadow on top of a bluff with broad views of the ocean.

Grande-Vallée to Murdochville— 86.9 Kilometers (54.3 Miles)

Petite-Vallée has no services other than roadside vegetable stands, but about 3 kilometers farther, after the obligatory climb over a sizable hill, the town of **Grande-Vallée**—with its population of 1560, one of the largest communities along the coast—has most services, including several motels (Hotel Grande-Vallée and Motel Richard; Motel Frigault has a dining room), bank, post office, and most significantly, a private campground. Located on open ground beside the road and rather run-down, this campground is not one of the prettiest, but it is situated on a bluff looking over the water and is virtually the only campground on this portion of the north coast. On the outskirts of the town, at the bridge over the Grande Vallée River, is a short side road leading to a provincial picnic area beside the river.

Just out of Grande-Vallée begins a major, 2.7-kilometer climb that is steep, winding, and exhausting. Near the peak is a picnic area with restrooms and water and an excellent view of the coast you've just traveled, with the town of

Grande-Vallée in prominent view in the foreground and receding hills and bluffs in the background.

Several other equally impressive views occur during the next few kilometers, during a roller coaster of ascents and descents, none as long as the one out of Grande-Vallée. This is wild, remote country now, with deep river valleys and huge hills descending from several directions at once. Most of the region is wooded, and there are, for a change, no villages in the coastal valleys, no doubt because the terrain is too irregular and rugged to allow easy development. The road continues to be fairly well paved, although patches and rough spots are common. Paved shoulders are intermittent, although they often appear in time to be useful on the ascents.

A very steep, 2-kilometer descent leads into the village of Rivière-la-Madeleine, where there are a store, service station, and several hotels with restaurants. Rocky, hilly terrain surrounds the town and the large river that flows through it, while low, grassy slopes lead down to the shore of the ocean. Some farming takes place here, but farms are modest and don't appear to be very active. A lighthouse perches on a grassy headland outside the village.

A 3-kilometer ride along relatively flat terrain leads into the village of Madeleine-Centre. The terrain has softened considerably here, with the hills much less imposing and the ascents longer and more gradual. A few kilometers after Madeleine-Centre, and following a one-and-a-half-kilometer descent that reaches a pitch of 8 percent, begins a remarkable stretch of coastal highway built at the base of a steep bluff. A sturdy seawall has been constructed along the shore to create enough space to accommodate the road and to protect it from crashing waves. As it stands, the seawall, built with concrete abutments about 4.5 meters from the edge of the road, also creates 16 kilometers of perfectly flat highway, with paved shoulders about 2.5 meters wide. Bluffs 91 to 122 meters high tower above the road, creating a minor risk of fallen rocks. Most of the bluffs are not sheer, although they're steep enough to create slides of sloughed off gravel and rock. Some trees cling to the face of the bluffs; unusual rock formations stand out elsewhere. It is certainly the strangest and most effortless section to ride along the coastal route.

Late in the day, at a roadside pull-off along the sea-wall, I struck up a conversation with a man and his three sons who were fishing from the rocks lining the water. Perhaps it wasn't exactly a conversation—they spoke no English, I very little French—but the message came across that they had earlier in the day caught a large codfish and were excited about their good luck. The youngest boy, who was about 10 years old, had captured the fish and was beaming proudly. When I tried to offer my con-gratulations, he took a deep breath and announced loudly, "Good morning!" It was obviously the only English phrase he knew, so I did not have the heart to correct him. Besides, it was my opportunity to repay the graciousness of the dozens of French Canadians who had waited patiently through my primitive French. I returned his "Good morning!" with enthusiasm, fielded a volley of "Good mornings" from his brothers and fa-ther, and continued on, looking for a place to camp for the night.

The seawall is interrupted briefly by the village of Gros-Morne, which has a small grocery store and a tav-ern, then ends finally near the village of Anse-Pleureuse and the junction with Hwy. 198. **Anse-Pleureuse**, which translates as "Crying Cove," is tiny, with few services, but has attained regional fame for its tales of wailing ghosts. According to legend, the cries of shipwrecked sailors can be heard at night in the wind-blown trees along the beach.

Cutting south and east from the intersection across the vast interior of the upper quarter of the Gaspé Pen-insula, Hwy. 198 is a two-lane secondary road in good condition but without paved shoulders. Almost imme-diately after the intersection it enters a narrow, sheer-sided canyon and proceeds upstream along the course of

This is one of the few stretches of flat highway along the remote and rugged north coast of the Gaspé Peninsula.

the Anse-Pleureuse River. After a short distance the valley widens somewhat to one-half to one kilometer wide, but the very steep, wooded mountains along the sides are spectacular, with sheer, layered rock in tightly spaced horizontal striations. The view up the valley is promising, with predominantly flat, mostly wooded ground protected from the wind for a considerable distance. Enjoy it. Such easy going does not last long.

About a kilometer and a half south of the intersection with Hwy. 132 is a picnic area on the shore of Lac de l'Anse Pleureuse, a small reservoir on the river. The road hugs the shore of the lake and is virtually flat. The rock formations on the valley sides continue to be remarkable, with horizontal striations—the geologic equivalent to the rings on a tree—that are in places warped upward or downward like the lines on a graph sheet, evidence of upheavals in the earth's surface. They give the rock a marbled, variegated look.

Even this near the intersection with Hwy. 132, it is evident that Hwy. 198 is not a heavily traveled route. The countryside along it, even in the flat, protected valley of the Rivière de l'Anse Pleureuse, is almost completely uninhabited, giving a foretaste of the remote country yet to come.

About 6.5 kilometers south of Anse Pleureuse is a flurry of short hills followed by another stretch of flat-lands. Three kilometers farther begins a short but fairly steep hill soon followed by a moderately difficult climb of one and a half kilometers. At the top, passing rolling highlands of hardwoods and poplar, you can look to the west and see the Chic-Chocs, a range of sharply outlined but predominantly wooded mountains dominated by 1,270-meter Mont Jacques-Cartier. They are at the heart of an enormous wilderness area, the near portion (bounded on the east by Hwy. 198 itself) protected by the Chic-Choc Wildlife Preserve, the more western area contained within Parc de la Gaspésie—Gaspé Provincial Park. Within the park and wilderness area are patches of subarctic vegetation, as well as populations of moose, deer, bear, and a sizable herd of woodland caribou.

Other hills follow the first, coming in a succession of ascents and descents that climb gradually to altitudes high enough to replace deciduous forests with spruce and fir. The road continues to be predominantly two lanes, with passing lanes built into most of the larger hills. The longest and most difficult climb in this stretch is a 5-kilometer ordeal that alternates moderately steep pitches with long stretches of gradual ascent. It takes you to a hilltop with a great view of the Chic-Chocs to the west and the long rolling hills of the interior to the south.

Also to the south is the first glimpse of Murdoch-ville. It is not a flattering view. This highly industrialized mining community is surrounded by kilometers of strip-mining operations that seem to have pillaged entire mountains and left the valleys filled with the discarded tailings. Mysteriously, all the largest conifers on the hills surrounding the mining operations have died, their dried, silver trunks sticking up from the forest like gray hairs. It's as if poisonous fumes from the mines have passed over them, selectively weeding out only the largest and stateliest trees. Perhaps reflecting the sorry state of the environment, the road is suddenly patched and cracked, in such poor condition that it becomes necessary to slow down and give careful attention to it.

Murdochville to Gaspé—91.7 Kilometers (57.3 Miles)

A 3-kilometer descent leads into the city limits of **Murdochville**, which was built in 1951 by Mines Gaspé around the substantial copper deposits discovered there. Incongruously, this industrialized city of 2,000 is a popular resort area, especially in winter when its impressive ski slopes are in operation (and when, no doubt, snow covers the ugliness of the mines). Tours of the copper mines are open to the public. Most services are available. A tourist information center is located along the highway near the center of town and is a good place to inquire about lodging. The only developed campsites available in the area are at a private campground 8 kilometers south of the city on Hwy. 198. Although primarily an RV park, it is set among attractive wooded hills, well away from the commerce and industry of Murdochville.

After Murdochville a long stretch of roller-coaster hills begins. This may be the most difficult stretch on the entire Gaspé route. The hills, though not as high as those on the north coast, are relentless, with steep climbs and descents of a kilometer to a kilometer and a half following one another with monotonous regularity. The pattern continues for about 16 kilometers, through remote woodlands with no evidence of houses or other development, at which point a 5-kilometer descent gives some relief. It drops into the valley of the York River, the major waterway in this part of the peninsula and a world-famous salmon river.

A one-and-a-half-kilometer ascent to the top of a ridge gives a good view of the valley of the York River.

After several more steep hills the road flattens out considerably and begins to travel parallel to the river through a lovely valley of hardwoods, birches, and poplars. The steep wooded slopes on both sides come down nearly to the river, which is fast and winding, with light rapids glittering between pools. The country is entirely uninhabited, and automobile traffic remains very light. Truck traffic between Murdochville and Gaspé is moderate but travels fast.

The final kilometers of the route continue through uninhabited, wooded terrain beside the York River. The road is primarily flat but descends with just enough gradient to allow for a leisurely, high-speed ride. The town of Gaspé officially begins at the upper end of the Basin du Sud-Ouest, where the York River widens into an inlet, but don't expect to enter the actual town until about 8 kilometers beyond the city limits.

10

Charlevoix and Ile d'Orléans

Begin/End: Baie-Ste.-Catherine to Québec City and Ile d'Orléans
Roads: Hwy. 138 and side trips
Accommodations: Hotels, bed-and-breakfast, private campgrounds
Length: 322.5 kilometers (201.6 miles)
Difficulty: Moderately difficult

Were you to believe everything written in tourism publications, you might be convinced most of the world is made up of places so beautiful, interesting, and photogenic they are barely suitable for mere mortals. In practice, of course, you tend to become a little skeptical about the loose enthusiasms of the travel bureaus. You start to doubt that *any* place can live up to its publicity photos.

Armed, then, with a dose of healthy skepticism, you realize quickly that, no, the Charlevoix region of Québec is not the most stunning place ever visited by earthlings. Nor is it quite, as one travel publication claimed, "an old sailor telling tales of the sea . . . the cry of the gull mingling with the roar of the waves."

Yet this region of sharply rolling hills along the north shore of the St. Lawrence estuary makes an interesting and enjoyable bike tour, through an area that has been popular with vacationing Québecers for more than 200 years. While far more developed than the wilderness reaches of Gaspé, and visited by many more people, Charlevoix is spacious and remote enough to remind you that it forms the southern fringe of some of the largest wilderness areas in North America. Within a short distance are wilderness preserves and vast parks, while villages and small cities along the coast offer some of the finest aspects of traditional French-Canadian culture— prospering from the tourist trade but without the need for gaudy enticements.

The region was named in honor of an early Jesuit historian, Father Francois-Xavier de Charlevoix (pronounced, approximately, Char-la VWAH). As early as 1760 the area was actively promoted as a tourist destination, and by the late nineteenth century was popular with wealthy Canadians and Americans who built elaborate summer homes in many of the communities along the coast.

Although the tourism promoters who call Charlevoix "Little Switzerland" are carrying the description too far, the long rolling hills and steep bluffs of the region are punctuated with many impressive cliffs, sheer valleys, and gorges. Within those hills are areas spared by the last ice age, so that protected valleys sometimes harbor remnants of vegetation usually found only in far-northern and arctic regions.

Here in the heart of Québec, French is spoken far more exclusively than in regions nearer the U.S. border. Don't be surprised to find yourself in situations where no one in attendance speaks more than a few words of English. Even campgrounds, hotels, and restaurants are frequently staffed by non-English-speaking Québecers.

If you're traveling from the eastern United States or Canada, the **Rivière-du-Loup** ferry is the most convenient way to reach the Charlevoix region. Those arriving from the other direction will find it no disadvantage to tour the region from Québec City north. Although I have described only the trip along the north shore of the river,

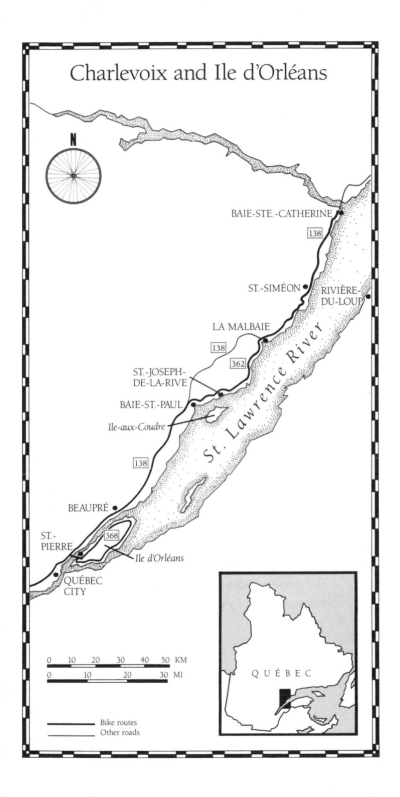

Charlevoix and Ile d'Orléans

N

BAIE-STE.-CATHERINE

138

ST.-SIMÉON

RIVIÈRE-
DU-LOUP

LA MALBAIE

138

362

ST.-JOSEPH-
DE-LA-RIVE

BAIE-ST.-PAUL

Ile-aux-Coudre

St. Lawrence River

138

BEAUPRÉ

ST.-
PIERRE

368

Ile d'Orléans

QUÉBEC
CITY

| 0 | 10 | 20 | 30 | 40 | 50 KM |
| 0 | | 10 | 20 | | 30 MI |

QUÉBEC

——— Bike routes
——— Other roads

a return loop can be made by crossing the St. Lawrence at Rivière-du-Loup (or Québec City) and following the southern shore of the river along Hwy. 132.

The ferry departs from the town of Rivière-du-Loup daily from April through November, with five to eight crossings made per day during the peak tourist season (June 22 to September 3) and two to three crossings during the off-season. The cost per adult is $7.20 one way, plus $2.60 per bicycle. Autos are charged $18.40. The crossing requires about 90 minutes. Be warned that during the busy tourist season of midsummer—I crossed during the busiest weekend of the year—the ferry, though large, is crowded. It's not unusual for automobiles to wait in line several hours before boarding.

ST.-SIMÉON
TO BAIE-STE.-CATHERINE
AND RETURN—
69.4 KILOMETERS (43.4 MILES)

From the ferry terminal in St.-Siméon north to Baie-Ste.-Catherine is a 35-kilometer tour through the remotest and least developed section of the trip. Since it involves a return trip over the same route, it is, of course, optional. However, this leg of the trip offers a good look at rugged Charlevoix terrain and several interesting highlights and is well worth the extra riding.

Most of the route is hilly, with the road winding back and forth over low mountains, dropping into river valleys, then climbing saddles of land. Hwy. 138 is a wide two-lane in good condition. Paved shoulders and passing lanes are common on the higher hills but unusual elsewhere. Traffic is light most of the season but can be quite heavy on summer weekends when residents of Québec City make mad dashes north to escape the city.

The first hill leading away from the north side of St.-Siméon is the toughest on the route: a 2.2-kilometer ascent that reaches gradients as steep as 11 percent on a section of road that offers neither paved shoulders nor passing lane. Once on top of it, however, you'll find the going is much easier as the road turns inland and travels along a high plateau and through a valley of meadows and woodlots, with long views of mountains and wooded slopes.

A picnic area and small swimming beach located on a roadside lake about 16 kilometers from St.-Siméon makes a good rest area, though it does not have drinking water. From here the road passes through narrow, rocky canyons with dark igneous outcroppings poking through the trees, and over some steep, rolling hills. Ponds tucked among the hills have the look of mountain lakes in the Rockies. A few colorful cottages on the far shores of the lakes seem accessible only by rowboat or canoe.

A final one-kilometer descent brings the road back into view of the St. Lawrence, with the shoreline ahead as rugged as the Gaspé shore, and leads into the outskirts of **Baie-Ste.-Catherine**. Scattered along the road are basic services, especially convenience stores and take-out restaurants. Across the mouth of the Saguenay River is the sister village of Tadoussac, accessible by free ferry.

Both Baie-Ste.-Catherine and Tadoussac are points of departure for excursion boats that make regular whale-sighting expeditions during the summer months. This area of the St. Lawrence and the lower Saguenay supports thriving populations of belugas, minkes, finbacks, and lesser populations of at least five other species of whales.

The St. Lawrence River can be divided into three distinct life zones: freshwater, brackish, and saltwater. The freshwater zone extends only as far downstream as Cap Tourmente, just below Québec City. Brackish water extends from there downriver to Baie-St.-Paul and is the portion of the river most rich in life. An incredible diversity and abundance of creatures live in the brackish water, which explains why the area around Baie-Ste.-

Catherine is preferred by beluga whales. One unfortunate footnote: because of contaminants working their way up the food chain and accumulating in the body tissues of the predators near the top, the St. Lawrence's belugas were recently declared to be among the most contaminated mammals on earth.

The fiord of the Saguenay River is probably the most spectacular natural feature of this portion of the coast and is the highlight of most whale excursions. Lined with escarpments and sheer cliffs averaging nearly 305 meters high, the rocky corridor of the river is preserved within the provincial park, Parc Saguenay.

Above the ferry landing, a rest area overlooks the mouth of the river from a high peak beside Hwy. 138. Known as Pointe-Noire, the overlook provides an excellent opportunity to view a resident population of beluga whales, as well as seals and marine birds. A pavilion with slide shows and exhibits staffed by naturalists provides information about the marine life of the region. An entry fee of $2.50 per adult is charged.

Retrace the same route to **St.-Siméon**, where all services are available. At least two private campgrounds are located near the outskirts of the community and are marked by roadside signs. In addition, a municipal campground is located within the village limits, reached via residential streets.

ST.-SIMÉON TO BAIE-ST.-PAUL— 87.2 KILOMETERS (54.5 MILES)

From St.-Siméon south are several kilometers of fairly level road along a plateau above the water, with a paved shoulder at least a portion of that distance. Although the terrain appears less rugged at first, with pastoral scenes of overgrown farmlands nestled among lower, less serious hills, major hills are yet to come. Still, the terrain has softened enough to encourage development: here, as else-where along the route to Québec City, scattered houses have settled in the countryside between villages.

A 2.4-kilometer descent inaugurates another section of long rolling hills. Some of the gradients reach 10 per-cent, and shoulders have usually been paved on both the uphill and downhill slopes of the major hills. From the tops are fine views of the entire St. Lawrence Valley, with the enormous estuary stretching away more than 16 ki-lometers to the rolling, less severe hills of the south shore. Here the St. Lawrence can be considered a river only with difficulty. Residents refer to it as "the sea," perhaps a proper reference considering the vastness of the river and the powerful tidal currents swirling upstream, flooding the estuary with saltwater.

Typically, when the road curves to the bluffs directly above the shoreline of the river, the hills are steep and long. They soften considerably when the road swings in-land, as it often does, and frequently diminish altogether as the road takes the course of least resistance through passes and valleys.

One large hill right on the coast requires a 3.5-kilometer climb. Although the ascent is not continuous—it flattens halfway up before beginning the last pitch—it's a tough climb up a major height of land. At the top is the community of St.-Fidèle-de-Mont-Morray with a gro-cery store, restaurant, and pizza take-out. The Crèmerie Saint-Fidèle is a cheese factory with a wide reputation for excellence. Again, the view of the St. Lawrence from the hilltop plateau where the community is located makes the difficult climb worthwhile.

There is no shortage of similar small communities along the remainder of the Charlevoix coast. Villages all offer the usual services, plus Victorian-style houses con-verted to bed-and-breakfast inns or restaurants. Even in the lightly inhabited stretches between the villages are frequent cafés, restaurants, take-outs, and motels.

A number of short side trips down from Hwy. 138 are possible on secondary roads. A loop right before La

Malbaie leads down to Cap-à-l'Aigle, a resort village notable for its quaint New England-style architecture and impressive restaurants.

Just after returning to Hwy. 138, a steep descent leads to the town limits of **La Malbaie**. The inlet here ("Bad Bay") was named by Samuel de Champlain in 1608, when his ship ran aground in the shallows. In the centuries afterward, the community that grew up near the site became one of the centers of the Charlevoix resort region. In the nineteenth and early twentieth centuries the town was known as Murray Bay and became a favorite vacation spot of U.S. politicians, including Howard Taft, who became twenty-seventh president of the United States. Many elaborate summer homes were built in La Malbaie during that era.

Today, this city of 4,000 is the unofficial capital of northern Charlevoix and offers all services. At least two private campgrounds are located on the Malbaie River upstream from town. The first, reached off Hwy. 138 just west of town, is definitely the better of the two. If it's filled (and it often is during summer weekends), backtrack to La Malbaie and follow the signs a few kilometers west on Chemin de la Vallée. In progress on the east side of the river mouth—you can't miss it—is a reconstruction of "Le Pélican," a 46-meter schooner that sank in a storm after battling the British in 1697.

At La Malbaie you have the choice of continuing on Hwy. 138 on an inland arc, or taking Hwy. 362 along the coast. I chose the coastal route, although larger, busier Hwy. 138 passes through fine country, mostly rolling farmlands and wooded hills.

Along the St. Lawrence south of La Malbaie is the neighboring community of Pointe-au-Pic, dominated by Hotel Manoir Richelieu, an enormous hotel with 390 rooms built at the turn of the century. It is also home to Musée de Charlevoix, a new art museum featuring regional artists.

Just outside Pointe-au-Pic, Hwy. 362 climbs a long, fairly steep hill and cuts inland a short distance, past diminishing numbers of houses, stores, and restaurants. That first climb—about a kilometer and a half—is made easier by a paved shoulder and ends on a hilltop looking out over the St. Lawrence. A private campground is located on the plateau, among steeply rolling farmlands and meadows.

An extremely steep, serpentine descent, highlighted by some of the most dramatic hairpin curves I've ever seen, ends at sea level in the village of Ste.-Irénée. This quaint fishing village is crowded close to the road, European style, with barely enough room on the road for trucks or even large cars to pass. Houses, stores, and a number of interesting bed-and-breakfast inns are built on terraces into the steep hillsides.

The climb out of Ste.-Irénée is drawn out somewhat longer than the descent into the town—expect a climb of 4.3 kilometers, with paved shoulders most of the way—and is not quite as steep. Fine views of the St. Lawrence are possible partway up. At the peak the road turns inland into rolling farmland scattered with woodlots and hay fields. For about 8 kilometers the route is nearly flat along a ridgetop that bends gradually back to the coast and passes through a number of tiny communities. The view of the St. Lawrence, again, is spectacular.

The town of Les Eboulements ("the landslides"—in reference to rock slides that resulted from a major earthquake in 1663) is perched on a steep slope above the river and is reached after a short, steep descent on Hwy. 362. It offers basic services but is remarkable for its numerous elegant cafés, inns, galleries, and arts-and-crafts shops. A side road leads down an incredibly steep 18-percent pitch toward the water's edge and the village of **St.-Joseph-de-la-Rive**. Some of the more interesting shops and galleries are located along the narrow street here, squeezed between the bluff and the river's edge.

At the end of the street in St.-Joseph-de-la-Rive is the ferry terminal to Ile aux Coudres. This 9.6-kilometer-long island in the St. Lawrence is an interesting side trip. It's name, "Hazel Island," was bestowed by Jacques Cartier, who anchored there in 1535 and found ripe hazelnuts in a grove on shore. A paved road circles the island, making a 24-kilometer loop, and leads to a number of inns and craft shops. At the southern tip of the island a museum celebrates an island history based on shipbuilding, whale hunting, and commercial fishing. Nearby, a windmill and watermill work side by side to operate a working blacksmithy and flour mill.

Back on Hwy. 362, there is an ascent of one and a half kilometers (with wide paved shoulders), which leads to a terrific view of the St. Lawrence and Ile aux Coudres. It is followed by several kilometers of difficult, tightly bunched hills, and finally by a series of long, steep descents that end in Baie-St.-Paul.

BAIE-ST.-PAUL TO QUÉBEC CITY— 98.7 KILOMETERS (61.7 MILES)

With its full array of services and a population of 7,300, **Baie-St.-Paul** is the largest city in Charlevoix. In the downtown area are many shops, galleries, restaurants, and inns, plus a hospital and public park. The Centre d'art de Baie-St.-Paul is a large art gallery with frequent exhibitions featuring regional artists. Nearby residential streets are lined with enormous shade trees and 200-year-old houses. Along the waterfront, the area around the old wharf is a popular promenade, with benches and picnic tables. On the outskirts of the city are small shopping centers and supermarkets.

Hwy. 362 ends at the junction with Hwy. 138 on the west side of Baie-St.-Paul. A difficult 5-kilometer climb on Hwy. 138 south out of Baie-St.-Paul, with the road widened to four lanes and a narrow paved shoulder in fair condition, takes the road inland and kicks off a series of major hills. It is followed by a brisk one-and-a-half-kilometer descent, then by another ascent that rises in stages a total of about 9 kilometers. The paved shoulder—almost as wide as a meter in some places—is intermittent but continues along most of the major climbs and descents.

From here, at the top of one of the highest elevations along the Charlevoix coast, is a good view of many kilometers of tumbling, forested hills. Portions of this stretch of highway follow the old "Chemin des Caps," a road in use before 1800 that reaches heights over 700 meters above sea level.

A few small communities in this hilly country have basic services. There are also scattered private campgrounds, more than are listed in the Québec tourism publications. Farmers' fields become more prevalent, many laid out in long, narrow strips separated by hedgerows or fencelines, reminders that it is traditional in Québec for a farmer to divide his property equally among his sons, creating more—and progressively narrower—farms from the land he himself inherited. In places the fields are not much wider than a suburban lawn, yet roll away inland far out of sight.

About 50 kilometers from Baie-St.-Paul, hilltop views on a clear day give the first glimpses of the Québec City skyline 48 kilometers to the south. From here to the city, the Charlevoix region grows tamer as towns expand into small cities and the spaces between them fill with suburbs and commercial zones.

A short distance beyond the town of St.-Tite-des-Caps, a driveway leads to a parking area near the Grand Canyon des Chutes Ste.-Anne. A modest admission fee gives access to hiking trails that proceed over swinging bridges to cliff-tops with views of a deep, rock-sided gorge of the Ste.-Anne River. A 73-meter waterfall is the highlight of the walk.

Just down the hill from the Ste.-Anne River Falls is the town of **Beaupré**. It and the communities to come have the flavor of extended suburbs. Avenue Royale turns toward the St. Lawrence and a shoreline wildlife preserve at Cap-Tourmente. Established to protect the habitat of snow geese, it is crossed by an 18-kilometer network of hiking trails from the banks of the St. Lawrence to the summit of Cap-Tourmente.

In spite of such natural attractions, the primary focus in Beaupré is a supernatural one. The basilica of Ste.-Anne-de-Beaupré, like Lourdes in France and Fátima in Portugal, is a Catholic shrine said to be the scene of miraculous healings. The present-day basilica, an enormous, spire-capped, Romanesque structure covering as much ground as a football field, is the fifth chapel built on the site to celebrate Saint Anne, the mother of Mary. The first structure was erected there in 1658 by French sailors who were caught in a storm on the lower St. Lawrence, and prayed to Saint Anne—the patron saint of seafarers—for deliverance, promising to build a chapel in her honor if they were saved. They landed safely, and true to their promise, built a humble chapel nearby. The miracles began immediately, starting with a settler named Louis Guidmont, whose crippling rheumatism was cured instantly when he struggled to place three small stones on the foundation wall of the chapel. Today pilgrims come from all over the world—as many as 1.5 million per year—to worship at the basilica. It has created a thriving tourist industry in the surrounding community, which is crowded with gaudy souvenir shops, cheap motels, fast-food restaurants, trailer parks, and auto dealerships. During the summer, and especially during the feast of Saint Anne between July 17 and July 26, the parking lots across the highway and beside the basilica are crammed with unbelievable concentrations of automobiles, recreational vehicles, and tour buses.

Cycling past this mess, you begin to wonder if you'll need a miracle to survive the traffic. Fortunately, the highway is four lanes wide here, and a narrow paved shoulder offers a bicycle lane just wide enough to allow slightly safer passage. Fortunately, also, the route here is on a low plain directly above the river and is virtually flat the remaining 32 kilometers to Québec City.

Once you're out of the congestion around Beaupré, the land opens up somewhat into farmlands, although dotted with frequent commercial enterprises. Across a channel of the St. Lawrence are the wooded hills of Ile d'Orléans. The road continues to be four lanes wide, and the paved shoulder expands to 2 meters. Although this is predominantly motel country, several terribly crowded RV parks offer an approximation of campsites.

On the east side of **Québec City**, a picnic area rests near the base of Montmorency Falls, a spectacular waterfall within sight of the highway. A paved bicycle path begins at the picnic area and winds between highways and along the river and offers the easiest and most enjoyable way to reach the interior of the city. An information pavilion near the falls offers city maps of the bike route as well as publications listing lodging, restaurants, museums, and other attractions of the city.

Québec City has often been called the most interesting city in North America and no doubt deserves an extended visit. The old walled city along the riverfront is like an enormous, living museum and includes (and is surrounded by) excellent parks, galleries, shops, hotels, and restaurants.

ÎLE D'ORLÉANS LOOP— 67.2 KILOMETERS (42 MILES)

Reached via a 2-kilometer suspension bridge that branches off Hwy. 138 just beyond the park at Montmorency Falls, **Ile d'Orléans** is a 32-kilometer by 8-kilometer island that divides the St. Lawrence into two channels downstream from Old Québec. With its fertile soil and a climate tempered by the St. Lawrence, the island was attractive to farmers who first settled there in the mid-seventeenth century and continues to be a center of agriculture.

Cyclists crossing the Pont de l'Ile d'Orléans from the

mainland must contend with the bridge's narrow lanes and heavy traffic. A sidewalk beside the lanes is the safest way across, although you'll probably have to walk your bike most of the way. Once on the island, a short, steep climb takes you to a busy corner crowded with service stations, restaurants, and an information pavilion. The island is a popular bicycling destination, with many local cyclists riding over from the city, but is not particularly well equipped for cyclists. Hwy. 368, which circles the island, is an average-sized two-lane, without paved shoulders. There is little advantage in traveling clockwise or counterclockwise, so I made the arbitrary decision to turn left on 368 and make a clockwise circuit of the island.

St.-Pierre, almost immediately east of the bridge area, is one of the oldest villages on the island and offers a quick look at some of the interesting architectural details of island buildings. The oldest buildings—many of which have been converted to cafés and inns—have their design roots in Normandy and other rural areas in France. Their brightly colored, sloping roofs and wide eaves give them a definite continental appearance. Église Sainte-Pierre, built in 1718, is the oldest existing church on the island and is open to visitors.

The road out of St.-Pierre travels along a bluff well above the river and is primarily flat. From here the mainland appears much more pastoral and undeveloped than it had seemed along the busy commercial corridor lining the highway. Farmers' fields descend from the highlands in variously colored and textured strips, are interrupted briefly by the road, and continue down to the shore of the river.

Although the fields between villages on the island are actively farmed for potatoes, corn, and strawberries, numerous houses break the fields into fragments. Among them are large, cottage-style stone houses covered with ivy and topped with brilliant red roofs. Spaced along the road are occasional bed-and-breakfast inns, cafés, and numerous fruit and vegetable stands selling fresh local produce.

Ste.-Famille, another very old farming village, is located an easy 16-kilometer ride east of St.-Pierre. It offers most services, including restaurants, cafés, bed-and-breakfast inns, service stations, and groceries. Open fields slope down from it to the bluff above the river and provide a good view of Ste.-Anne-de-Beaupré on the mainland. Many of the houses in Ste.-Famille are outstanding, even for Ile d'Orléans, with elaborate trim work and enormous flower gardens accenting their traditional architecture. Again, farms are tucked in wherever there is space, and they blend with the cottage effect of the houses and yards.

The flat terrain and easy riding continue to the east end of the island, where the road turns across the base of the point and travels through light forests and farmlands. A picnic area at the end of the island is a good rest stop and is equipped with a three-story-high observation tower that gives an outstanding view of the rolling mountains of the Charlevoix region downstream of the island. It offers a good view, too, of ship traffic on the St. Lawrence, with large Great Lakes ore carriers passing so close to the island's south shore they appear to brush against a fringe of trees growing there.

The village of St.-Francois, at the southeast corner of the island, has a few services, including a small grocery, a cáfe, and pizza take-out. The private campground just outside the village on the shore of the river is the only campground on the island.

This portion of the south shore is less developed than the north. Farmers' fields are larger, and houses are more widely spaced. The road continues to be mostly flat.

The village of St.-Jean was considered the capital of the island until the construction of the bridge in 1935. It is dominated by a large stone church built in 1732 and by houses built in the nineteenth century by maritime pilots and navigators who made the town their home. Near the church is the Manoir Mauvide-Genest, a Norman-style manor built in 1734 by the surgeon of

The southern tip of Ile d'Orléans, and the St. Lawrence River downstream.

Louis XV. It has been recently converted into a restaurant and museum. Also in St.-Jean is the island's first significant hill, a short but steep (14-percent gradient) descent into the center of the village, where houses and shops crowd the road. Services and businesses include restaurants, cafés, galleries, gift shops, and a public pool. The village seems much larger than its population of 840 warrants, evidence that many of the stately homes are summer cottages.

After St.-Jean the road continues quite flat along the edge of the river. Cottages line the water most of the length of this shore in the resort center of the island. The town of St.-Laurent has a grocery, restaurant, gift shops, and bank. Like the other communities along the south shore, it is a resort town and is crowded with fine summer homes.

A couple of fairly steep, one-kilometer hills follow St.-Laurent and take the road away from the river back into the farmlands of the interior. At Prévost Road you have the choice of turning north on a hilly shortcut to the bridge, or continuing west to the tip of the island at Ste.-Pétronille. This village, locally known as "Bout-de-l'île" ("End of the Island"), has basic services and a good view across the river of the city of Québec and Montmorency Falls. The English general James Wolfe commanded a garrison of artillery and infantry here in 1759, building a fortress from which he bombarded the walled city across the river. It was the most popular resort area on the island in the nineteenth century and is dotted with elaborate summer homes built by wealthy merchants from Québec.

·ONTARIO·

Home to the national capital of Ottawa and with more residents than any other province, Ontario is both the economic and political center of Canada. Though it leads the nation in industrial production, most of its industry and agriculture, as well as 90 percent of its population, are concentrated in the relatively small Great Lakes/St. Lawrence lowlands in the southeastern corner of the province. As is true in Québec and the provinces west of it, the vast majority of Ontario's 1,068,587 square kilometers (412,582 square miles) is found in the northern reaches, a land of mostly undeveloped wilderness crossed by thousands of rivers and lakes.

In the early centuries of European settlement, the St. Lawrence River and Great Lakes opened an immense and highly lucrative trade in beaver and other animal pelts from "Upper Canada," as Ontario was known (to differentiate it from Québec, or "Lower Canada"). The potential for wealth was so great that France and England were quick to battle for possession of it, a rivalry that stirred conflict as well among the Huron, Iroquois, and other native residents of the region. France finally relinquished its North American territories after the Treaty of Paris in 1763, and both Ontario and Québec came under control of the British Empire. Within another decade, when the United States won its independence from England, about 10,000 pro-British Loyalists migrated to English-speaking Ontario, particularly the fertile farmlands of the St. Lawrence basin.

Today that region is the most populated and commercially developed in all of Canada. Yet, though it is home to such major metropolitan centers as Toronto, Ottawa, London, and Windsor, it remains predominantly rural, with farmlands and woods surrounding small communities in a pattern similar to that of rural New England.

In contrast, the northern portions of the province, including the Lake Superior country described in Chapter 12, remain some of North America's most extensive wilderness regions.

Weather

Climate in Ontario is tempered by the Great Lakes, which tend to cool the coastal areas in the summer and warm them in the winter. The Lake Superior shoreline can be particularly cool—the lake never warms enough for comfortable swimming—and at that northern latitude frosts are recorded every month of the summer. Southern Ontario is much warmer during the summer months and averages a few degrees warmer than the ocean-fronted Maritimes.

Language

English is the predominant language in Ontario, although French is spoken in many communities near the Québec border. Road signs and tourist publications are typically bilingual.

Traffic Laws

Freeway speed limits are 100 kilometers per hour, while most other highways and county roads have limits of 80 or 90 kilometers per hour. Roads in urban areas generally have limits of 40 to 60 kilometers per hour. Bicycles are considered vehicles and must obey the same traffic laws as motorists.

For More Information

For maps and other general information about travel in Ontario, contact the Ontario Ministry of Tourism and Recreation, Queen's Park, Toronto, Ontario, Canada M7A 2E5. The phone number from anywhere in Canada and the continental United States is 1-800-668-2746.

For detailed information about the St. Lawrence Parks Commission, write RR#1, Morrisburg, Ontario, Canada K0C 1X0; or phone 613/543-3704. Reservations at Parks Commission campgrounds can be arranged by calling 613/543-3704.

For more information about Lake Superior Provincial Park, contact the Ministry of Natural Resources, P.O. Box 1160, Wawa, Ontario, Canada, P0S 1K0; phone 705/856-2396 or 705/856-2284.

11

St. Lawrence Shore and Thousand Islands Parkway

> **Begin/End**: Cornwall to Kingston
> **Roads**: Hwys. 2, 675 (Thousand Islands Parkway), and side trips
> **Accommodations**: Campgrounds, motels, inns
> **Length**: 177.8 kilometers (111.1 miles)
> **Difficulty**: Easy

That portion of Ontario bordering the north shore of the upper St. Lawrence River, between the Québec border and the river's outlet from Lake Ontario, is one of the most popular and longest-settled vacation destinations in eastern Canada. Canadian and U.S. vacationers have visited the Thousand Islands region of the St. Lawrence since the American Civil War, traveling there by water via the St. Lawrence and overland on a long-established system of riverside roads. The lowlands bordering the river on both the Ontario and New York shorelines are fertile farmland that long ago attracted settlers. This predominantly flat region creates interesting bicycling opportunities—opportunities that are further enhanced by frequent paved highway shoulders and bicycle paths.

The east-to-west orientation of the trip is designed for convenience only. If you plan to cycle the route one-way, and have arranged a shuttle-ride back to your starting point, it may be most logical to begin in Kingston and travel east to Cornwall, taking advantage of summer's mostly southwest winds. However, if you plan to retrace the route to return to your vehicle, it is probably wiser to cycle against the wind on the first leg of the trip, then return with it at your back. Though winds are not the problem along the St. Lawrence they can be in more open country, be prepared for continuous light headwinds during the east-to-west ride described below.

CORNWALL TO BROCKVILLE— 95 KILOMETERS (59.4 MILES)

Cornwall, with a population of 46,425, many of whom speak French predominantly, is Ontario's easternmost city and is considered the headquarters of the St. Lawrence Seaway in Ontario. All services are available in this riverside city, but give special attention to the downtown pedestrian mall, where interesting shops, galleries, gardens, and open-air concerts make it the nucleus of the community in summer. Bicycle repairs and supplies are available at Kalrim Cycle and Sports on Boundary Road, and at Rhodes Cycle Boutique on Pitt Street.

A two-lane, paved bicycle trail originates near the center of the city and winds down along the edge of the St. Lawrence, past the R. H. Saunders Generating Station, an enormous hydroelectric facility, to Guindon Park, a 200-hectare municipal picnic and recreation area along the river. The trail then parallels Hwy. 2 west along the St. Lawrence for a total distance of about 20 kilometers. Within Guindon Park (which will eventually have campgrounds, although none were completed as of this writing) a number of unpaved trails are open to mountain bikes.

At the end of the bicycle trail on Hwy. 2 is the town

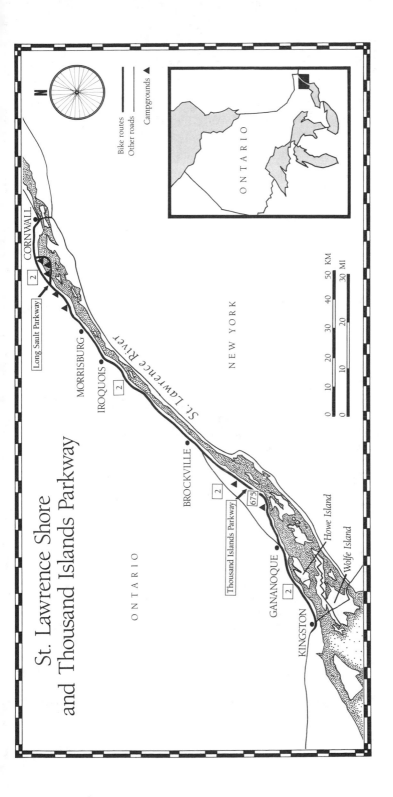

St. Lawrence Shore
and Thousand Islands Parkway

Bike routes ——
Other roads ——
Campgrounds ▲

N

CORNWALL

2

Long Sault Parkway

MORRISBURG

IROQUOIS

2

St. Lawrence River

BROCKVILLE

2

Thousand Islands Parkway

675

GANANOQUE

2

KINGSTON

Howe Island

Wolfe Island

ONTARIO

NEW YORK

ONTARIO

0   10   20   30   40   50 KM
0   10   20   30 MI

of Long Sault. Turn left here to **Long Sault Parkway**, a paved road that follows a network of eleven islands, joined by bridges and causeways, that form a loop into the St. Lawrence. Administered by the St. Lawrence Parks Commission, the parkway passes through a region flooded before the 1959 opening of the St. Lawrence Seaway, when a system of dikes, channels, dams, and locks made it possible for the first time for oceangoing vessels

This road, part of the Long Sault Parkway, was partially submerged when the St. Lawrence Seaway was built in 1959.

to travel the entire length of the St. Lawrence River into the Great Lakes. Several "lost" towns are now submerged beneath the water along this stretch of the seaway, and some of the old paved roads that lead to them are visible beginning and ending abruptly at the water's edge on islands that were once hilltops along the river.

Long Sault Parkway is a pleasant and relaxing bike ride of 11 kilometers. Except for a couple of short stretches of gravel on side trips out to points on the islands, the roads are paved and in good condition. The islands are low and alternately wooded or open grasslands, and they attract large numbers of Canada geese and other waterfowl that habitually stop in the area during their spring and fall migrations. Three large, well-equipped campgrounds are scattered along the parkway, all offering showers, picnic areas, swimming beaches, and access to hiking and nature trails. Campsites are open from May 18 to September 3 (except the westernmost campground, McLaren, which is open until September 30). Day-use permits are required for automobiles ($5.25 each), but cyclists are able to enter the area free of charge.

At the end of the Parkway, Hwy. 2 proceeds west along the river and follows the primary land route used in the nineteenth century to link Québec and Toronto. Here it is an average-sized two-lane highway in good condition, with a paved shoulder almost a half meter wide. Although the route is not heavily developed, much of it is lined with scattered houses and small businesses, most of them built after the seaway flooded the lower regions of the area in the late 1950s. Traffic is moderate to moderately heavy; most through-traffic and trucks are routed on Hwy. 401, a controlled-access expressway that runs parallel to Hwy. 2, a few kilometers inland.

The town of Ingleside, immediately beyond the western entrance to the Long Sault Parkway, has most services, including stores and restaurants clustered in a small shopping center.

The road continues entirely flat along the river, although a strip of marshlands often separates the road from the actual edge of the river. The St. Lawrence here is broad but frequently braided into channels and dotted by dozens of irregularly shaped, wooded islands. It has the look of a northern-Ontario lake in some places, an effect instantly shattered when you see monolithic Great Lakes ore carriers cruising slowly past the islands.

The Upper Canada Migratory Bird Sanctuary, about 5 kilometers west of Ingleside, is a 1,400-hectare area of wetlands, cornfields, and marshes that is the summer home of a flock of 2,000 Canada geese and is a stopover for thousands more geese and ducks during spring and fall migrations. Eight kilometers of self-guided nature trails pass through the sanctuary and offer a good opportunity to view wetland wildlife habitat. The paved road that winds through the sanctuary ends on Nairne Island, where there is a campground. A visitors' center near the highway has interpretive displays and information.

A little more than 3 kilometers from the bird sanctuary's interpretation center is Upper Canada Village, a Parks Commission facility that recreates a village from the 1860s. Fully operational saw and flour mills, a woolen factory, artisan shops, and working farms are open to visitors. A reconstructed restaurant serves foods of the period, while more modern fare is available at a cafeteria and snack shops.

A kilometer west of Upper Canada Village is Riverside-Cedar Park and Campground, a 412-site campground with excellent beaches and all facilities.

Morrisburg has restaurants, motels, stores, and a bike shop, Charlie's Sport Shop, located on the highway at the east end of town. Part of this community of 2,300 was moved to higher ground after the flooding of the seaway project.

After Morrisburg the paved shoulder shrinks to about a third of a meter wide, but the pavement remains in good condition and the entire route continues to be virtually flat. The St. Lawrence is visible in glimpses through fringes of woodlands and marsh. Small farms and woodlots fill most of the rural country between the towns along this stretch of the river.

The town of **Iroquois** has the usual array of services and a private tent-and-trailer park, but is most notable for having been entirely relocated by the seaway project. It is also the location of the Iroquois Seaway Locks, a major lock system where visitors can observe oceangoing ships at close range as they are lifted or dropped through channels and locks.

The excellent riding conditions are diminished somewhat after Iroquois, where the paved shoulder ends and the road drops to only fair-to-good condition, with patches and cracks. The terrain remains predominantly flat, although a few low hills begin here. The road passes through mostly rural lands and sometimes bends very close to the St. Lawrence, where you can see the river's many islands and channels.

After the town of Cardinal, expect a few more rolling hills. Some of the brick and stone houses along the road date back to the early 1800s, and because they are on higher ground, were unaffected by the flooding of the St. Lawrence.

In the town of Johnstown, where most services are available, a bridge crosses the river to a rural section of upstate New York, the first such bridge since Cornwall. Beyond Johnstown and the industrial port town of Prescott, the road continues to depreciate in quality, with increasingly lengthy stretches of rough, patched, and broken pavement. The route is still relatively flat, though low rolling hills are common. Commercial roadside development is fairly continuous from Johnstown, Prescott, and Maitland to Brockville.

BROCKVILLE TO KINGSTON— 82.7 KILOMETERS (51.7 MILES)

With a population of 21,000, **Brockville** is the largest community in the middle region of Ontario's St. Lawrence waterfront and advertises itself as the "City of the Thousand Islands." The oldest incorporated city in Ontario, founded by United Empire Loyalists in 1784, Brockville was originally known as Buell's Bay but was renamed for General Isaac Brock, a British hero of the War of 1812. Hwy. 2 passes through the downtown district (where it is known as King Street), past blocks of shops, galleries, restaurants, and hotels. The waterfront area has public parks and a sizable museum and is the departure point for boat excursions through the Thousand Islands region of the St. Lawrence. An excellent bookstore, Leeds County Books, located downtown, has a collection of local titles. For cycle repairs, visit Dave Jones Sports. Some of the neighborhoods surrounding the downtown and waterfront regions are worth a side trip just to see the English Tudor-style homes built on riverfront estates by well-to-do refugees who came here in the late eighteenth century to escape the newly formed United States. Several of the houses have been converted to stately and impressive bed-and-breakfast inns, including Brockville Bed-and-Breakfast. On the western outskirts of Brockville is a municipal campground.

Outside Brockville, Hwy. 2 is a four-lane divided highway in fairly good shape (watch for some cracks and patches). Not quite 10 kilometers past the turnoff to the municipal campground, the highway joins with Hwy. 401. Follow this busy four-lane highway for about a kilometer and a half, to the exit onto Hwy. 675, the Thousand Islands Parkway, a paved secondary road that follows the shoreline of the river closely while Hwys. 2 and 401 continue a few kilometers inland.

At the intersection with the Thousand Islands Parkway is the eastern end of the Thousand Islands Bikeway, a bicycle trail that parallels the road for its entire 37-kilometer length. Constructed of asphalt, and about one meter wide, the trail parallels the road on its right (north) side, approximately 15 meters off the shoulder. A parking area near the intersection has an information board where orientation maps and other information are available.

Although most of the route is flat, rolling hills are more common here than along the river to the east, and some minor ascents and descents are to be expected. The route follows the shore of the river closely, but views of the water are often obstructed by fringes of woods.

Brown's Bay day-use park, 4.3 kilometers from the beginning of the bike path, has a picnic area and swimming beach. The road here is nearly at water level and offers a clear view of many islands visible out in the river. Brown's Bay Park is administered by the St. Lawrence Parks Commission, whereas some of the islands here in the heart of the Thousand Islands group are under the jurisdiction of the St. Lawrence Islands National Park. Others are privately owned and developed with small, attractive cottages or, in a few cases, with magnificent large houses. Others, too small for development or recreation, are hardly more than rocks emerging from the river, perhaps sprouting a few trees.

After Brown's Bay the road continues flat and low, only a few feet above water level, and is lined with marsh grasses, willows, and other lowland plants. Frequent small picnic areas are the best places to stop for unobstructed views of the river and the islands.

Mallorytown Landing is the land base of St. Lawrence Islands National Park and the main docking area for boaters wishing to explore the islands. The park, the smallest national park in Canada, focuses primarily on the islands but offers bicyclists on the mainland a few services as well. Across the road from Mallorytown Landing is a large campground with tent sites, water, and washrooms, but no showers. At the river is a picnic area, swimming beach, and visitors' center with information and exhibits of natural and cultural interest.

The islands of the St. Lawrence, with their hot, dry southwest sides and cool, shaded northeast sides, produce interesting microclimates where a great variety of plants and animals thrive. Composed primarily of Precambrian rock more than 600 billion years old, the islands—and there appear to be at least a thousand of them—are rugged and rocky but support dense growths of both northern conifers and southern hardwoods.

Soon after the American Civil War, when the expansion of the railroads made transportation easy and inexpensive, the Thousand Islands region became a vacation area popular with both Americans and Canadians. Islands that were purchased by those resorters still support some of the vacation homes built during the era. Other visitors were served by steamships that carried them to dozens of resort hotels that grew up on the mainland and the islands.

Today some of those same resorts are still in business, although bed-and-breakfast inns have replaced many of the old-fashioned resort-hotels. The island cottages—including impressive structures as large as mansions—remain mostly in private ownership.

The town of Rockport has most services, including bed-and-breakfast inns, an RV park, and boat tours of the islands.

West of Rockport, wooded hills with granite outcroppings become larger than anywhere else on the trip and create some moderately difficult climbs. Use caution crossing the interchange with Hwy. 81, which leads south across the Thousand Islands Bridge to the United States. Visible from here is the Skydeck Observation Tower on Hill Island, a 122-meter-high structure that provides a 64-kilometer view of the Thousand Islands Region.

Past the interchange is Ivy Lea Campground, a St. Lawrence Parks Commission park with 131 campsites, showers, picnic area, and beach. Camping is permitted from May 18 to October 8.

The village of Ivy Lea has most services, including motels and restaurants. Residential streets near the river are lined with fine late Victorian-style houses.

An islet in the Thousand Islands region of the St. Lawrence River.

At the western end of the Thousand Islands Bikeway, before the town of Gananoque, is a picnic area with washrooms and swimming at Gray's Beach. The Thousand Islands Parkway and the bicycle trail end at the junction with Hwy. 2.

Take Hwy. 2 into **Gananoque**, a commercially busy town of 5,000 with many motels, restaurants, and gift shops. The highway leading through the town's commercial zone is two lanes wide and broad enough for comfortable cycling, even in the midst of heavy summer traffic.

West of Gananoque, Hwy. 2 is an average-sized two-lane with gravel shoulders and is in fair to good shape. It moves away from the river into farm country, where the St. Lawrence is visible only in glimpses.

An interesting side loop is possible by taking Howe Island Ferry Road a short distance south to the river and the terminal for a toll ferry to Howe Island. Hwy. 22 leads across the island to another ferry at the west end, where the road rejoins Hwy. 2 near Pitt's Ferry.

Between the ferry roads, Hwy. 2 expands to include paved shoulders one meter wide. From here to Kingston is easy riding on the smooth shoulders, through lightly rolling farm country. Some of the farms in this area are active, though not necessarily prosperous, but many others are overgrown and neglected.

Coming into **Kingston** you'll see the extensive grounds surrounding the reconstruction of Old Fort Henry, a British installation first built during the War of 1812 in the face of possible invasions by U.S. forces across the St. Lawrence. A museum houses military artifacts, and a "guard" of park employees in period costume perform daily parades, drills, and marches. The St. Lawrence Parks Commission maintains a restaurant and a gift shop on the grounds.

Kingston is a bustling city of 60,500 and offers all services, including at least two bicycle shops: J-and-J Cycle (corner of Bath and Days roads) and Alfords Sporting Goods, on Princess Street, downtown. Located at the junction of the Rideau Canal—which connects Lake Ontario with the Ottawa River at Ottawa—and the mouth of the St. Lawrence at Lake Ontario, it was of strategic importance during the War of 1812. Its British historical roots have given rise to numerous museums and monuments.

A ferry that departs from the wharf in downtown Kingston provides an opportunity for a return route east to Cornwall. Operating on an approximate one-hour schedule, the 25-minute crossing to Marysville on Wolfe Island is toll-free. Hwy. 95 crosses the island about 11 kilometers to another ferry, a 10-minute crossing to Cape Vincent, New York, that costs $5 per automobile and $1 per passenger. From Cape Vincent go northeast on Hwys. 12E, 12, and 37 to Rooseveltown and the International Bridge across the St. Lawrence to Cornwall. At least eight New York state parks offer camping along the route.

12

North Shore, Lake Superior

Begin/End: Sault Ste. Marie to Minnesota border
Roads: TransCanada Hwy. 17, Hwy. 61
Accommodations: Provincial and private campgrounds, motels
Length: 779.2 kilometers (486.3 miles)
Difficulty: Moderately difficult to difficult

Defined loosely, northern Ontario is that majority of the province found north of Lakes Superior and Huron, an immense wilderness area that extends hundreds of kilometers north to James Bay and Hudson Bay. While the Lake Superior shoreline is dotted with communities, including the busy cities of Sault Ste. Marie and Thunder Bay, much of the shoreline is as wild as the vast country to the north of it.

At the heart of this tour on the edge of the Ontario wilderness is the lake itself. First-time visitors to Lake Superior are often astonished at its size and potential for violence. At 82,106 square kilometers in area and reaching depths of 400 meters, it is the largest freshwater lake in the world. But it is not just a lake—that implies close boundaries and a tamed spirit. It is a small ocean capable of almost unbelievably violent tantrums, able to produce 9-meter waves that can break up and swallow the enormous, oceangoing ships that cross it with loads of iron ore, grain, and coal. When the winds are up, the surf along the north shore is beautiful and humbling, pounding a shoreline lined with jumbled, water-worn boulders deposited by the last glacier 10,000 years ago, and the raw, jagged sheets of the Canadian Shield—at 600-million years old, among the most ancient rock on the surface of the earth. In its quiet moods it can be traveled (at the edges) by canoes and sea kayaks; in less tranquil moods it cannot be traveled at all. The land around the lake is so remote, wild, and sparsely inhabited that a cyclist can't help feel a certain vulnerability. There's an almost overwhelming sense of enormity: you're clinging to the edge of the massive, all but uncharted country stretching north to Hudson's Bay and the vast, inhospitable lake stretching as far as you can see to the south.

The uncertainty of weather in this latitude adds to the feeling of vulnerability. Superior, one moment glass-calm and serene, can blow up into 2-meter whitecaps in an hour or less. The lake is rarely warm enough for swimming, even during the hottest summers, and it has a powerful effect on the weather. A day that begins with warmth and sunshine can change almost without warning to cold, wind-driven rain or sleet.

The beaches and rocky coast paralleled by Hwy. 17 are among the most interesting in North America, thrown down by forces that left the area in geologic chaos. Intermingled with beaches of sugar sand are harsh rock outcroppings containing sometimes three or four distinctly different rock formations, all bordered by dense northern coniferous forests. The Canadian Shield begins here: millions of acres of forests erupting with rocks and dotted with thousands of lakes and rivers.

Hwy. 17 forms the northern portion of the Lake Superior Circle Tour (it continues through Minnesota, Wisconsin, and the Upper Peninsula of Michigan). On-

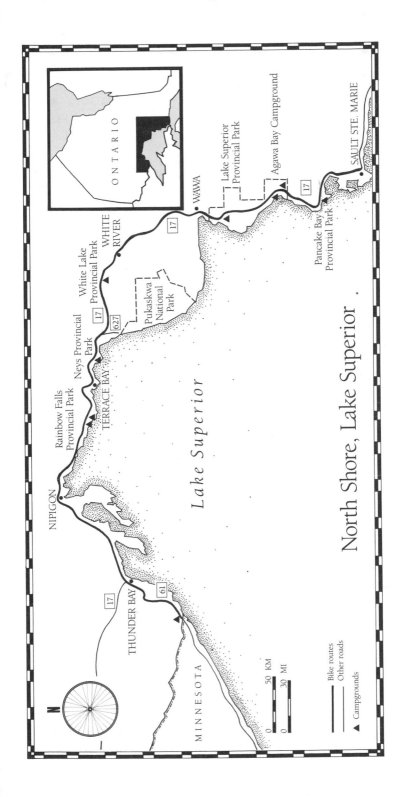

North Shore, Lake Superior

Lake Superior, along the north shore, in a typically rollicking mood.

tario gives the road the subtitle "The Route of the Voyageurs," in reference to the expeditions of the French Canadian trappers and traders who paddled the North Shore in 12-meter birchbark canoes during the seventeenth and eighteenth centuries. While the route is very civilized by the standards of the voyageurs, the road passes through wilderness areas large enough to make camping equipment a necessity on this trip. It is difficult to depend on finding lodging in motels and bed-and-breakfast inns, especially in such remote sections of the route as the one between Wawa and White Lake Provincial Park, where small towns may have no lodging available and long stretches of forested terrain have no services at all.

Winter comes early and stays late along the North Shore, and the tourist season lasts only from about the end of June to the end of August. Earlier or later than that campgrounds and other services tend to be closed or operate only on a reduced basis. On a positive note, motels advertise reduced rates during the off-season, and weather, although highly variable, can be pleasant then, especially in early to mid-September.

SAULT STE. MARIE TO PANCAKE BAY PROVINCIAL PARK— 72 KILOMETERS (45 MILES)

At the southeast end of Lake Superior, where the lake drains into the lower Great Lakes over the rapids of the St. Mary's River, the city of **Sault Ste. Marie**, with a population of 81,700, has grown and prospered into one of northern Ontario's busiest cities. Established by French missionaries in 1669, it had long been an important gathering place for Indians and trappers portaging the rapids on their way to or from Lake Superior. Cyclists beginning a trip here will have the usual urban complications of busy streets, lack of secure long-term parking, and a fringe of shopping centers, malls, and six-lane highways. Hwy. 17, the TransCanada Highway, is the only major road in and out of the city and is well marked, even in the twisting, potentially confusing complex of streets in the old inner city.

The downtown district offers easy access to viewing platforms, walkways, and pedestrian parks lining the Soo Locks, the most famous canals in the St. Lawrence/Great Lakes lock system. The first of them, built in 1895, finally made it possible for large ships to bypass the dangerous rapids of the St. Mary's River and enter Lake Superior. Two-hour excursion cruises pass through the American locks and offer a view of the Canadian locks. In the downtown area, two bicycle shops offer supplies and information: Collegiate Sports and Duke of Windsor Sport Shop, both on Queen Street East.

Approximately 6 kilometers from the downtown area, Hwy. 17 shrinks from a busy four-lane to a less-busy three-lane with paved shoulders one meter to one and a half meters wide. Development ends rather abruptly, and the road enters wooded terrain with short hills. Within another 3 kilometers the road reduces to two lanes, but a fine 2-meter-wide paved shoulder makes for easy riding. About a kilometer and a half later begins a long, gradual climb of 8 kilometers, through hilly country with occasional outcroppings of dark or pink granite. The surrounding hills are rough and irregular, but covered with deciduous trees that make this region spectacular in autumn. Occasionally, small rocky rivers cut through the valleys.

Near the top of the ascent the paved shoulder ends. Here and elsewhere along the route, the steeper hills are approached with a passing lane. A fairly steep descent of 2.4 kilometers follows.

From here the two lanes are wide enough for fairly relaxed biking, and the road is in good condition, though chuckholes and cracks are not uncommon early in the spring, after the ravages of the not-inconsiderable North Shore winters. Also, be warned that the highway, though not busy by most standards, is a trucking route. Canadian truck drivers are a free-spirited lot, intensely proud of their trucks and not afraid to put the pedal to the metal. Trucks loaded with Vancouver lumber products gain speed far to the west on the downside of the Rockies, plummet eastward across the plains, and are still going strong when they pass Lake Superior.

The first 24 kilometers of highway outside Sault Ste. Marie travels north cross-country, so you won't see Lake Superior until the road approaches Batchawana Bay. After crossing the Goulais River, a 7-kilometer ascent—gradual, for the most part, with long grades that are seldom difficult—rises to a peak overlooking Lake Superior's Batchawana Bay. Ranges of low, rocky mountains parallel the shore a few kilometers inland. A 3-kilometer descent leads nearly to water level along the bay.

The Batchawana Bay area is a popular resort region and is dotted with cottages and summer homes. Motels, a restaurant, and grocery store are clustered on the south shore of the bay. The shore itself is irregular and fairly rocky, with tiny inlets creating protected beaches. Sheltered from wind and relatively shallow, Batchawana Bay is one of the few areas in Lake Superior where the water warms enough for comfortable swimming in summer. The road along the bay is flat and wide—three lanes much of the way, with paved shoulders about half a meter to a meter wide—and passes numerous rock formations and views of rolling, tumbling hills to the northwest.

Near the north shore of Batchawana Bay, a roadside plaque is located at the halfway point of the Transcanada Highway—3,888 kilometers from St. John's, Newfoundland, and 3,888 kilometers from Victoria, British Columbia. Completed in 1962, the highway crosses 2,325 kilometers within Ontario alone, more than in any other province.

Batchawana Bay Provincial Park, located 64 kilometers from Sault Ste. Marie, is a large day-use park where picnic areas, drinking water, and swimming beaches are available for free use. Several motels, restaurants, and rental cabins are located along the highway in the vicinity of the park.

Camping is available about 10 kilometers beyond Batchawana Bay Park at **Pancake Bay Provincial Park**. This large campground has 338 campsites located on a low bluff very close to the water along a 3-kilometer-long sandy beach and is equipped with hot showers. Services in the area, within walking distance of the park, include a motel, restaurant, and grocery. Pancake Bay itself earned its name because it was the last stop for voyageurs paddling east from Grand Portage at the far end of the lake and was the traditional site of a final feast of remaining supplies before the voyageurs replenished their stocks in Sault Ste. Marie.

PANCAKE BAY PROVINCIAL PARK TO AGAWA BAY CAMPGROUND (LAKE SUPERIOR PROVINCIAL PARK)—62.7 KILOMETERS (39.2 MILES)

Beyond the protection of Batchawana Bay, the lake opens quickly to its full size. From this point forward expect winds to increase as they blow unencumbered across the lake. Predominant south winds in summer are at your back and won't be much of a problem.

The shoreline from here is very rocky and has been formed into elaborate sculptures by waves and weather. Generations of sightseers and fishermen have developed pull-offs and campsites on the rocky bluffs and beaches along this portion of the lake. During much of the summer those places, whether used for lunch stops or overnight stays, are highly attractive. Winds from the lake help keep the blackflies and mosquitoes down, and wild blueberries and huckleberries grow in profusion in shaded areas near the water. Keep in mind, however, that Ontario's strict Crown Land camping permit system requires campers to pay a $3.50 daily fee, in advance, for camping on the 87 percent of Ontario that is owned by the provincial government. Because of the complications of the system—and the stiff fines for ignoring it—it might be wisest to plan on camping only at designated campgrounds.

Numerous rivers and streams cross the highway beyond Batchawana Bay, many tumbling over sets of waterfalls into Lake Superior. Short hikes up rivers like the Montreal and Agawa can lead to spectacular falls. Hiking along the same rivers downstream leads to shoreline where rocks are becoming larger and more prominent, on a coast that becomes progressively wilder and more rugged.

In the long stretch of wild coastline between Pancake Bay Campground and Lake Superior Provincial Park, expect a number of significant hills. Most range from 1½ to 3 kilometers in length and are moderately steep, with frequent stretches of relatively flat road partway up. Passing lanes are common on the largest hills, as are paved shoulders about half a meter to a meter wide, although the shoulders are often in poor condition, crumbling at the edges and covered with gravel. Services along this remote stretch are infrequent and scattered. Occasional failed restaurants and motels, their windows boarded and parking lots sprouting weeds, are reminders of how difficult life is in the region. Tourist dollars obviously don't go far enough, a fact made especially significant when you notice how little traffic there is, even during the summer "busy" season.

The Montreal River—where a deep gorge and falls are visible to the right—is followed by a major climb of 2.7 kilometers. Again, a passing lane helps considerably on the ascent. From the top are good views of the interior, with rugged hills in the distance looking, in profile, like tumbled scoops of ice cream.

A steep descent, followed by 3 kilometers of flat road, leads into Lake Superior Provincial Park.

AGAWA BAY CAMPGROUND TO WAWA— 97.9 KILOMETERS (61.2 MILES)

Lake Superior Provincial Park, with 1,580 square kilometers of territory and 53 kilometers of Lake Superior shoreline, is one of the largest provincial parks in Ontario and is the most utilized parcel of public land on the north shore of Superior. Three campgrounds provide a total of 274 unserviced campsites, each with drinking water, picnic tables, and toilets. Hiking trails cross the park's interior and follow a long section of otherwise inaccessible shoreline.

Crescent Lake Campground, right inside the park entrance, offers forty-eight sites on the shore of Crescent Lake and is open only in the heart of summer, from June 23 through September 3. The next campground is 8 kilometers farther at **Agawa Bay Campground**, on the shore of Lake Superior, and is the headquarters of most activity in the park. It offers 164 sites scattered along the fine sandy beach of the bay and is open from May 18 to September 30. Rabbit Blanket Lake Campground at the north end of the park has sixty-two sites and is open from May 4 to October 28. In addition to the three campgrounds, half-a-dozen day-use parks are scattered along the 80 kilometers of highway in Lake Superior Provincial Park.

Services are limited in the park, but a store, restaurant, and gas station ("Last Gas for 80 Kilometers," according to the sign out front) are located along the highway about one and a half kilometers south of Agawa Bay Campground. Although each of the three campgrounds are pleasant, I was particularly taken by Agawa Bay because it is located right on the shore of Lake Superior, while the other two are located on comparably tame inland lakes. Campsites are situated beneath a fringe of red pines and hemlocks just above the beach, an easy stone's toss from the water, and within easy earshot of the waves. The good clean sandy beach is scattered with driftwood (you'll need to collect it if you want a campfire—there are no wood vendors nearby and the floor of the woods had been picked clean). Lulled by the sound of the waves and by spectacular sunsets over the lake, you'll find it's a great place to sleep, although the occasional semitruck passing on the highway can break the spell.

North of Agawa Bay campground, after a stretch of flat highway that extends beyond the bridge over the Agawa River, a steep, sizable hill climbs above the lake and offers clear views of the tumbled, chaotic hills of the interior and the island-studded expanses of Lake Superior. At the top of the hill, a gravel road on the left (west) leads 2 kilometers downhill (and it is a steep and winding descent, not recommended for road bikes) to a parking area and small picnic site. From here a half-kilometer foot-trail leads downhill to the shore, where granite cliffs are painted with about sixty ancient Ojibwa pictographs, relics of a civilization that dates back to at least 9000 B.C. Painted on the walls in red ochre are such memorable scenes as a canoe with two paddlers, a sturgeon, a moose, dancing figures, birds, and various signs and symbols. The largest paintings, on Agawa Rock, are said to represent the crossing of Lake Superior by about fifty men in canoes, led by one Chief Myeegun. Their 4-day crossing, from the Porcupine Mountains of Michigan's Upper Peninsula, was blessed by a deity known as Misshepezhieu, represented in the paintings as a horned, lynxlike being.

The rest of this section of shoreline is remarkable for its great number of unusual rock formations. Ridges of rock rise from the water like vertebrae. One of them, a 15-meter-high promontory known as Devil's Chair Island, was worshipped by the Ojibwa as the place where the god Nanabozho landed after leaping over the lake, and was the source of legends about the creation of the earth. Devil's Warehouse Island is also rich in legend, and may have been the site of an ochre deposit where the Ojibwa mined the paint used in their rock painting.

After following Lake Superior for about a third of the distance through the park, the highway cuts inland and begins a long series of fairly steep descents and ascents. Some of the stretches through the highlands are relatively flat, passing ponds tucked among the hills and through forests of mixed conifers and hardwoods. The wide two-lane highway continues, and passing lanes make the hills less troublesome.

At the northern end of the park, after Rabbit Blanket Lake Campground, the highway descends nearly 6.5 kilometers, some of it quite steep, before approaching the lake again at Old Woman Bay. The picnic area there is followed immediately by a very steep climb of one and a half kilometers, then a series of lesser hills that continue to the northern boundary of the park.

The Michipicoten River, a kilometer and a half beyond the park, was a major canoe route to James Bay long before the coming of white fur traders, and the area around its mouth was frequently used for campsites and trading. Bluffs, cliffs, and small islands rim the shoreline there, which is backed up by sand beaches and receding rows of dunes. Today the lower river forms a portion of the canoe trail—a series of rivers and lakes connected by short portages—that leads through the interior of the provincial park.

Supplies and lodging are available in the community of Michipicoten River, or 8 kilometers north at the much larger town of Wawa.

WAWA TO WHITE LAKE PROVINCIAL PARK— 131.2 KILOMETERS (82 MILES)

Wawa—Ojibwa for "wild goose"—is the unofficial capital of the eastern half of the North Shore and the jumping-off point for wilderness trips to the north and east of the lake. A population of 4,000 makes it a very large community for this portion of Ontario, and one well equipped with all services and supplies. Motels, restaurants, and stores are spread out for a few kilometers before and after the downtown district (which is on Hwy. 101 just east of Hwy. 17). Except for a KOA campground on Hwy. 17 at the northern outskirts of town, lodging is limited to motels.

North of Wawa, Hwy. 17 cuts inland across the base of the enormous Pukaskwa Peninsula, and crosses through some of the remotest and least visited country along the North Shore. Much of the terrain is relatively flat and is wooded with spruce and tamarack that sprout in thickets among numerous ponds and expansive marshes. From Wawa to the town of White River, a distance of more than 96 kilometers, expect to see few houses or services. The predominantly flat terrain allows for good progress, however, on a two-lane road (sometimes widening for no apparent reason to three lanes) in good condition.

About 56 kilometers north of Wawa is a grocery, motel, and gas station, virtually the only place to find supplies and lodging along the center of the route.

Obatanga Provincial Park, located midway between Wawa and White Lake Provincial Park, makes a good alternative stopover. The park offers 132 campsites, as well as showers, laundromat, interpretation building, and access to a system of hiking trails and a canoe route of thirty-two interconnected lakes.

The terrain beyond the provincial park remains similar, although hills begin to grow in size and frequency. Most hills of any significance—and none, for now at least, exceed one kilometer in length—have passing lanes and often a paved shoulder on both the ascent and descent. The country remains wild and undeveloped and, typical of northern Ontario, liberally dotted with lakes and rivers.

The town of **White River**, home to about 1,000 residents, has most services, including restaurants and motels. Its primary claim to fame comes from being mentioned in an interesting footnote in the history of children's literature. According to local historians, a black bear cub was purchased in the town at the outbreak of World War I in 1914 by an officer in the Canadian army as he passed through on his way to Québec. The soldier, Captain Harry Colebourn, named the cub Winnipeg—soon to be shortened to Winnie—and carried it with him across the Atlantic to London. When Captain Colebourn was called to the front lines soon after arriving in England, he donated the bear to the London Zoo. During the war it became the favorite attraction of many children, including a frequent visitor named Christopher Robin Milne. Years later Christopher Robin's father, A. A. Milne, would remember his son's relationship with the bear from Ontario and would use it in his children's classic, *Winnie-the-Pooh*.

The long stretch of remote, mostly flat country between White River and White Lake is broken only by an isolated outpost offering a general store, RV park, and housekeeping cottages. A few kilometers farther is White Lake Narrows, where Hwy. 17 crosses a neck in large White Lake. Just beyond the bridge is an access road leading to White Lake Provincial Park.

WHITE LAKE PROVINCIAL PARK TO NEYS PROVINCIAL PARK— 79.7 KILOMETERS (49.8 MILES)

A narrow, winding, paved two-lane road leads 5 kilometers south from Hwy. 17 to **White Lake Provincial Park**. Spread out in the woods adjacent to the lake, the park is equipped with 200 sites (serviced and unserviced), hot showers, a laundromat, picnic area, interpretive center, and comfort station, and is in operation from May 18 to September 30.

White Lake is roughly the halfway point of the North Shore route. From here Hwy. 17 turns slightly to head mostly west toward Thunder Bay. After the campground the terrain remains similar but development is more common. A few kilometers west are a restaurant, convenience store, and housekeeping cottages; just beyond them are another restaurant and motel. The road here is in fair condition, rough in places and bumpy; its paved shoulder is about half a meter to a meter wide, with crumbling edges. The condition improves somewhat on hills, where the shoulders are wider and in better shape.

Within 24 kilometers of White Lake the terrain becomes moderately hilly for a short distance, with small mountains visible in the distance and rock outcroppings again common. A fairly steep, one-kilometer-long ascent is followed by a longer descent and a 16-kilometer stretch of virtually flat highway. At the end of those 16 kilometers a long descent leads to the bridge over the Pic River, which is immediately followed by a 3-kilometer, fairly gradual ascent to the village limits of Marathon. Just beyond the river, Hwy. 627 leads a few kilometers south to the entrance to massive **Pukaskwa National Park**, a wilderness reserve accessible primarily by hiking trail or canoe.

The town of Marathon is located on the Lake Superior shore, 3.8 kilometers off Hwy. 17 on Hwy. 626. Services near the intersection of the highways include several motels, restaurants, and service stations.

Beyond Marathon, and for the next 19 kilometers, the highway crosses a roller-coaster series of hills offering views of Lake Superior and cuts in and out of canyonlike passes of sheer rock. The range of hills is rocky, but heavily forested throughout, and creates fairly steep ascents and descents as long as 2.5 kilometers. The road is in generally good condition; its paved shoulder is about half a meter to a meter wide the entire distance, except on the insides of curves, where it's a meter and a half. A final, very steep descent of about one kilometer drops into a steep-sided canyon and leads, nearly at lake level, to Neys Provincial Park.

NEYS PROVINCIAL PARK TO RAINBOW FALLS PROVINCIAL PARK—79.2 KILOMETERS (49.5 MILES)

Located among sand dunes along the shore of Lake Superior, **Neys Provincial Park**, with 144 serviced and unserviced campsites, is reached by a short two-lane paved road off Hwy. 17. Open from May 18 to September 16, the park's facilities include hot showers, a laundromat, interpretive building, comfort station, and picnic areas. An excellent white-sand beach runs the length of the park.

Positioned near the end of the Coldwell Peninsula, the park is set among unusual hills and rock formations that have been dramatically shaped by the forces of the lake and its weather. Because of its proximity to the cooling effect of the lake, the Coldwell Peninsula is one of the southernmost regions in North America where subarctic plant life can survive. In addition to thriving populations of moose, bear, and other mammals common to Ontario, it supports one of the few remaining herds of woodland caribou found in this portion of mainland Canada. At the site of what is now the park's trailer campgrounds, a prisoner-of-war camp housed German officers during World War II.

The next 80 kilometers of highway, much of it paralleling the shore along the northernmost region of Lake Superior, is one of the hilliest stretches of the entire Lake Superior route. Just beyond Neys Provincial Park, a bridge crosses the Little Pic River where it flows through a deep, rocky canyon before emptying into the lake. The road here, and for the next 34 kilometers, is in very good condition, with paved shoulders over 2 meters wide. As elsewhere on Hwy. 17, all recently paved sections of the road have wide paved shoulders. It's conceivable that in the near future, once the entire route has been resurfaced, it will be possible to ride paved shoulders all the way from Sault Ste. Marie to Thunder Bay.

The first climb after the Little Pic River is a major one and is followed by a continuous series of steep, winding ascents and descents up to about one and a half kilometers in length. At times the road cuts close enough to the lake to offer good views of the water and the islands scattered along shore; other times large hills block the view or the road slices through canyons of raw granite and conglomerate rock.

Thirty-eight kilometers west of Neys Provincial Park, the road drops one and a half kilometers down an extremely steep hill, flattens out along the lakeshore, and suddenly loses its paved shoulder. From here it continues in only fair condition: bumpy, busted, and patched. Expect to find paved shoulders only on the insides of sharp bends, especially on hills. A side road leads down to the shore and the ghost town of Jackfish, where there is a long, sandy beach along a Lake Superior Bay known as Jackfish Lake. Established in 1871, the town is the site of what is thought to be the first gold mine discovered in northwestern Ontario. Although that mine is long abandoned, other gold mines in the region are still active.

The town of **Terrace Bay**, with a population of 2,700, has most services (including a hospital, bank, and post office) in the main business district just off Hwy. 17. A 1.3 kilometer biking trail leads through the center of town and offers good views of the unusual sand and gravel terraces—source of the town's name—that were left as the lake level receded after the last ice age. A short distance offshore are the Slate Islands, where a wildlife preserve supports a population of woodland caribou. As with many communities in this part of Ontario (and elsewhere in Canada), don't expect to find any businesses until almost 2 kilometers after the first city-limit signs.

Schreiber, about 11 kilometers beyond Terrace Bay, follows a section of moderately hilly, rocky terrain. Motels, restaurants, and service stations are scattered along the highway in the vicinity of this small but apparently prosperous community.

Outside Schreiber, paved shoulders 1.5 to 2 meters wide line both sides of the road through close to 10 kilometers of flat or moderately hilly country, past several inland lakes. The paved shoulders continue to Rainbow Falls Provincial Park.

RAINBOW FALLS PROVINCIAL PARK TO NIPIGON— 79.7 KILOMETERS (49.8 MILES)

Named for a mist-shrouded waterfall on the Whitesand River, **Rainbow Falls Provincial Park** is open from June 1 to September 3 and has 113 unserviced sites located near the shore of Whitesand Lake, a short distance inland from Lake Superior. On the opposite side of Hwy. 17, and almost 5 kilometers to the west of the main park, is Rossport Campground, with 40 unserviced sites along the Lake Superior beach. Both campgrounds have showers and other conveniences, and the larger Rainbow Falls facility is equipped with a comfort station and laundromat.

Hiking trails radiating from the park lead to Rainbow Falls, near the outlet from Whitesand Lake, and to the peaks of a number of hills where lookouts provide good views of the surrounding forests and lakeshore. The North Superior Hiking Trail passes through the park and leads to nearby Worthington Bay, where several Ojibwa pictographs are visible on rock outcroppings.

Immediately after the provincial park, Hwy. 17 climbs major hills with views of an island archipelago that extends to Nipigon. The islands in the group are known by geologists as cuestas and are characterized by the steep, granite escarpments on their north sides and gentle wooded slopes on their south sides. St. Ignace Island, by far the largest in the archipelago, contains fifty lakes and four waterfalls and is capped by a 568-meter mountain peak, the highest in the Great Lakes. The interior waters of Nipigon Bay, protected by the islands, are considerably calmer than elsewhere along the North Shore.

Rossport is a small fishing village on the shore of that protected water. Similar in some ways to the classic fishing villages of the Atlantic coast, it has a small commercial area lined with shops, cafés, and galleries. Chartered fishing trips can be arranged at the docks. A good choice for dinner and an overnight stay is the Rossport Inn, a remodeled 100-year-old railroad inn on the shore of the lake.

The remainder of the distance along Nipigon Bay is characterized by long, not particularly steep hills up to a kilometer and a half in length, and by stretches of flat riding immediately above the water. Numerous picnic tables and parking areas provide good rest stops. The rock formations along the lake here are smaller and less spectacular than those found in more open areas along the lake. The road is in good condition most of the distance, with wide paved shoulders.

From the Indian Reservation at Pays Plat (where roadside vendors, in season, sell wild strawberries, raspberries, and blueberries), a series of long, quite difficult hills crowd the coast. Some of the climbs are as long as 5 kilometers, though they are usually not relentlessly steep. For the next 64 kilometers the road alternates traveling virtually flat along the water to climbing into the hills and through canyons cut through bright pink granite. The road continues to be in good shape, with paved shoulders that vary from one-half meter to 2 meters in width.

Services are scarce along this stretch, but watch for a motel, restaurant, and store combination near the Gravel River. A bit farther, near the village of Gurney, a resort and private campground offer basic services.

NIPIGON TO THUNDER BAY— 98.7 KILOMETERS (61.7 MILES)

The community of **Nipigon**, on the Nipigon River near its mouth in Nipigon Bay, is a busy resort town of 2,500. This was the site of the first permanent settlement of

Europeans along the North Shore and was for decades an important trading post. Services in the town include motels, restaurants, grocery stores, and Boomer's Bakery and Coffee Shop (good pastries and homemade soup). About 5 kilometers west, on Hwy. 17, is a private campground.

A 96-kilometer section of Hwy. 17–11 between Nipigon and Thunder Bay is officially designated the Terry Fox Courage Highway, in tribute to the one-legged runner who attempted a 5,120-kilometer marathon across Canada to raise money for cancer research. Fox ended his trip along this section of the TransCanada Highway, when illness made it impossible for him to continue.

Beyond Nipigon the route changes somewhat. The road is in only fair condition, loses its paved shoulder (except in isolated stretches), and passes through much flatter terrain. From Nipigon to Thunder Bay the land is more heavily developed than the remote country to the north and east. While still remote and uncivilized by most standards, scattered residences give the impression of blending one town in with the next. Light forests of spruce, poplar, and tag alders cover both the flatlands and the low hills between settlements. Although relatively developed, towns remain small and offer only limited services. One of the larger towns in the stretch is Dorion with a population of less than 500 and offering only a gas station, restaurant, private campground, and country store.

About 6.5 kilometers west of Dorion a turnoff to the north leads a few kilometers to Ouimet Canyon Provincial Park. Although the park is for day-use only, Ouimet Canyon itself is a spectacular chasm measuring approximately 3 kilometers in length, 150 meters across, and lined with sheer 100-meter cliffs. A 2.5-kilometer path follows the rim of the canyon and gives access to several fenced viewing stations.

About 22.5 kilometers west of the turnoff to Ouimet, following a stretch of slightly hilly but otherwise unremarkable wooded countryside, a large truck stop with a motel, restaurant, and store is located at the intersection with Hwy. 587. Sibley Provincial Park is at the end of Hwy. 587, 33.5 kilometers out at the tip of the Sibley Peninsula. Within the park are trails leading to high cliffs along the western shore of the peninsula and a mountain peak 356 meters high. According to Ojibwa legends, the cliffs, known as the Sleeping Giant, were the site of silver mines awarded to the Ojibwa by the deity Nanibijou, who promised that any white men learning of its location would be killed. The legend contends that an Ojibwa man betrayed his people by promising to lead white profiteers to the mine, but when their canoe neared the Sleeping Giant a sudden storm swept across the lake and all were drowned.

The remaining 32 kilometers to Thunder Bay are probably the least attractive on the North Shore route. Terrain continues to be mostly wooded, with low hills, and development is light, but a wide swath of the woods has been cleared to make room for the road and for enormous metal towers that carry high-tension wires along the side of the highway. The road continues to be in fair condition, but paved shoulders, where they exist, are only about a third to a half meter wide and in poor condition.

THUNDER BAY TO MINNESOTA BORDER— 77 KILOMETERS (48.1 MILES)

Fooled into thinking that any city located on the shore of northern Lake Superior would have to be small, I entered the center of **Thunder Bay** on Hwys. 11B and 17B and became promptly and completely lost. With a population of 112,500, Thunder Bay qualifies as a bona fide metropolis. It is Canada's third-largest port and is said to be the world's largest grain-handling port, serving as the eastern terminus for the massive agricultural output of Canada's plains. The city sprawls along the flanks of low hills leading down to the waterfront and is surrounded by a sizable fringe of malls, shopping centers, and expressways, creating the usual bicycling hazards. Traffic is heavy, especially during rush hours, and few highways and streets are well designed for bicycles. Bicycle shops include High Country Cycle-Southside on East Victoria Avenue, and High Country Cycle on S. Cumberland Street.

To cross through the city, as I did, remain on 11B/17B until the junction with Hwy. 61 south out of the city. Within the city of Thunder Bay are a number of interesting things to see and do, including Lake Superior cruises, museums, galleries, city parks, summer stock theater, and a reconstruction of Old Fort William. From vantage points within the city you can look across Thunder Bay to the Sleeping Giant, the enormous limestone cliffs at the end of the Sibley Peninsula.

To avoid as much of the metropolitan area as possible, stay on Hwy. 17 as it skirts the city and becomes a busy four-lane divided highway. Follow it to the junction with Hwy. 61, then take the smaller highway south.

Hwy. 61 outside Thunder Bay diminishes quickly from four busy lanes to two busy lanes, without paved shoulders. Residential and commercial development spreads out soon after the suburban outskirts of the city, and the country opens into farm country. An unusual formation of rocks parallels the road to the east. Similar to the "table" rocks of the American Southwest, the sheer-sided, flat-topped formation appears as if everything around it simply fell away, exposing rock. The valley floor stretches several kilometers away from the rocks and is virtually flat.

Within a few kilometers of the city, farms grow in size and prosperity and numerous roadside stands offer vegetables and strawberries for sale. Fields and pastures have been carved from woodlots of poplar and maple.

Gradually, as the valley floor becomes hillier, houses and farms appear less frequently and the woods become more prevalent. The road continues the same, two lanes without paved shoulder, but 32 kilometers outside Thunder Bay the traffic is considerably lighter. Within 64 kilometers of the city, hills up to one and a half kilometers in length (but not very steep) roll away among dense forests.

About 3 kilometers from the Minnesota border, Hwy. 593 leads north 2 kilometers to Middle Falls Provincial Park, where twenty-five unserviced sites, a picnic area, and hot showers are open from June 1 to September 3.

The final stretch of steep, hilly, wooded country ends with a one-and-a-half-kilometer descent to the Pigeon River and the border crossing into Minnesota. Not far beyond the U.S. border is a restaurant and small motel. A few kilometers farther is the town of Grand Portage, with limited services. The next sizable community, offering a full array of motels, restaurants, stores, and outfitting shops, is 72 kilometers south of the Canadian border at Grand Marais. Hwy. 61 in Minnesota has paved shoulders about 1 to 2 meters wide, is mostly flat, and follows closely along the shore of western Lake Superior virtually the entire 245 kilometers to Duluth.

· RESOURCES ·

One of the secondary pleasures of touring by bicycle is discovering new restaurants, cafés, hotels, and bed-and-breakfast inns. Still, there are times when it is useful to know about a few of those places in advance, so I've put together a list of some of my own favorites from each of the twelve tours described in this book.

ANNAPOLIS VALLEY, NOVA SCOTIA

Among several outstanding bed-and-breakfast inns in the town of Annapolis Royal is the Queen Anne Inn, a beautifully restored 125-year-old Victorian mansion with 10 guestrooms (all with private baths). *Address*: 494 Upper St. George Street, P.O. Box 218, Annapolis Royal, Nova Scotia, Canada, B0S 1A0. *Phone*: 902/532-7850.

Near the Queen Anne Inn in Annapolis Royal, Historic Gardens is a kind of gardening theme park with expansive, trail-accessible grounds divided into such interesting areas as the Victorian Garden, the Spring Color Garden, the Perennial Garden, and the Rock Garden. Adjoining the gardens is Gardens Restaurant, which serves lunches, afternoon tea, and dinner in a restored Victorian house. *Address*: Annapolis Royal Historic Gardens Society, P.O. Box 278, Annapolis Royal, Nova Scotia, Canada, B0S 1A0. *Phone*: 902/532-7018.

The town of Wolfville has a number of interesting possibilities for lodging and meals. I was especially impressed with Blomidon Inn, a Victorian-era sea captain's mansion converted into a hotel and restaurant. *Address*: 127 Main Street, Box 839, Wolfville, Nova Scotia, Canada, B0P 1X0. *Phone*: 902/542-2291.

Chez La Vigne, also in Wolfville, is a café offering country French cuisine as well as regional specialties and fresh seafood. Not for low-budget travelers. *Address*: 17 Front Street, Wolfville, Nova Scotia, Canada, B0P 1X0. *Phone*: 902/542-5077.

CABOT TRAIL, NOVA SCOTIA

Many bed-and-breakfast inns on Cape Breton Island are part of a unique program that demands the same standards of quality and a common rate schedule. For a list and description of inns on and around the Cabot Trail, contact the Cape Breton Tourist Association, 20 Keltic Drive, Sydney River, Nova Scotia, Canada, B1S 1P5. *Phone*: 902/539-9876.

The Inverary Inn Resort in Baddeck makes an excellent home base while touring the Cabot Trail. Located on 11 acres on Bras d'Or Lake, the resort has a hotel, housekeeping cottages, a restaurant, tennis courts, and swimming pools. *Address*: P.O. Box 190, Baddeck, Nova Scotia, Canada, B0E 1B0. *Phone*: 902/295-2674.

The Harbour Restaurant in Chéticamp is a good choice for seafood dinners. It's located in the heart of town, on the shore of the harbor, and has a pleasant outdoor patio. *Address*: P.O. Box 400, Chéticamp, Nova Scotia, Canada B0E 1H0. *Phone*: 902/224-2042.

On the east side of the Cabot Trail, luxurious accommodations and dining are available at the Keltic Lodge in Ingonish Beach. The sprawling lodge is located on the waterfront and is surrounded by golf courses, tennis courts, beaches, and a swimming pool. Lodging is available also in the adjacent White Birch Inn. *Address*: Keltic Lodge, P.O. Box 70, Ingonish Beach, Nova Scotia, Canada, B0C 1L0. *Phone*: 902/285-2880.

GROS MORNE NATIONAL PARK, NEWFOUNDLAND

There's not much choice of accommodations in the Gros Morne region, but you can find clean rooms, good service, reasonable rates, and a passably good dining room at the Ocean View Motel in Rocky Harbour. *Address*: P.O. Box 129, Rocky Harbour, Newfoundland, Canada, A0K 4N0. *Phone*: 709/458-2730.

In Port-au-Choix try the Sea Echo Motel. *Address*: P.O. Box 179, Port-au-Choix, Newfoundland, Canada, A0K 4C0. *Phone*: 709/861-3777.

AVALON PENINSULA, NEWFOUNDLAND

St. John's has many good restaurants and hotels, especially in the downtown and waterfront regions. In the suburban area, I stayed in the Château Park Hotel, where the rooms and the dining room are satisfactory, and the employees are extraordinarily friendly and helpful. *Address*: 7 Park Avenue, Mount Pearl, Newfoundland, Canada, A1N 1J1. *Phone*: 709/364-7725.

Accommodations and restaurants are rare along the Avalon tour itself, but the Trepassey Motel and Tourist Home offers adequate facilities (including a dining room) at about the halfway point of the trip. *Address*: Route 10, Trepassey, Newfoundland, Canada, A0A 4B0. *Phone*: 709/438-2934.

Dining and accommodations are available near the

ferry terminal in Placentia at the Harold Hotel. *Address*: Main Street, P.O. Box 142, Placentia, Newfoundland, Canada, A0B 2Y0. *Phone*: 709/227-2107.

BLUE HERON DRIVE, PRINCE EDWARD ISLAND

Some of the best restaurants in the Maritimes are found in Charlottetown. Especially noteworthy for seafood (the chowder is terrific) is the Claddagh Room in the historic downtown region known as Old Charlottetown. *Address*: 129 Sydney Street, Charlottetown, P.E.I., Canada, C1A 3W6. *Phone*: 902/892-9661.

In the same neighborhood, Olde Dublin Pub serves authentic Irish pub food and does many imaginative and delicious things with potatoes. *Address*: 131 Sydney Street, Charlottetown, P.E.I., Canada C1A 3W6. *Phone*: 902/892-6992.

Luxury accommodations in downtown Charlottetown are available at the CP Prince Edward Hotel. *Address*: 18 Queen Street, P.O. Box 2170, Charlottetown, P.E.I., Canada, C1A 8B9. *Phone*: 902/566-2222.

One of the best known of P.E.I.'s famous lobster suppers is at St. Ann's Church in Hunter River. *Address*: R.R. #1, Hunter River, P.E.I., Canada, C0A 1N0. *Phone*: 902/964-2385.

KINGS BYWAY DRIVE, PRINCE EDWARD ISLAND

Bayberry Cliff Inn is an interesting bed-and-breakfast located a few miles from the Wood Islands Ferry Terminal. Perched on the edge of a 12-meter cliff, it has great views of the Northumberland Strait. Breakfast is one of the best I've had at a bed-and-breakfast. *Address*: R.R. #4, Little Sands, P.E.I., Canada, C0A 1W0. *Phone*: 902/962-3395.

In the northern region of this tour, the Mathew House Inn has rooms with private baths in a large house overlooking Souris Bay. Canoe and bicycle rentals are available, and good swimming beaches are within walking distance. *Address*: 15 Breakwater St., Souris, P.E.I., Canada, C0A 2B0. *Phone*: 902/687-3461.

For excellent—and abundant—servings of seafood, try the Lobster Shanty North in Montague. *Address*: Main St. South, Montague, P.E.I., Canada, C0A 1R0. *Phone*: 902/838-2463.

FUNDY NATIONAL PARK, NEW BRUNSWICK

Except for the chalets and cabins available in the national park itself, Fundy is definitely camping country. One alternative is Broadleaf Farms, a farm vacation bed-and-breakfast located at the northern end of the loop that starts at Fundy National Park. *Address*: Hopewell Hill, Albert Co., New Brunswick, Canada, E0A 1Z0. *Phone*: 506/882-2349.

GRAND MANAN ISLAND AND THE QUODDY LOOP, NEW BRUNSWICK

In St. Andrews, anybody who is anybody stays at the Algonguin Hotel, an immense (and expensive) seaside facility equipped with swimming pool, tennis courts, two golf courses, and a dining room. *Address*: St. Andrews by-the-sea, New Brunswick, Canada, E0G 2X0. *Phone*: 506/529-8823 (1-800-828-7447 from the U.S.).

For smaller budgets and simpler tastes, the Pansy Patch is an attractive bed-and-breakfast inn, located near the water in St. Andrews, with guest rooms furnished with period antiques. Pool and tennis privileges are available, and a downstairs antique and rare-book shop makes for great browsing. *Address*: 59 Carleton, St. Andrews, New Brunswick, Canada, E0G 2X0. *Phone*: 506/529-3834 (May–October), 203/354-4181 (before May 15).

On Grand Manan Island, the Compass Rose is a fine

bed-and-breakfast inn located on the harbor in North Head. Breakfasts are complimentary, lunches and suppers extra. *Address*: North Head, Grand Manan Island, New Brunswick, Canada, E0G 2M0. *Phone*: 506/662-8570 (after May 1), 506/446-5906 (before May 1).

GASPÉ PENINSULA, QUÉBEC

The town of Percé is bursting with good restaurants and pleasant hotels. I enjoyed my stay at Hotel La Normandie, which is located virtually on the beach in the heart of the town and has a fine dining room whose many windows offer a great view of Percé Rock and the morning sun. *Address*: P.O. Box 129, Percé, Québec, Canada, G0C 2L0. *Phone*: 418/782-2112.

For outstanding French (and Irish!) cuisine in a unique, seafront setting, try Auberge Le Coin du Banc. *Address*: Percé, Québec, Canada, G0C 2L0. *Phone*: 418/645-2907.

In Gaspé, lodging at reasonable rates is available at the Auberge Ash Inn, a small inn near the center of the city. *Address*: 186 rue de la Reine, Gaspé, Québec, Canada, G0C 1R0. *Phone*: 418/368-6320.

CHARLEVOIX AND ÎLE D'ORLÉANS, QUÉBEC

The Hotel Saguenay et Cabines offers lodging (nothing fancy, but the price is right) near the whale-watching tours at the mouth of the Saguenay River in Baie-Ste.-Catherine. *Address*: 294, route 138, Baie-Ste.-Catherine, Québec, Canada, G0T 1A0. *Phone*: 418/237-4271.

The grandest and most elegant hotel in the Charlevoix region is probably Manoir Richelieu, a 390-room affair with the look of a European manor house, located in the town of Pointe-au-Pic, near La Malbaie. Facilities include dining rooms, a golf course, tennis courts, and indoor and outdoor pools. Not for travelers on a tight budget. *Address*: 181 Richelieu, Pointe-au-Pic, Québec, Canada, G0T 1M0. *Phone*: 418/665-3703.

On Ile d'Orléans, Auberge La Goéliche is a renovated and moderately priced hotel at the south end of the island, with a good view of the river and the city of Québec. Facilities include a dining room and swimming pool. *Address*: 22 avenue du Quai, St.-Pétronille, Québec, Canada, G0A 4C0. *Phone*: 418/828-2248.

ST. LAWRENCE SHORE AND THOUSAND ISLANDS PARKWAY, ONTARIO

In downtown Cornwall, Travelodge is a decent, reasonably priced motel that makes a convenient location for starting (or ending) a trip on this tour. Facilities include a dining room and a lounge. *Address*: 1142 Brookdale Ave., Cornwall, Ontario, Canada, K6J 4P4. *Phone*: 613/932-4213.

Brockville's largest and fanciest hotel is the Royal Brock, equipped with a good dining room, indoor pool, lounge, exercise and aerobics room, squash courts, and other facilities. *Address*: 100 Stewart Blvd., Hwy 29 S. at Hwy. 401, Brockville, Ontario, Canada, K6V 4W3. *Phone*: 1-800-267-4428 (in Canada), or 613/345-1400 (in the U.S.).

In Gananoque, try the Golden Apple Restaurant for lunch or dinner. Set in a turn-of-the-century building, it's been in operation since 1928 and offers an interesting menu at reasonable prices. *Address*: 45 King St., W., Gananoque, Ontario, Canada. *Phone*: 613/382-3300.

NORTH SHORE, LAKE SUPERIOR, ONTARIO

The Rossport Inn, at the northern end of Lake Superior, is an interesting restaurant and inn occupying a 100-year-old railroad station overlooking Rossport Harbour. The six guest rooms often require reservations in summer.

The dining room specializes in locally caught fish. *Address*: Rossport, Ontario, Canada, P0T 2S0. *Phone*: 807/824-3213.

For comfortable lodging (and a taste of luxury) try the Stel Red Oak Inn in Thunder Bay. A large solarium encloses a swimming pool, whirlpool, and saunas. Other facilities include a lounge, a coffee shop, and a dining room. *Address*: 555 W. Arthur Street, Thunder Bay, Ontario, Canada, P7E 5R5. *Phone*: 807/577-8481.

·INDEX·